THOTH
THE HERMES OF EGYPT

A STUDY OF SOME ASPECTS
OF THEOLOGICAL THOUGHT IN ANCIENT EGYPT

BY

PATRICK BOYLAN M. A.

PROFESSOR OF EASTERN LANGUAGES, UNIVERSITY COLLEGE, DUBLIN,
AND PROFESSOR OF SCRIPTURE, ST. PATRICK'S COLLEGE, MAYNOOTH

Thoth:
The Hermes of Egypt

Published 2011
Research Associates School Times Publications
Frontline Distribution Int'L Inc.
Published in the Caribbean by: Miguel Lorne Publishers & Frontline

First Published in 1922

Library of Congress Control Number: 2009944075
ISBN: 0-948390-654

Thoth:
The Hermes of Egypt

Published by:
Research Associates School Times Publications
&
Frontline Distribution International Inc.
Chicago. Jamaica. London. Republic of Trinidad and Tobago.
5206 S. Harper Avenue, Chicago, Illinois, 60615

CONTENTS.

PREFACE.

The purpose of this essay is to indicate the chief tendencies of ancient Egyptian speculation in regard to the god Thoth. Taking as the basis of his work a fairly complete examination of the chief references to the god in Egyptian literature and ritual, the author has tried to distinguish the more important phases of Thoth's character as they were conceived by the Egyptians, and to show how these aspects, or phases, of his being help to explain the various activities which are assigned to him in the Egyptian legends of the gods, and in the ritual of tombs and temples. An attempt has been made, in many instances, to discover the simple concrete meaning which often underlies characteristic epithets of the god, and the need of seeking groupings among epithets which can in any way be associated with well-defined activities or aspects of the god has been emphasised. The author has not aimed at anything like a full analysis of the individuality of the god. That would have demanded a much closer and more detailed study of Egyptian religious literature, and a more extensive recording of results, than Egyptological scholarship has hitherto attempted in regard to any problem of ancient Egyptian religion.

It will be noticed that texts derived from the Egyptian literature of the Graeco-Roman period have been freely used throughout this essay. Every student of Ptolemaic texts becomes rapidly convinced that those texts contain a considerable amount of theology, which, though it cannot, perhaps, be always paralleled from the older texts, seems to be fully in line with genuine Egyptian thought of the early — sometimes of the very early — period. Hence, whenever the Ptolemaic texts seemed to promise any assistance in explaining aspects of Thoth, they have been used as authentic documents of Egyptian speculation and belief.

For the theological thought of the early period, the Pyramid texts have, of course, been minutely examined. Considerations of space and expense have excluded the printing of quotations from the Pyramid texts, but frequent references to the numbered *Sprüche* of Sethe's *Pyramidentexte* will enable the reader to follow and control the writer's use of the Pyramid literature. Passages from the Book of the Dead, in like fashion, have been, for the most part, referred to, rather than quoted. The references are generally to Naville's *Totenbuch* (in the text of which, however, certain slight emendations based on *Wörterbuch* material, have sometimes been incorporated).

The theme of this essay was suggested to the writer some time before the outbreak of the Great War by Professor Erman. The subject had already been treated by the Russian scholar Turayeff in his Богъ Тотъ which was published in 1898. Though that study was the outcome of painstaking work on the part of the distinguished Russian Egyptologist, it was, on the one hand, inaccessible to most students of Egyptology and Comparative Religion, and, on the other, it needed to be largely supplemented and modified in view of the great advance in Egyptological research since 1898. Most of the results of that advance were stored up in the material which had been gradually accumulated for the Berlin *Wörterbuch*, and Professor Erman made the composition of this essay possible by procuring permission for the writer to make free use of that material. The writer's gratitude is due to Professor Erman not only for procuring that permission, but also, and still more, for the unfailing generosity with which he put at the writer's disposal his great store of knowledge and his keen critical ability whenever he was consulted on any question arising out of textual or other difficulties connected with the study of the character and worship of Thoth. To Professor H. Schäfer, and to the other officials of the Egyptian Museum at Berlin, and to many of the young scholars who were engaged on work connected with the *Wörterbuch*, the author is greatly indebted for much courtesy and kindness.

The thanks of the writer are due in a very special way to Professor Hermann Junker of Vienna. To him he owes his initiation into the Egyptian script and literature of the Ptolemaic period, and to Dr. Junker's published work on the religion of the Ptolemaic period many points in the present essay are due, directly or indirectly. During the passage of this essay through the press, Dr. Junker has found time, in the midst of his academical duties in Vienna, to read the proofs, and to make many useful suggestions. For all his kindly help the writer is deeply grateful. To Dr. W. Till of Vienna who helped to prepare the MS for the printer, and assisted constantly in the proof-reading, much thanks is also due.

The title of the essay has been chosen partly to suggest from the beginning an important and intelligible aspect of Thoth to the general reader, and partly to remind the student that a god who, at first sight, might seem to be a divinity of purely Egyptian importance, was, nevertheless, associated with such a widely flowing current of ancient thought as the speculation of the Hermetic writings.

St. Patrick's College,
Maynooth.
January 1922.

P. B.

CORRIGENDA.

Page 3, note 1, read Nav. 94.
" 4, " 1, " *Rylands.*
" 16, " 3, " *Mystères ég.*
" 64, " 5, " makes.
" 84, " commands the *šꜣi* [instead *ḥśb*].
" 85, " 6, " *Šꜣi* [twice].

Chapter I.

The name of Thoth.

The name of the god with whom this essay is concerned occurs with considerable frequency in the texts of the Old Kingdom. In the oldest texts, however, it is written mainly with the familiar symbol of the god — an ibis on a perch, and only very rarely do we find in the most ancient texts the fully written form of the name. The Old Kingdom gives us as a *scriptio plena* of Thoth's name .(1) This form of script is common also in the funerary texts of the Middle Kingdom, and is especially frequent in the inscriptions of the nomarchs of El-Bersheh. In addition to this script the texts of the Middle Kingdom show the following forms of the name;

(a)  Lacau, Sarcophages 1, 212. Lacau, Textes religieux, p. 79. The same form without the determinative; Lacau, Sarcophages 1, 201, and often in El-Bersheh. Cf. Petrie, Kahun, Pl. 5.

(b) 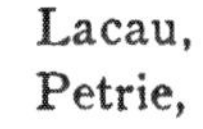 Lacau, Sarcophages 1, 206.

(c)  Lacau, Sarcophages 28111 (vol. 2, p. 89) (in the personal name . A Middle K. sarcophagus in Leipzig shows the same form. See P. S. B. A., 1914, p. 36, for same script-form from El-Bersheh.

(d) 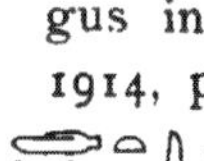 Lepsius, Älteste Texte, 46, n. 1. Ibid. Tafel 2, 22 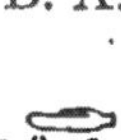.

---

(1) Common in the name of the festival . Cf. Maspero, *Trois années de fouilles. Mission* I, 2, p. 200, and L. D. often.

In the New Kingdom and later periods the following scripts occur;

(a) Cairo Ostrakon, Dynasty 20; Wb., no. 71.

(b) Newberry, Ushabtis, nos. 13: 46532.

(c) Ptolemaic period. Edfu, Roch. I, 419, 3, 6.

(d) Claimed to have been read by Brugsch in a Papyrus belonging to the Consul, Herr König. Vid. ÄZ. 1868, p. 72.

The symbolic or non-phonetic method of writing the name is far the most common in all the periods. The Pyramid script — an ibis on a perch, maintained itself in the texts of every age of Egyptian literature. Probably the script most widely used in all the later periods is . This compromise, as one might call it, between a symbol, or ideograph, and a fully written out form of the name appears even as early as the Middle Kingdom (Cairo, 20519, Stela of the M. K.). The non-phonetic script appears in the various periods in the following forms;

1. Old and Middle Kingdom.

(a) Pyr., El-Bersheh.

(b) Brit. Mus. 581. Stela M. K. (Griffith regards the ibis without perch as simply = heb, ibis. See Griffith, Hieroglyphs, p. 21).

(c) (perch and feather) Cairo, 20473, M. K.

(d) Blackden and Fraser, Hatnub, 1, 2—3 (Early M. K.).

(e) El-Bersheh 1, 15.

(f) El-Bersheh, often: Cairo, 20520 (Early M. K.).

2. New Kingdom and later.

All the above non-phonetic forms of the O. and M. Kingdoms recur in the later periods. The combined form of script — ibis and — is, as was said above, the most familiar script of the later texts. In this form an ibis-headed man often takes the place of the ibis on perch — thus, (Naville, Totb., Kap. 44, 3 : 95, 1, etc.). A parallel and rare script substitutes the ape for the ibis (cf. Champollion, Pantheon, pl. 30 G). (1)

The Ptolemaic period commonly gives us such forms as (usual); : : (Mar., Dend. III, 68 u), , .

In late texts, especially those of the Graeco-Roman period, we find the following strange looking forms of the god's name, (Book of Breathing, 2, 18); ("Complaint of Isis and Nephthys", 63); (Mar., Dend. II, 14); (2) Schäfer has shown, however, that these forms are due to an inaccurate hieroglyphic reproduction of the hieratic group for . (3) The hieratic sign for closely resembles the hieratic sign-group . The ape has in later puzzle-script the value , (4) and so also has the symbol . This, together with a misreading of the hieratic determinative, explains the script .

The name has been preserved to us in Coptic in the ancient Sahidic form ⲐⲞⲞⲨⲦ. (5) In Bohairic the name

(1) In Book of Dead, Nav. 44, 4, there is a curious variant to viz., . In Lacau's *Text Rél.*, on the coffin of , appears as a variant for the name Thoth (Textes Rél., p. 79). The coffin of is from El-Bersheh. A somewhat similar case of variants from the same district is and Annales du Service, Vol. II, p. 213 f. Cf. Pyr. 425 e, variant for .

(2) Cf. , Athribis. Pl. XXV.

(3) Ä. Z. 40 (1902/3), p. 124. A similar reading of for , Brit. Mus. 807. *Cf.* also the Turin Stela, no. 157. Cf. article by Gardiner and Sethe, Ä. Z. 47, p. 58.

(4) Cf. *Große Oase* 17 (Brugsch), = .

(5) So in the Paris Magical Papyrus. Cf. Ä. Z. 21 (1883), p. 100 f. (art. by Erman).

appears as ⲐⲰⲞⲨⲦ. (1) A form ⲐⲀⲨⲦ also appears in Coptic. (2)

In Aramaic the name appears as תחות (Sachau, Aramäische Pap. aus Elephantine, passim). In Neo-Babylonian we find the form *Tiḫut* (Ranke, Keilinschriftliches Material, p. 41).

In Greek several forms of the name have been handed down. Pietschmann (Hermes Trismegistos, p. 31 f.) has brought together the chief types:

Θευθ (Plato, Phaedrus, 274 c: Philebus 18 b).

Θουθ (Rosetta Stone, l. 49).

Θεθ (in the proper name Θεθμωσις. Cf. Parthey, Ägyptische Eigennamen, 117. Θεθ is the toneless form of Θωθ).

Θωθ (Syncellus, ed. Dindorf, p. 72).

Also, Θως, Θωτ, Θατ. Spiegelberg has attempted (3) to explain these various forms from the Coptic. From ⲐⲰⲦ, which is a contraction of the Bohairic ⲐⲰⲞⲨⲦ (like ⲦⲰⲚ from ⲦⲰⲞⲨⲚ, cf. Sethe, Verbum I, 171), Spiegelberg derives, several forms:

(a) Θουθ — an Achmimian form of ⲐⲰⲦ [cf. Ä. Z. 24 (1886), p. 130].

(b) Θατ — a Faiyum form, like ⲘⲘⲀⲦⲈⲚ for ⲘⲘⲰⲦⲈⲚ.

(c) Θετ — a toneless form, as in θετμωσις. The form ⲐⲞⲨⲦ in compounds, according to Spiegelberg, arises from the toneless form *Tḥʿwt* (from ⲐⲞⲞⲨⲦ): *u* naturally becoming *ʿw*.

(d) Θοτ (as in Θοτορταιος) is an older form, and not so toneless as Θετ.

(e) θευθ — This Platonic form Spiegelberg confesses he cannot explain. He conjectures, however, that it has arisen from an Egyptian (Coptic) dialectic form.

(f) θωυθ and θωυτ are the same as the Coptic ⲐⲰⲞⲨⲦ. (4) The various Greek forms of the name would be, thus, due

---

(1) Recueil, 1901, p. 199.

(2) Is this Sahidic? Cf. Ryland, *Demotic Pap.* III, p. 186. Crum, *Ostraca Ad.* 44.

(3) Rec. 1901, p. 199 f.

(4) Philo of Byblos quoting Sanchuniathon speaks of Τάαυτος — ὃν Αἴγυπτοι μὲν ἐκάλεσαν Θωύθ, Ἀλεξανδρεῖς δὲ Θώθ. Cf. Reitzenstein, *Poimandres*, p. 161. Clement of Alexandria (Strom. I, p. 356. Migne, vol. 8, col. 769) calls Thoth, Θωύθ. Eusebius says (Praep. ev., cap. 9, p. 31—32) Θωύθ οἱ Αἴγυπτοι, Ἀλεξανδρεῖς Θώθ, Ἑρμῆν δὲ Ἕλληνες.

directly to dialectic forms, or to differently stressed forms in Coptic.

In Latin the name appears as Theuth (Cicero, De nat. deorum III, cap. 22, 56), and Thoyth (Lactantius, *Instit. div.* I, 6, 3, vol. I, p. 13, ed. Fritzsche).

From the foregoing textual and traditional material it is possible to reconstruct the Egyptian pronunciation of the god's name. The Sahidic ⲐⲞⲞⲨⲦ belongs to the class of Coptic substantives ending in Ⲧ, in which the chief vowel stands before the consonant that precedes the Ⲧ. It would suggest, therefore, an Egyptian form like *Ḏe-ḥowti* or *Te-ḥow-ti* (cf. Steindorff, *Kopt. Gramm.*^{2}, p. 60). The form ⲐⲞⲞⲨⲦ, again, with its short Ⲟ reminds one of *nisbe*-forms; and these *nisbe*-forms present, as Sethe has shown, the same general appearance as substantives with pronominal suffixes. As ϢⲀϤⲦ and ϢⲀⲚⲦ come from  and , ϨⲢⲀⲒ – ϨⲢⲎⲒ from , ⲢⲀϨⲦ from ⲢⲰϨⲈ, so, in like manner, the apparently *nisbe*-form *D*^{e}*ḥowti* would be derived from *Ḏḥwt*.

If ⲐⲞⲞⲨⲦ has arisen from a *nisbe* of *Ḏḥwt* the name Thoth would mean "He of *Ḏḥwt*", "the one from *Ḏḥwt*", or "the Dweller in *Ḏḥwt*". Spiegelberg has very rightly compared the names ⲐⲞⲞⲨⲦ and ⲤⲒⲞⲞⲨⲦ. (1) ⲤⲒⲞⲞⲨⲦ is "He of Siut", and ⲐⲞⲞⲨⲦ on this analogy must be "He of *Ḏḥwt*".

The divine name 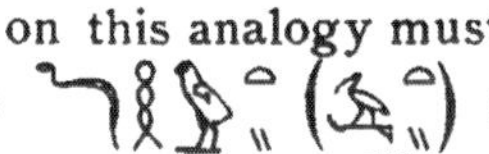 may be paralleled with such other names of deities as  (Harris, I, 61 a, 8);  (Harris I, 59, 5); 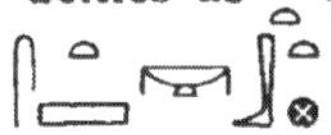 (Pyr. 1145);   [var. 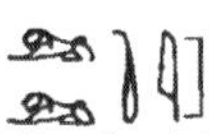] (Pyr. 2081 — *Ruti* = "he of the lion", *i. e.* Atum);  ("the god of Sepa" = Anubis); 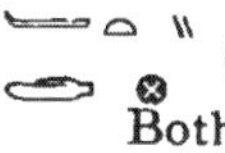 ("god of Edfu" = winged Horus).

Both from the form of the name, therefore, and the existence of obvious parallels, these seems to be good reason for regarding  as a *nisbe*, or place-adjective derived from a place-name 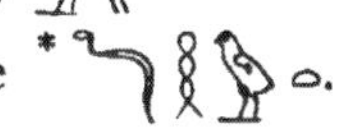. It must be admitted, how-

(1) Recueil, 1901, p. 199; cf. Ä. Z, 1883, p. 95. Cf. Bubastis, *Sedfestival Hall of Osorkon* II, Festival Hall, Pl. II.

ever, that, while places like Sepa and Siut and Edfu etc., are well known, a town or district named is not familiar. We find a district named mentioned in Ptolemaic texts. (1) Possibly this might be read as . The town-name "the town wherein is Thoth", mentioned in the Pyr. texts (1271 c), may imply that the town in question was called directly *Dḥwt*. But there is nowhere in Egyptian texts any clear and indubitable evidence that any Egyptian town or district was called by that name. Of course, just as *Ruti* is "He of the lion", the *nisbe* ⲐⲞⲞⲨⲦ might be derived from something other than a place name. Here, however, we meet again the difficulty that no substantive *Dḥwt* is known in Egyptian. While it seems probable, then, that ⲐⲞⲞⲨⲦ is a *nisbe*-form, it is impossible, in the existing state of our knowledge, to determine any thing further in regard to its derivation. For the sake of completeness, and to illustrate by a history of failures how difficult it is to explain the name Thoth, I add here a brief account of some of the most plausible attempts which have been made to solve the problem of the origin and meaning of the name.

(a) Naville (2) regards as an adjectival form from a substantive (= stork, or crane). He explains the name as meaning, "le dieu à tête de grue".

Loret (3) has put forward a similar view. He explains the god's name as = "le dieu en forme d'ibis", and postulates the existence of a word = ⲈⲦⲈϢⲒ, ⲦⲒϨⲒ (sic!) "ibis".

Piehl (4) follows Naville, assuming that means "crane-headed" and that the epithet is derived from a word = crane or ibis.

---

(1) Mar., Dend. II, 27, 15; II, 39 d; Düm., *Geogr. Inschr.* III, 22; Edfu *Roch.* I, 333.

(2) Ä. Z. 1877, 28 ff. If Naville thought that the primitive symbol of Thoth was the ibis-headed *man*, he had no basis in the texts for the view.

(3) Bulletin de l'inst. franç. d'arch. or., vol. 3, p. 18. *Cf.* Brugsch, *Rel. u. Mythologie*, p. 439 f. (4) *Sphinx* II, p. 51.

(b) Maspero (1) derives the god's name from — the name of some sort of bird. He gives no text however, in which this bird-name occurs. He seems also inclined (2) to connect the god's name somehow with , and to explain it as "le dieu ibis".

In an article in the *Recueil* (3) Ahmed Bey Kamal identifies the word with and with the Coptic TIϨI. He seems also (*ibid.*) to find a close relation between Thoth and (= Thagout, Ḳor'ān c. IV, 54).

(c) Goodwin (4) explained as a dual of (= TIϨI "*grus*"). He explains the dual as an intensive form, and suggests that the god's name means "Great Ibis".

At an earlier period Goodwin derived the name from which he explained as "artist" or "craftsman". (5) The ending , being a "dual of excellence", would make the artist κατ' ἐξοχήν. Levi in his dictionary, accepting apparently this view, gives us the word on Goodwin's authority.

(d) Pietschmann (6) agrees with Goodwin in regarding as a dual ending, and explains the god's name as "double ibis", or "ibis κατ' ἐξοχήν". He points out that the (so-called) dual ending is omitted when the "superlative" epithet "twice-great" is used with the name. Pietschmann admits, however, that the superlative force of the ending is sometimes forgotten by Egyptian scribes. Pietschmann, like Goodwin, then, supposes the existence of a word or meaning "ibis".

(e) Lieblein (7) thinks that the name suggests the lunar character of the god. is connected with

(1) *Biblioth. ég.*, vol. 28, p. 119 f. (2) *ibid.*
(3) 1902, p. 21 f.
(4) Ä. Z. 1874, p. 38.
(5) Ä. Z. 1872, p. 22 f.
(6) Hermes Trismegistos, p. 3.
(7) *Gammelaegyptisk religion*, p. 72 f.

, and this word means either the yellow topaz, or jasper. The word refers mainly to the yellow, or pale-yellow, colour of the stones. The ending is adjectival, and the name should mean the yellow, or pale-yellow, god. This would be a name for Thoth as moon-god, and would suggest the peculiar appearance of the moon. Lieblein seems also to think that might mean the yellow coloured bird, *i. e.*, the ibis. He lays stress in this connection on the point that Thoth as moon is usually depicted with a yellow-coloured head. (1)

(f) Lefébure (2) long ago connected with (= lead) and sought support for this view in the expression (Bk. of D. Nav. c. 134, 4—5). Unfortunately for this view, however, ⲦⲀϨⲦ (= lead) and ⲐⲞⲞⲨⲦ do not seem to be in any way really connected.

Against all the above attempts at explanation stands the fact that there exists, so far as we know, no Egyptian word for crane or ibis of the form or . Neither is it possible to find a proof of the existence of Maspero's . We find, indeed, in an Edfu text (3) . But the bird is, apparently, the same as the bird in , *i. e.*, Baklieh in the Delta (near Hermopolis Parva). I have not been able to discover any text which would justify Maspero's reading of as .

The suggestion that the god's name is based on a word meaning 'ibis', is a mere assumption. There is really no such word as with the meaning ibis. Ibis is , not

(1) *Ibid.*, p. 74. Cf. Pietschmann, *Hermes Trismegistos*, p. 7.

(2) *Mythe Osirien*, p. 208. A somewhat similar view is put forward by Petrie in *Ancient Egypt* 1917, p. 116. Petrie thinks that *Dehuti* means "he who is the moon" — the root of the word being *zehat* (*i. e.*, apparently) which = the white metal, *i. e.*, lead. Petrie supposes also that *Dehuti* may be connected with the Hebrew צח.

(3) Edfu Roch. I, 307. is probably to be read simply as *bnw*.

. It is, however, quite true that in late texts Thoth is occasionally called . We find as a name of Thoth in Dendereh, (1) and, at times, his name is written as . We have here, however, no more than a mere epithet of the god. is the tongue of a balance, and Thoth appears in many familiar scenes of the Book of the Dead in very close relation with the scale or balance in which the heart of the deceased is weighed against the feather of Truth. From his rôle in the Judgment-scene, Thoth has become, familiarly, the tongue ( ) of the balance, just as he has become, from his rôle in the same Judgment-scene, . In the judgment-scenes of the funerary texts we sometimes see the ape of Thoth represented actually as the tongue of the scales of Judgment. When is used as a name for Thoth, it is used, then, as a mere *epitheton*, and is in no wise connected with .

It is well known that the first month of the Egyptian year was called in the later period Thoth. It might, then, seem not improbable that there should be some connection between this circumstance and the early name given to the first month of the season. (2) Is there, then, some etymological connection between and as month-names?

The name seems to refer to the Feast of the Drunkenness of Hathor (3) which was celebrated in the first month, and thus gave its name to the entire month. There is, therefore, no need to assume an etymological connection between the two month-names in question. The name seems to have been given to the first month before Thoth's name was connected with that month in the time of the XVIIIth Dy-

(1) Mar., *Dend.* I, 39 d. In Mar., *Dend.* II, 41 a, the king is described as = "the balance-tongue of Thoth".

(2) Ramesseum L. D. III, 170—171. Medinet Habu, Treasury of Ramses III. Sethe, Heft 15, 119 (unpub.). Tomb of Min, *Mission* V, 365.

(3) See text pub. in *Mission*, V, 365, and *cf.* Theban tomb of (copy by Sethe 10, 60).

nasty. (1) The connection of Thoth's name with the first month seems to indicate the steadily growing importance of the "Lord of time" in the New Kingdom. (2)

It seems, then, to be impossible to connect the name of the god with any word , , or . It is no less impossible to connect, as Naville proposes to do, (3) a postulated with ϴΗΟΥ — as if Thoth were so-called because he was a wind-god. If the name is to be explained by derivation from the designation of some familiar object, that designation must, at least, be known as an element of the Egyptian vocabulary.

It would seem, then, that the only reasonable probability which emerges regarding the name of the god is that it presents a *nisbe*-form resembling the familiar *nisbe*-titles of the gods of Sepa, of Edfu, of Siut etc. The apparent confusion of the consonants , and in the Egyptian forms of the name raises no difficulty of importance. The Egyptian often passes into , and later into . (4) That the Greek form of the name ends or begins sometimes with τ, and sometimes with θ is due, in large measure to the want of fixity in the Egyptian consonants, and partly also to the tendences of Greek τ to pass into θ and *vice versa* in the transliteration of foreign, especially Egyptian, names.

---

(1) See article by Gardiner, *Ä. Z.* 1907, p. 136 ff. Cf. art. by Erman, *Ä. Z.* 1901, p. 128 f. dealing with month-names on the reverse of Ebers Papyrus.

(2) A contracted form of the god's name sometimes occurs. Thus in a Berlin Pap., in a proper name, ("Thoth-comes"). With this may be compared the play on words in the Turin Pap. 238 f. I am Thoth : "The hearts of the gods are made sad by his mouth in this his name Thoth".

(3) *Ä. Z.* 1877, p. 29.

(4) See Maspero in *Rec.* 1915, p. 160 f. becomes , and then . So , (= ה and, hence, תחות). A close parallel to > etc. is — — noted by Maspero, *ibid.*, p. 168.

Chapter II.

Thoth in the legends of Osiris and Horus.

Of all the numerous myths and legends to which ancient Egyptian monuments and texts refer there is but one which we can reconstruct with reasonable completeness. It is the legend or myth of Osiris. This legend, however, would have remained for us as incomplete and fragmentary as the multitudes of others alluded to in passing, or vaguely outlined, in Egyptian rituals or calendars, had not the divinity which supplied its theme, become, in virtue of the most vigorous of ancient religious propagandas, and of historical accidents which are but obscurely known, the most powerful and venerable of the Egyptian gods. Another circumstance — quite external — has contributed greatly to make the Osiris-legend of decisive importance for modern students of Egyptian religion: Plutarch selected that legend to illustrate by its various phases his theories on the nature and growth of religious beliefs. Plutarch has thus given us a moderately systematic account of the worship of Osiris, and of the origins of that worship; and in Plutarch we find, grouped together to form a single picture, many features of the Osirian legend which would otherwise have remained for us without bond of connection, scattered here and there throughout the literature of Ancient Egypt. But, while Plutarch has thus systematised for us much that would have remained without him empty of meaning and reference, his very tendency to systematise, and his preoccupations of theory often diminish the value of his work for modern students. He seems, at times, to confuse fact and symbol, and his groupings of incident are often, no doubt, due more to the needs of logical construction, than to the realities of ancient Egyptian belief. Yet, however much Plutarch's philosophy may colour his description of fact, we may take his account of the Osirian legend as largely reliable. The control which native Egyptian texts — especially very ancient ones — supply, is, in the main, a ground of trust in Plutarch's account.

The legend of Osiris, as outlined in Egyptian texts, and in Plutarch, may well be taken as the best starting-point for the study of the most ancient organised Egyptian theology. It will serve here to supply important points of view in regard to Thoth. To discover the real place of our god in the Osirian Cycle is to ascertain his importance in the most ancient religious thought of Egypt. It is necessary to discuss whether Thoth belongs to the legend of Osiris essentially or merely extrinsically; wether his importance as a divinity preceded, or was mainly due to, the growth of Osirian cult. It must obviously be of importance to show whether there are any outstanding aspects of Thoth which owe their origin solely or chiefly to the story and the religion of Osiris. And, as the legend of Osiris is closely involved with those of Horus the son of Isis, and Horus the Sun-god, it will be necessary to investigate Thoth's rôle in relation to the two Horuses. If we succeed in defining, even vaguely, Thoth's place in these ancient legends, we shall have reached some notion of his importance among the gods of Ancient Egypt, and some idea of his character as it was primitively conceived.

a) Thoth in the legend of Osiris.

In the Osirian legend of Plutarch there are five chief *dramatis personae* — Osiris, the prudent king who procured for Egypt the blessings of peace, well-being, and civilisation, Isis his faithful spouse, Horus his son and heir, Typhon (Set) his unscrupulous and energetic rival, and Hermes (Thoth) who appears chiefly as the friend and legal advocate of Horus. Plutarch speaks of a great law-suit which Horus had to sustain against Typhon in which the strong support of Hermes secured a victory for Horus. (1) The aim of Typhon in the law-suit was to prove the illegitimacy of Horus, and, thus, to deprive the latter of all right of succession to the throne of Osiris. Through the brilliant support of Thoth the legitimacy of Horus was established, and his right of succession

(1) *Is. et O.* ch. 54, 3—4 : 19, 8.

to Osiris confirmed. This victory of Horus over Set through the advocacy of Thoth Plutarch calls a victory of reason (*Logos*) over disorder and evil.

Plutarch's description of this great law-suit, though we can follow it in its main features, is confused in detail. It is obvious that Plutarch had not sufficient data to give a perfectly clear and consistent narrative of the legal conflict between Horus and Set, or of the part played in it by Thoth. There are gathered together in his narrative strands from several ancient legends. With the help of the native Egyptian texts, however, we can complete the Plutarchian version of the Osirian legend and of Thoth's place in it.

It is clear from his work that Plutarch did not really regard Osiris as an ancient king who had founded the civilisation of Egypt, and had been opposed, and, at last, destroyed by his rival and brother. Osiris is for Plutarch a symbol either of the all-fertilising Nile, or of the moist reproductive powers of nature (1). He is satisfied that Osiris is somehow symbolic of generative or reproductive power in nature, for he finds that Osiris and Dionysos have been identified. He, further, raises with the *Mathematikoi* the question whether Osiris and Set (Typhon) are not to be contrasted with each other as sun and moon. (2) In this reference Plutarch finds many points in Osiris which suggest, strangely enough, his identification with the moon.

Plutarch, then, is not seriously concerned with the idea of Osiris as a king. Whether, however, Plutarch was led to explain the Osirian legend symbolically rather than historically, because he had closely studied the native Egyptian teaching on the matter, or because a symbolical interpretation fitted in best with his theories of religious developments, we cannot determine. He is wrong, at all events, in attempting, as he does, to reduce every feature of the legend to symbolism. In the legend of Osiris, as in most ancient myths, popular constructive fancy and priestly speculation have added many details of importance to the primitive myth. And these additions have not always been made in the spirit

---

(1) *Is. et O.* c. 32, 2 ff. : c. 33.

(2) *Is. et O.* c. 34. *Cf.* cc. 36—39 : 41—42.

of the legend's primitive symbolism. Hence, in order to ascertain Thoth's true rôle in the Osirian story, we must seek to disentangle that story from the accretions made to it by the popular, and priestly mind. We cannot hope, however, to set up more than a purely tentative reconstruction of the primitive myth of Osiris. But it is obviously only by discovering the primitive form of the legend that we can decide whether Thoth was, in reality, one of its *dramatis personae*.

1. The primitive Osiris-myth.

The Osirian religion appears as well established in the oldest religious literature of Egypt — the Pyramid texts. It is, indeed, the dominant religion of that literature. That the Osirian cult had passed through a long period of development before it appears in a stereotyped form in the Pyramid period must be assumed. But, even in the oldest texts, the primitive form of the myth, the nucleus out of which Osirian religion had grown, is almost forgotten. Even in the oldest texts we can see that a large mass of heterogeneous detail has already been built up about and above the primitive myth. Yet sometimes in the Pyramid texts the ideas of the primitive Osiris-myth show through the details superadded by century-long speculation. From these occasional glimpses of the primitive myth which the early literature gives us, much support can be derived for Plutarch's symbolic interpretation of the Osirian legend, and, particularly, for his view that Osiris represents somehow the reproductive forces of nature.

It is well known that the ritual of the Osirian cult resembles, even in the oldest texts, the ritual of the so-called "mystery"-religions, (1) and we know that in the ancient world the "mysteries" were, as a rule, attempts to dramatise occurrences in nature. It would be reasonable, therefore, to regard the "mysteries" of Osiris, or the "Passion" of Osiris as a dramatisation of some event in nature, — possibly of the death of nature in late autumn and winter, and its revival in spring. If the primitive cult of Osiris was based on the recurrence

(1) Herodotus II, 170 f. speaks of the representation of the passion of Osiris at Sais as μυστήρια. Plutarch also speaks of the dramatisation of Osiris' sorrows as τελεταί (*Is. et O.* 27). Cf. Moret, *La Passion d'Osiris*, *Revue de Paris*, 1909, p. 615—660.

of natural events, it will have had associated with it, very probably, some of the practices of sympathetic magic. That there is a well-pronounced magical element in the oldest Osirian texts seems fairly evident. But, so far, scholars have given little attention to this feature of early Osirian theology.

The data at hand to determine the meaning of the primitive myth of Osiris are few. This essay is concerned with them only in so far as they help to throw light on the growth of the cult of Thoth. We give, therefore, no more than the general heads of the Egyptian evidence for the Plutarchian or symbolical theory of the Osirian cult.

Osiris is represented in the Pyramid texts (1) as carrying off the dead as his booty, *i. e.* in his capacity as earth-god, or Geb. (2) It appears, again, from ancient texts (3) that Osiris was sometimes worshipped as a tree. Schäfer has given reasons (4) for connecting Osiris with the *pḳr*-tree in Abydos by means of the notion of tree-worship. This *pḳr*-tree stands in the closest connection with Osiris. It is mentioned in the "mysteries" of the god. It is not impossible that the *motif* of the legend in which the coffin of Osiris is discovered in the erica tree (5) is derived from the cult of Osiris as a tree.

In many places Osiris appears quite unambiguously as god of burgeoning nature, or of vegetation. He it was, as we learn from Greek sources, (6) who discovered the vine, and taught men how to cultivate corn. This would not, of course, make Osiris a primitive corn-god, or vine-god — for he was not anything so definite as this to start with. (7) But the ancient Egyptian texts certainly bring him into close relation with developing plant-life. (8) He is lord of the vine when it is luxuriantly abundant (Pyr. 1524). We find Osiris sending

(1) Pyr. 145 : 350.

(2) Cf. Erman, *Religion*, p. 104.

(3) Pyr. 1285—87 : Cf. *Is. et O.* c. 20.

(4) *Ä. Z.* 1904, p. 109. *U-Pḳr* — "the District of the *Pḳr*-tree", was the name of Osiris' burial-place in Abydos.

(5) *Is. et O.* c. 15. Cf. Pyr. 1285–7.

(6) Diodorus I 14 : 15, 8 : Plut. *Is. et O.* 13, 1.

(7) Cf. *Journal of Hellenic Studies*, Vol. 29 (1909), p. 86. Art. by Scott-Moncrieff.

(8) Pyr. 699 : 1019.

the dead king as herald of a year of plenty. (1) A calendar-note of the late period for the 25th of the month Thoth points in the same direction: "On this day nothing must be eaten which bears any resemblance to the grape of Busiris." (2)

With this aspect of Osiris as symbol of nature in its growth we may well connect the custom of planting corn-seed in clay images of Osiris, and also the custom of outlining the figure of Osiris with corn-seeds planted in the soil. (3) When the corn sprouted in the clay image of the god, and when the green of the sprouting corn outlined the figure of the god, he could readily be seen to stand for nature in its reproductive power. A similar custom existed of sketching the figure of Osiris on a piece of stuff, strewing the outlined figure with earth, and planting corn in the earth thus strewn. (4)

These customs seem to point clearly to an association of Osiris with the life of vegetation. It may, therefore, perhaps, be safely assumed that, in some, at least, of his primitive aspects, Osiris was regarded as the fructifying principle of nature in its growth. It falls in well with this view, that, according to Plutarch, (5) the feast of the death of Osiris was celebrated on the 17th Hathor (November). The Papyrus

(1) Pyr. 1194/5, Cf. Osiris' title , Sharpe and Bonomi Seti I, XVIII c. 5.

(2) Wreszinski, *Tagwählerei im alten Ägypten. Archiv. für Rel.*, Vol. XVI, p. 90 f.

(3) Brugsch, *Ä. Z.* 1881, p. 80—82 : Murray, *Osireion*, p. 28. Moret, *Mystères gé.*, p. 41. Naville, *Totb.* 101, 10—12. Cf. Egypt. Explor. and Arch. Report, 1902/3, p. 5 : 1898/9, p. 24.

(4) Daressy, *Fouilles dans la vallée des Rois*, p. 26. For the whole question of Osiris's character as at once Nile-god, earth-god, and god of vegetation, see Breasted, *Development of Religion and thought in ancient Egypt*, p. 18—23. The pertinent Pyramid texts are carefully quoted in this work. Cf. also E. Meyer, *Ägypten zur Zeit der Pyramidenbauer*, p. 19; Baudissin, *Adonis und Esmun*, p. 191. The theory of the connection of Osiris with vegetation is supported by Frazer (*Adonis*², p. 269 ff.) : E. Meyer, *Gesch. d. Altertums*, Bd. I², p. 70 : Erman, *Religion*², p. 21 f. A strong attack on this view, and an attempt to make the primitive Osiris a god of the dead, from the pen of Scott-Moncrieff, may be read in the *Journal of Hellenic Studies*, 1909, p. 86. An important statement of some aspects of the Osirian problem, tending to weaken the evidence for the vegetation-theory has been made by Gardiner, in Davies and Gardiner, *Tomb of Amenemhet*, pp. 55 ; 81—93.

(5) *Is. et O. c. 42, 1.*

Sallier assigns the "weeping of Isis" to this same month. (1) Thus, at the time when the Nile was sinking, when the trees shed their foliage, when nature was visibly tending to decay, when the south winds (Typhon) began to prevail over the pleasant winds from the north, — at this time of general death, Osiris also died. His death synchronised with the death of nature.

With the symbolism of Osiris as representing the reproductive powers of nature is connected his identification with the Nile. Thus, it is said, Pyr. 589: "Horus comes: he perceives his father in thee, fresh (2) as thou art, in thy name fresh (living) water." In Edfu there is an unmistakable passage. Osiris is represented as spewing forth the Nile, and the accompanying text says: "I hide my body to make thy fields prosper." (3) With this we may connect the frequent designation of the Nile as the "outflow of Osiris". (4) In the Shabaka text Osiris appears as "He to whom the waters of the inundation belong, and who is drowned himself therein"; and one must agree with Erman when he says of this passage: "His (i. e. Osiris') rôle as god of the cultivated fields and of vegetation, could scarcely be expressed more clearly." (5)

The dramatic element, which is known to have been anciently present in the cult of Osiris, points, as was suggested above, to the probability that that cult developed from a nature-myth. Further, it has been shown that Egyptian literature gives clear, if not frequent, indications that Osiris was regarded anciently both as a Nile-god, and as an earth-god. It is not a very great assumption, then, to suppose that in the primitive myth of Osiris, this god represented, or was identified

(1) From the 18th to the 25th Hathor were made the Osirian barley-beds. Indeed it would seem as if all the chief Osirian festivals were celebrated in the month of Hathor. Cf. Davies and Gardiner, *Tomb of Amenemhet*, p. 115. Whether the feast of "Earth-hacking", which was held on the 22nd Hathor, points to agricultural aspects of Osiris, is uncertain. Cf. *J. of Eg. Arch.*, 1915, p. 121 ff. (Review of Frazer's *Adonis, Attis, Osiris* by Gardiner). Is there any connection between the Osirian barley-beds and the נִטְעֵי נַעֲמָנִים of Isaiah 17, 10?

(2) Cf. with this the Pyr. texts 2111 and 848.

(3) Edfu, R. II, 48.

(4) L. D. IV. 13 b (Ptolemaic).

(5) Erman, *Ein Denkmal memphitischer Theologie*, p. 934.

with, the fructifying and generative element in nature, (1) — whether we take him as vine-god, tree-god, or god of corn, or god of the earth or of the Nile. This idea of Osiris may possibly underlie the legend of the dismembering and restoration of his body. As in other lands, so also in Egypt, the waning and rebirth of nature furnished *motifs* for religious dramas. With the "Passion" of Osiris one is forced to compare the saga of Tammuz, and the cult of Dionysos and Attis.

The ancient nature-dramas — Semitic, Asiatic, Greek — agree substantially in the number and rôles of their *dramatis personae*. There are present in all the dying nature-god, his spouse who bewails him, and his malicious foe and rival who brings about his destruction. How many actors do we find in the drama of Osiris?

Isis appears in the drama obviously as the female counterpart of Osiris. (2) Both are children of Heaven and Earth. If Osiris is the fructifying principle of nature, Isis must be the fructified nature that brings forth. She is, according to Plutarch (3) the female principle of nature. Isis is Γένεσις, just like Osiris, and from the two proceed the γεννητικαὶ ἀρχαί. To put it another way: Horus, according to Plutarch, (4) is the child of the Nile, and of the inundated soil, and hence his birthplace is the marshland, Buto. Isis, further, in her aspect as Selene, is regarded as mother of the Kosmos. (5) When everything seems to sink into the sleep of death in the shortening days of autumn, Isis bewails her dying spouse, — nature unfructified bewails the passing of the life which would have kept her living and productive.

Thus Osiris and Isis, as the fructifying and the fructified elements of life and nature, belong, of necessity, to the primitive nature-myth. Is the god Typhon, or Set, an equally necessary figure in the drama?

---

(1) Plutarch says (*Is. et O.*, c. 51, 4) that Osiris was represented ithyphallically, "because of his generative and luxuriant nature". Cf. chapters 33—35 *ibid.*

(2) For the Greeks Isis was, at times, identical with Demeter: Cf. Herodotus II, 59; Diod. Sic. I, 25, 96. For Isis as goddess of fertility and corn-growing, cf. Augustine, *De civ, Dei*, VIII, 27.

(3) *Is. et O.* c. 53, 1.

(4) *Is. et O.* c. 38, 3.

(5) *Is. et O.* c. 43. Cf. Reitzenstein, *Zwei religiöse Fragen*, p. 106.

The god of nature dies: his death, however, comes not from himself, but from an enemy. Set is this enemy. He is the brother of Osiris because the rivalry of brothers is the most obvious, and the most widely known. From the cosmic standpoint he is the power which brings the moisture and life of nature to an end. He is the evil principle which brings distruction to the source of fertility, to the "good god", the . He is not the ocean which swallows up the Nile, (1) but rather a symbol of what dries up and destroys (2). He symbolises all things which hinder or destroy the generative powers of nature. (3) With the destructive burning glow of the south wind (4) he fights against his brother. When the Nile failed to reach the wonted level of inundation, this was ascribed to the hindering power of the hostile Typhon. Every influence, indeed, which made difficult, or impossible, the tilling of the fields, or the growth of the crops, was incorporated in Set.

All this is not stated, of course, about Set in the ancient Egyptian texts, and much of the above is based on Plutarch's philosophising. In some such way, however, we must reconstruct the part of Set in the original myth of Osiris. As we shall see presently, however, the story of Osiris is so inextricably interwoven with that of Horus, that the features of the Osirian Set are quite obscured by details derived from the legend of Horus.

It remains now to inquire what part — if any, can have been played by Thoth in this primitive nature-myth of Osiris, this dramatic rehearsal of the phenomena of nature's growth and decay. Were Thoth primitively an astral deity, one might infer his right to some place in the drama in question, for the heavenly bodies — particularly the sun and moon, might be looked on as influencing greatly the growth of nature, and the phases of agricultural life, both as life-giving, and as time-determining factors. Yet, so far as we can see, the old Osirian legend had just as little to do with the heavenly

---

(1) *Is. et O.* c. 32, 2.
(2) *Is. et O.* c. 33, 1.
(3) *Is. et O.* c. 49, 4.
(3) *Is. et O.* c. 39, 2.

bodies as had the parallel nature-myths in the ancient world. No doubt, as thought developed, there were interwoven with the Osiris-legend many other myths which were concerned with the sun and moon. But these myths had little or nothing to do with the primitive cult of Osiris. An astral Thoth does not, therefore, fit into the primitive Osiris-legend, and the other aspects of Thoth, which we shall have to discuss, seem to fit him just as little as his astral qualities, to play a part in the drama of a vegetation-deity.

Yet it cannot be denied that Thoth appears in a striking way in the saga of Osiris. This is evident, not merely from Plutarch, but from ancient native Egyptian texts. There is, however, the possibility that this activity of Thoth in the Osirian legend is due to secondary factors, — that, while having no part in the primitive nature-myth, Thoth becomes nevitably connected with a more developed form of that myth.

2. The Saga of Osiris as King.

It was more or less inevitable that a nature-myth like that of the dying Osiris should gradually be built up into a semi-historical drama; and the story of Plutarch shows us the semi-historical form into which the Osirian legend developed. The transformation of the primitive myth must have begun very early, since, even in the oldest religious texts, it has gone so far as to obscure almost completely the original story. In the Pyramid texts Osiris appears usually, not as a dying and revivified god of nature, but as a half-human, half-divine king of ancient Egypt, who succumbs to the malice and intrigues of his brother, is bewailed by his faithful spouse, and, finally, avenged by his posthumous son and successor, Horus.

The chief shrines of ancient Osiris-cult seem to have stood in northern Egypt, and we may, therefore, possibly conjecture a northern origin of the developed form of the legend. To the ancient nature-myth Horus, the son of Isis hardly belongs. But in a drama of rivals contending for the throne of Egypt such a son of Osiris and Isis was quite in place. This drama in its historico-political form was dominant in ancient Egypt, as the oldest texts show, and from this circumstance we can easily explain the importance and popularity in ancient Egypt of the "Son who avenges his father".

or Reason against Set. The trial referred to by Plutarch seems to have been held before the gods of Heliopolis. The trial described in the Egyptian funerary texts, in which Osiris was pronounced "justified", seems to have been pictured by the Egyptians as a sort of exemplar death-trial, or judgment. The Bk. of the Dead puts this trial in the "Princes' House" at Heliopolis; (1) but the localisation is probably to be explained by the growing preponderance of Heliopolitan theology. It is only very vaguely that the Pyramid texts speak of a trial of Osiris and Set, (2) and they give no idea of the place where it was held. Indeed the idea of a legal conflict between Osiris and Set decided before a divine tribunal is, to say the least, unobtrusive. (3) It is not impossible that this conflict is a purely secondary detail borrowed from the Horus-Set story.

That Osiris should be brought before the gods to be judged is explicable enough when one remembers that Osiris with his Abydos title "Prince of the Dead" has to serve, in all things, as exemplar of those who should follow him to the "west". This trial or judgment of Osiris is, therefore, not essentially primitive. It does not become prominent until Osiris appears clearly as god of the dead. (4) In such typical,

---

(1) Nav., *Totb.* c. 1, 7—10. (2) Pyr. 956—960: 316—318.

(3) A passage like Pyr. 957, where Set is accused before a tribunal of having struck down Osiris, may possibly be such a reference. But the situation in the passage is obscure.

(4) The question might be raised in general whether Osiris is ever pictured as model of the dead until he becomes lord of the dead through his assumption of the position of 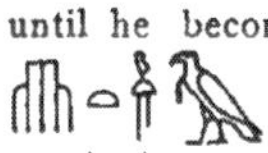 at Abydos. This would be towards the close of the O. K. For important suggestions on Osiris as *king vid.* Davies and Gardiner, *Amenemhet* p. 55. It is there put forward as a possibility *(note 1)* that Osiris was, in the first instance, a type of the dead king, and that it was only after the time of the O. K. that he became a god of the dead. The connecting link between the two ideas — dead king and god of the dead — would be the ever-growing custom of using the royal funerary ritual for nobles and burghers, as well as for kings. Thus, while in the O. K. the king *alone* was identified with Osiris, it became customary at a later time to identify all the dead with Osiris. This view is very important. It does not seem, however, to take sufficient account of the influence on the cult of Osiris of the identification of Osiris with the Abydene god of the dead, the "Prince of the Westerners". Further, no explanation is offered of the identification of the dead king with Osiris in the O. K. It is true that it is the dead king, and not the living king, who is identified

or exemplar, trial as that to which Osiris, as first of the dead, was subjected, Set would, properly speaking, scarcely have found a place. On the other hand, a trial or legal process of such earnestness as the judgment of the dead, could not be imagined otherwise than after the fashion of the great state-tribunal of Heliopolis. Thus the trial came to be located in Heliopolis, and to be conducted before the Heliopolitan gods — of whom, as we shall see, Osiris himself actually was one. Then the old mythical rival of Osiris, the wicked Set, was introduced to provide the necessary rôle of plaintiff in a great lawsuit.

---

with Osiris. But does not this circumstance suggest a view like that put forward in the text, — that the "Passion" of a nature-god has been gradually transformed into a semi-historical drama in which the king of Egypt is slain by his rival brother? The slaying of the king would, of course, be the chief incident in a funerary ritual. If Osiris came to be regarded as a king of ancient Egypt, what he did and suffered would naturally become exemplaric for all kings of a later time, and then, in the fashion suggested by Gardiner, for all Egyptians. Junker in his recent remarkable work *Die Onurislegende* (Wien, 1917) is inclined to think that some features of Osiris as a king of Egypt rather than as a god of nature may be due to such considerations as the political preponderance of the Osirian nome, Busiris, in the ancient period. The ancient local god of that nome *'nḏti* wears the peculiar ornament of the two ostrich feathers on his head. (Pyr. 614 a : 220 c : 1833 d). These ostrich feathers appear then later in combination with the diadem of upper Egypt to form the *ꜣtf* crown. The two ostrich feathers appear also in the nome-signs of This and Elkab, and are found also in connection with the cult-symbol of Chati, and with the insignia of Sobek and Tatenen in Memphis. All this seems, according to Junker (*op. cit.* p. 65), to suggest the probability that some ancient chief, whose home was Busiris, succeeded in establishing an extensive kingdom in upper Egypt in the pre-dynastic period. The ancient god of the Busiris nome, *'nḏti*, had his worship recognised throughout the territory which became subject to the victorious chief of the *'nḏti* nome. Junker notes the interesting fact that the sacred lake in 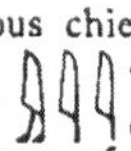 was called 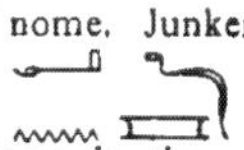 — a further indication of the political importance of the Busiris nome in the pre-dynastic period. There can be little doubt that political influences of the most varied types worked together to bring about the great extension of Osirian cult in ancient Egypt. It was possibly a result of political movements that the cult of Osiris was established in Abydos, and that Osiris thus came to be identified with *H̱nti imntiw*, the Abydene god of the dead. The breaking up of the body of Osiris Junker is disposed to regard, rather as an echo of the ancient custom of dismembering the dead body of a defeated foe, and distributing the sundered limbs among the victors (cf. Pyr. 1863 ff. and Pyr. 1543—50), than as a feature derived from a nature-myth (*Onurislegende*, p. 55). Junker's theory of the political expansion of the Busirian nome and, with it, of Osirian cult supposes without much show of explanation the identification of Osiris with the local god *'nḏti*. But this identification is itself a problem.

An eloquent advocate was just as necessary in the case as a vigorous plaintiff. Thus Thoth came to play his part in the lawsuit. But it is to be noted that, as before in regard to the reuniting of the limbs of the dead, so here also, Thoth's character fitted him for his special functions. Thoth was, as we shall see, quite apart from the trial of Osiris, connected with the dead, especially in relation to the Judgment. His peculiar eloquence, and the magical power of his words fitted him to be the advocate and general helper of the dead. Hence, in the great exemplar trial Thoth must be thought of as the advocate of the "First of the dead". Because, again, the Osirian trial was constructed popularly after the fashion of a case in the High Court of Heliopolis, Thoth's activity in the trial was inevitably conceived after the manner of a High Court Assessor, Advocate, or Scribe.

The growth of popular imagination in reference to the Trial of Osiris will have been connected by action and re-action with the innumerable representations of the judgment-scene depicted on the tombs and coffins of the Middle and the New Kingdom. Out of a saga grew the pictorial setting, and this, in turn, helped to develop the saga. The popular notion of Thoth's intervention in the trial of Osiris must have gathered not a few of its details from Egyptian funerary art.

In view of the foregoing, then, it may be said that Thoth's part in the semi-historical form of the Osirian drama is chiefly due to essential and independent features of Thoth's own character. That implies that Thoth is not in any way a creation of the Osirian myth, and that we must not take the Osirian drama as a starting point in the analysis of Thoth's personality. He seems, indeed, in many ways to be as ancient and as independent a god as Osiris himself.

We find in Egyptian sources many references to other activities of Thoth in regard to Osiris which also seem to follow from the anciently conceived independent character of the god. Thus we learn that Thoth acted as vizier for Osiris (1) — probably when the latter was carrying on his campaign of civilising the world. Thoth appears also as Secretary or

(1) Mar., Dend. II, 33 c. Cf. Diod. Sic. I, 17, 3: Lepsius, *Totenbuch*, 145, 3 refers to a time when Thoth acted as vizier for Horus.

Scribe of Osiris. (1) This idea is a detail borrowed from the legends of the sun-god. Thoth is the scribe of Re, and when Osiris, the great type of the Dead, comes to be identified with Re, Thoth becomes the secretary of Osiris (= the dead).

In the passage of the Book of the Dead just referred to, (2) the dead is represented as seated at the side of Osiris, in the capacity of Thoth the Scribe. There is obviously a reference here to the voyages of the sun-god in his barque. But it looks strange, at first sight, that the dead should be likened to Thoth rather than to Osiris. There is here, however, merely a confusion of religious thought, due partly to an old theory which identified the dead with the moon-god, (3) and partly to the idea that the dead becomes one of the attendants of Re in his "barque of millions". Even the Pyramid texts give to the dead king the position of Scribe in the solar barque; (4) and, at times, the official scribe of the sun-god is represented as ousted from his place to make way for the royal dead. (5)

Thoth appears, then, very prominently in the legends of Osiris. In many legends which centred round Isis he was also prominent. (6) Most of these legends deal either with the perils of Isis during her pregnancy, or with the terrible struggles between Horus, her son, and Set.

One of these legends is that referred to by Plutarch (*Is. et O.* 19, 6—7), according to which Hermes (Thoth) crowned Isis with a crown of horns after she had been deposed by Horus. The Papyrus Sallier (IV, 3, 5—6) evidently refers to the same legend, when it tells how Horus cut off the head of Isis, and how Thoth then — probably by his magic formulae — set upon her shoulders the head of a cow so that she became the "First of the Kine" *i. e.* the goddess of Atfih. This is clearly a local legend of Atfih explaining how the divinity worshipped there was really identical with Isis.

(1) Nav., *Totenbuch* c. 69, 11—12. Diod. Sic. calls him ἱερογραμματεύς of Osiris. I, 16, 2. Philo of Byblos (according to Eusebius, *Praep. evang.* I, 924. 10 [14. 17]) spoke of Hermes (Thoth) as γραμματεύς of Kronos.

(2) Nav., *Totenbuch*, c. 69, 11—12.

(3) Cf. Pyr. 1233. (4) Pyr. 490. 491.

(5) Pyr. 954. 955.

(6) Note that Diod. Sic. I, 17, 3 makes Hermes the friend and chief adviser of Isis during the absence of Osiris.

There are a few scarcely intelligible Egyptian texts which seem to refer to an improper connection of Horus and Set the fruit of which would have been, if one can trust some obscure texts of the later period, the god Thoth himself. The texts in question, however, are too few, and too difficult in their isolation, to afford a basis for any view of Thoth's relationship with the gods of the Osirian cycle. (1)

There can be little doubt that the prominence of Thoth in the more developed form of the Osirian drama is largely due to the increasing popularity of Thoth himself. The more familiar he became to the religious mind of Egypt, the more striking was the rôle assigned to him in the most popular cult of the country — the cult of Osiris.

If it is true, as Maspero suggested, (2) that the Osirian Saga had its beginnings in the Delta, we may suppose it to be possible that the ibis-god Thoth was brought into the Saga at first partly by geographical considerations. The Ibis-nome of Lower Egypt is so near many of the chief scenes of the Osirian tragedy, that the god of that nome would pass easily into the cast of the tragedy.

The presence of Thoth in the cycle of Osirian legend is, therefore, due mainly to external reasons. When, therefore, we find the two gods Osiris and Thoth standing together, apparently in close relationship, in such ancient texts as the funerary inscriptions of the M. K., we must not suppose that the two are essentially related to each other, or that Thoth

---

(1) There seems to be a reference to this legend in an Edfu text Roch. II, 44 where Thoth in his name  is said to have sprung from the skull of the "Enemy" 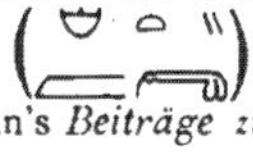 who may be Set. See a full treatment of the pertinent texts in Erman's *Beiträge zur ägyptischen Religion*. Sitzungsber. d. k. Pr. Akademie 1916, p. 1142—1144. Erman thinks that the more or less unintelligible texts which bear on this matter (Turin, 74; Pap. Turin 25, 5; Griffith, *Hieratic Papyri from Kahun and Gurob*, pl. 3, p. 4) refer to some kind of action by which conquerors expressed their contempt for those whom they had defeated. Erman refers (*ibid.*, p. 1144) to the text in *Totb.* 134, 9 dealing with Thoth which says that he is: 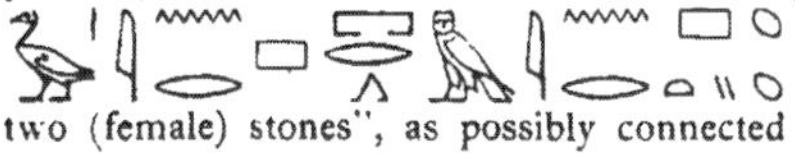 "Son of the stone, sprung from the two (female) stones", as possibly connected with some unknown myth.

(2) *Études de Myth.* II, p. 10, 39 etc. Cf. *Ä. Z.* 1904, pp. 77—107. Art. by E. Meyer on the growth of the cults in Abydos.

owes his ancient character and importance solely or mainly to the Osirian cult.

As our study of Thoth's character proceeds it will become more and more evident how inevitably his own personal gifts fitted him to take a part in the semi-historical drama which was grafted on to the "mysteries" of the primitive nature-myth. (1) As the god of law and right Thoth would naturally become the ally of Osiris in his contest with Set, and his advocate in his trial as "First of the Dead" before the gods of Heliopolis. Thoth's other functions in regard to Osiris, — the preparation of the god's (king's) body for burial (with Anubis), the bringing together of the god's limbs, the equipping of Osiris against the perils of the world beyond the grave, the offering of the due funeral sacrifices, and the carrying out of the ritual prescribed for burial — all these activities were equally required for every case of burial of king or noble. Indeed the details of the developed Osirian legend are little more than an echo of the main features of the life and death of the Pharaohs of the Old and M. Kingdoms. Every rite performed for the Pharaoh in historical times must have been performed also for the model Pharaoh, Osiris, in the far off past. The functions of Thoth in the legend are such as he must naturally have performed outside it. Thoth was, in all probability, a god of the dead and of sacred ritual prior to his connection with the drama of Osiris. But, though it is true that Thoth's character and functions are not due to his connection with the Osirian legend, the central cult of Egypt, with its elaborate ritual, with its literature, and pictorial representations, could not fail to give a more concrete definiteness to the deities associated with it. Some measure of moulding and influence, and much help towards popularity must, therefore, have been derived by Thoth from the Osirian cult, though in himself he is already a definite individuality

---

(1) It is obvious, of course, that the theory of the growth of a nature-myth into an historico-political drama in which a god of vegetation becomes a king of Egypt, is largely an assumption. Yet it is as likely to be correct as the view which regards Osiris as primitively the dead Pharaoh. In our view Osiris becomes identified with the dead king in the developed form of the nature-myth. Later still Osiris becomes identified with every Egyptian whose wealth permitted the celebration of funerary rites.

before the Osirian nature-myth becomes a semi-human, semi-divine tragedy. We shall see, in the course of this study how Thoth acquired a number of standing epithets through his association with scenes in the later forms of the Osirian legend, and we shall see from these epithets something of the manner in which Egyptian theology tended to develop.

b) Thoth in the legends of Horus.

We must make careful distinction between Egyptian sagas dealing with the sun-god Horus and his enemy Set, and the legends of Osiris. Even Plutarch seems to know something of this necessary distinction when he speaks (1) of the birth of the "ancient" Horus (Haroëris), thus implying that this Horus is other than the son of Osiris and Isis. Just as the primitive myth of Osiris the nature-god was enlarged as time went on, and greatly altered in *motif* by accretions due to popular and priestly theologising, so, in the legend of Horus and Set, an earlier and later stage can be distinguished.

The subject cannot be fully investigated here, but the distinction of the earlier form of the legend from its later developments must be briefly explained so far as it affects the position, in ancient theology, of Thoth.

In this legend, as in that of Osiris, the starting-point is to be sought in certain cosmic happenings. (2) In the primitive myth of Horus, the sun and moon on the one hand, and darkening influences on the other seem to be the chief factors. In brief, it may be said that the primitive myth deals with the conflict of the powers of light with the powers of darkness.

In due course this myth was enlarged into a legend of struggles between antagonists — half-human, half-divine. The primitive myth can be traced somewhat more easily here than

(1) *Is. et O.* 12, 6.

(2) It is assumed here that one of the oldest forms of the ancient Horus (Haroëris) is Horus the god of heaven, or god of light, the god whose two eyes are the sun and moon, *Ḫnti irti*, "He on whose forehead are the two eyes". The possible existence of another equally ancient form of Horus as warrior-god, who as falcon led the early tribes of Egypt to victory, and was later regarded as incarnate in the Pharaohs, need not be here discussed. The two aspects of Horus, as god of light, and as warrior-god, or god of battles, are close enough to be regarded merely as different aspects of the same divinity arising naturally from the transformation of a cosmic into a political or semi-political legend.

in the Osirian legend. Here the contending parties are outlined with a considerable amount of distinctness, whereas the chief feature of Osiris is his vagueness and elusiveness.

In the older form of the legend there is question mainly of the apparent defeat of the powers of light in time of eclipse of sun or moon, during the waning of the moon, at the setting of the sun, during the advance of darkling storm-clouds. The men of primitive times had puzzled over these cosmic events, and had sought to find their causes. For the ancient Egyptians the light which shone in sun and moon was thought of as the flashing of two eyes — the eyes of heaven. The god of heaven they called *Ḥor* — thinking of heaven, perhaps, as a great face (), with sun and moon as its two eyes.(1) When day passed into night, when the sudden storm burst, and, possibly, when the clouds were marshalled in the skies, the Egyptians thought of all this as the work of a power which was hostile to light. This power was regarded as evil and at some early period was identified with a local storm-god called Set. It is not possible to reconstruct all the features of the ancient legend. When we first meet it, it is no longer merely cosmic. It has been added to, and modified by priestly speculation and popular fancy, so that the primitive myth of a conflict between light and darkness has become the story of an unceasing struggle between two adversaries half-human, half-divine. Myths tend, of course, to develop in this manner. The popular mind seeks naturally to transform the divinities of its legends into beings partly, at least, of flesh and blood, and to express cosmic events in the language of human history. Hence in the developed anthropomorphic form of the Horus-legend we find historico-political *motifs* which have nothing to do with the primitive saga. Interwoven with the saga are many features that recall incidents of the struggles between Upper and Lower Egypt in the pre-dynastic period. Details of all kinds have been added to the legend to give it a reasonable human aspect, and thus it is somewhat difficult, at times, to determine what is purely cosmic, and what is merely anthropomorphic in the story.

(1) Compare the name of the Letopolitan god  *Ḫnti irti*, or *Mḫnti irti*.

It is a remarkable fact that the enemy of Horus the god of light, bears the same name as the rival of Osiris. Set is the foe of Horus, as well as of Osiris. It is difficult to decide whether Set displays similar qualities in both legends. A fully satisfactory explanation of the origin of Set's cult, and of his connection with Osiris and Horus in the primitive period has not yet been discovered. It is possible that the similarity in name, and possibly, identity in personality of the Osirian Set with the enemy of the sun-god Horus, is largely responsible for the confusion of the Osirian legend with that of Horus. (1) The Osirian drama has supplied many features to the legend of Horus — so many that it is often uncertain whether a particular text deals with a conflict between Osiris and Set, or with a struggle between Horus and Set. And it is equally clear, on the other hand, that features of the Horus-legend have passed over into that of Osiris. It must be left to other inquirers to disentangle fully the two sets of myths. The task of determining Thoth's rôle in either is complicated by the general confusion as to the borrowings of both.

The great importance of sun-worship in ancient Egypt may be inferred from the comparatively large number of centres of sun-cult which existed there. There was, for instance, the ancient shrine of the winged sun-disc in Edfu, where the glories of the rising sun were worshipped; then there was the primitive shrine of the sun-god at Heliopolis, and there were other centres of sun worship at Thebes and Memphis. The god of these shrines was, certainly, not Horus the son of Isis. (2) Even before the cult of Osiris began to spread

(1) Cf. Meyer, *Seth-Typhon*, p. 19. Plutarch (*Is. et O.* 55; 51 *et pass.*) describes Typhon (Set) as a destructive being. As a primeval storm-god, or god of the weather, Set could, obviously, be at once the foe of a vegetation-god and of a god of light, of Osiris and Horus. As a weather-god Set would naturally be widely worshipped in the early period. Several Egyptian terms which refer to the phenomena of storms are determined by the symbol of Set. It is clear from several passages in the Pyr. texts that Set was not regarded in the ancient period merely as a malicious being. The detestation with which he was later regarded was due to the growth of legend, and, probably, in no small measure, to the growth of the legends of Osiris and Horus.

(2) Haroëris the falcon-headed war-god had a very great number of cult-centres in ancient Egypt. Indeed the local deity in every district of any importance was early identified with some form of Horus, as well as with Re.

widely in Egypt the "ancient" Horus was honoured in many a shrine of the Nile valley. There is no reason for thinking that the different sagas of the sun-god had any connection primitively with the saga of Osiris. In the beginning Haroëris was rather the god of heaven than the sun-god: sun and moon were indeed the eyes of Horus. But so fickle is popular fancy that the god of heaven became identified at an early period with the greater eye of heaven, and his original character was almost forgotten.

The rôle of Thoth in the different stages of the legend seems to be intrinsic and necessary to the saga. In the very ancient form of the legend, where the chief *motif* is the cosmic struggle between Horus and Set, Thoth acts as friend and protector of Horus, and of his eye. To this activity of Thoth may be referred the Pyramid passages (Pyr. 594—597) which tell how the eye of Horus separated from its owner, was found by Thoth as it wandered on the further shore of the lake *Nh̲ꜣ*, and was carried back to Horus on the ibis-wings of Thoth. With all this should be compared the Pyramid texts, 947, 976, 1176, 1377, 1429.(1) The eye of Horus which Thoth cares for is, to judge by the literature of the later period, the left eye — the moon. The disappearance of the moon in eclipse and in the interval before the appearance of the new moon was a cause of anxiety to the Egyptians and to other ancient

(1) Compare the strange passage Pyr. 1742, where the eye of Horus is borne on the wing of Set. Pyr. 84 speaks of the "eye of Horus which is on the forehead of Set", but the reference here is obviously to the diadem which Set through usurpation or momentary victory, wears, the 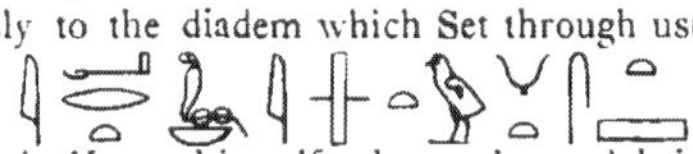 of Pyr. 979 b. In one form of the legend it is Horus himself who seeks and brings back his eye; but according to Pyr. 976 the eye of Horus is carried on the wings of Thoth "on the east side of the divine ladder". The legend of the flight of the eye and its return is obviously similar in many respects to the legends of the Destroying Eye of Re, of the angry eye which became the serpent on the diadem of the sun-god, of Onuris who fetched the divine lioness from the eastern desert, and of Hathor of Byblos. All these legends are intricately interwoven — so much so, indeed, that it is often difficult to decide to which of them a particular feature or *motif* primitively belongs. Thoth is certainly associated primitively with the astral legend of the moon-eye that vanished and was found again. The primitive astral myth contains no suggestion of an angry eye of Horus. Thoth's function as pacifier of the eye is connected with the more reflective legend of the Eye as Serpent on the crown of Horus (in which Sechmet appears as the Eye in her form *nsr.t*, and Thoth is the *sḥtp nsr.t*).

peoples. (1) To explain this disappearance, probably, the Egyptians devised the idea of a flight of the eye of Horus from its owner. The aim of the flight would be to escape the hostility of Set, and the exile of the eye would continue as long as there was a possibility that Horus might be overcome by Set. During its absence the eye was naturally under the protection of the moon-god Thoth. To Thoth also would fall the task of bringing back the eye to Horus when the season of danger was past. The place of the eye's sojourn, and the fashion of Thoth's care for it are variously described in the texts. In one prominent set of texts the eye is spoken of as having fled over a lake called *Nḫ3* (2) which is located in the eastern side of the heavens. On the shore of this lake Thoth is said to have found the eye, and to have brought it back to Horus, bearing it across the lake *Nḫ3* on his ibis-wings. In many texts, particularly those of the Ritual, it is implied that Thoth had to make a long search for the eye before he found it; in other texts it is insinuated that the eye came of itself to the moon-god, as if seeking his protection. Thoth's activity in the search for, care of, and fetching home of the eye is described in a number of technical terms;  (= probably, "restore", "hand over"), . (3) The eye is sought for at two seasons 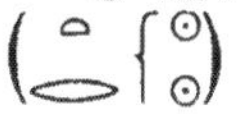 perhaps, the time just before the new moon,

(1) In Babylon the waning and vanishing of the moon were attributed to evil demons. By Marduk, whom Bel commissions for the purpose, the moon-god, Sin is rescued from his foes. Cf. Combe, *Sin*, p. 21 f.

(2) For the position of Lake *Nḫ3*, and its position in the legends of the Eye of Horus cf. Junker, *Onurislegende*, pp. 79, 138. According to Junker the lake is east of Egypt. It is mentioned in the legend of the fetching of the Eye of Horus from *Kns.t*. During the struggles between Horus and Set, therefore, we are to think of the Eye of Horus as hiding itself away in the east.

(3) See Moret, *Rituel du culte divin*, pp. 82—86; cf. p. 34. Cf. also the familiar text quoted by Junker (*Onurislegende*, p. 138).: I am Thoth 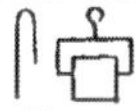

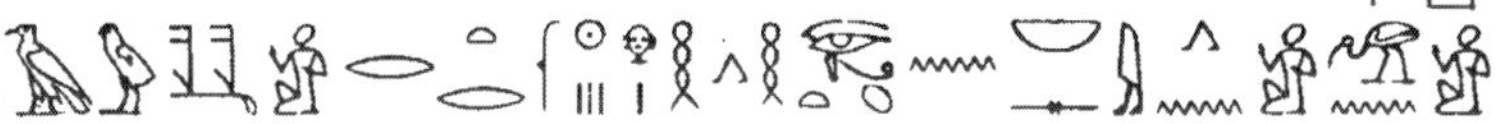

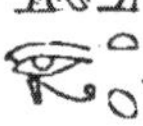. Cf. *Edfu*, R. I, 25.

and the time of lunar eclipse. These two "seasons" seem to be called occasionally . (1)

When the moon reappears after its waning or vanishing it shows the traces of violent hostile attack. It is only at full moon that it appears again with full splendour on the face of heaven. It is then , "healthy", "perfect"; and it is Thoth who has made it sound and whole; and it is he, also, who has restored it to its owner (Horus). From the legend of a healing of the damaged eye has arisen the name of the eye, (usually,). (2) Thoth is, therefore, *śwḏ3 wḏ3.t*, "He who makes whole the Eye". Further, it is Thoth who brings back the eye that had vanished: he is (Pyr. 58), "He who brings it" (the Eye) (3) — thus acquiring for himself the epithet "He who brings It". (4) When in the Pyramid-ritual the dead king brings to Horus the eye of the latter, he does so of course, as Thoth. But Thoth not merely restores the eye to Horus: he avenges it on its enemy (Pyr. 1233): but we are told nothing about the

---

(1) *Vid.* Moret, *Rituel*, p. 97 f.: Berlin P. 3055, col. 8, 9 — 9, 1 says: "I am Thoth who wanders at the two seasons seeking the Eye () for its lord. I come: I have found the *wḏ3.t*; I have handed it over () to its lord." See Lefébure, *Le mythe Osirien*, p. 87. with Set-determinative is used for the raging of the Apophis, Nav., *Totb.* 130, 22. Moret (*loc. cit.*) regards as the "distress" caused to the Eye of Horus by eclipse. The danger of lunar eclipse was great at the beginning of the month, and at the full moon, so that Moret believes that these seasons are the *tr n nšn*. Cf. *Totb.* c. 112 and 148: cf. also Plut. *Is. et O.* c. 43—44. *Nšn* is also used to describe the attitude of the Eye of Horus when, because of its anger with Horus, it abode far from him in anger (See Junker, *Die Onurislegende*, p. 136 ff.)

(2) For the *wḏ3.t* in the Pyr. texts see Pyr. 450 ff.: 1642: 21 a. 55 a etc. Junker points out (*Onurislegende*, p. 139) that *bṯķ.t* is used in the Pyr. as a parallel to *wḏ3.t* (Pyr. 118 b).

(3) Cf. Edfu R. I. 25: Thoth "who brings the *i3ḫw.t* eye to its lord" — which is also written in the same text: .

(4) Pap, Leyden 347, 12, 2 - 4 (N. K.). See below, p. 73 f. In the texts it is sometimes Horus himself who seeks his Eye. Min and Shu also seek it, at times.

nature of the vengeance taken. When Thoth restores the left eye of Horus he sets it in its due place on the face of the god: (Edfu, R. II 16): he, further, (1) "makes it (restores it to its owner) and causes it to shine brilliantly" (Dend. M. D. III, 19 n). The bringing back to Horus of his Eye by Thoth has brought the latter into connection with several Egyptian legends of the Eye of Horus. It is thus that he has been associated with the legend of the angry Eye of Horus which refused to be reconciled with its lord. In this legend the angry eye becomes identified with the goddess Sechmet in her character as *nsr·t* and Thoth's function in her regard is *šḥtp nsr·t*, the pacification of the *nsr·t*. In somewhat similar fashion Thoth has been brought into relation with the legend of Onuris. The name of this god *Ini ḥri·t*, "He who brings the one that was far away", refers probably to the bringing to Egypt from the mountain lands of the eastern deserts of a goddess in leonine form who was forced or induced to leave her desert home by an ancient battle-god in lion or falcon form. This ancient god was Horus the warrior-god who, because he brought to Egypt the stranger goddess received the epithet *Ini ḥri·t* (Onuris) — "He that fetches her that was far away". Later this *Ḥri·t* came to be identified with the *wḏꜣ·t* and *Ini ḥri·t* was explained as "He that brings the Eye that was far away". Thus the name of Onuris came to be written (as Thoth's could be, and sometimes was, written) as a deity carrying the *wḏꜣ·t*, . Thus, too, the identification of Thoth and Onuris became possible, with results which we shall see later. The legend

(1) Cf. Leyden V. 1. is predicated of Thoth. Mar. *Abyd.* I 37 a speaks of Thoth as : and the Abydos-Ritual speaks of him as (Ch. II): Cf. Naville, Goshen, *Shrine of Saft el-Henne,* Thoth with in his hands is described, . cf. Edfu R. I 25: Thoth . In some cases, of course, Thoth brings back to Horus (or Re) the right eye, or the Sun. This activity of his seems to be secondary or borrowed in the legends of the sun-god Re: it is based on his more primitive activity in connection with the moon.

of Hathor's coming to Egypt from Byblos, which underlies the story in the D'Orbiney Papyrus, is closely related in *motif* to the legend of Onuris, and it also has been, to some extent, interwoven with the cosmic legend of Thoth as the bearer of the *wḏ3·t*. (1)

Thoth seems to have rescued the eye of Horus, not merely from Set, but from numerous other foes. The Ritual of Abydos (ch. 36: plate 20) speaks of Thoth having rescued the eye of Horus . Who these enemies were can be gathered from the Book of the Dead, Nav., *Totb.* 183, 42—44. (2) The passage refers immediately to the deceased (= Osiris); but it seems to contain echoes of the Horus-saga: "I am Thoth who acquitted (or, justified) the voiceless one, who protected the weak one, and stood forth in defence of his belongings:  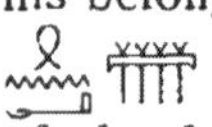 "I have banished the darkness and removed the veil of clouds". Plutarch tells us (*Is. et O.* c. 44, 9) that the Egyptians called the earth-shadow, which darkened the moon in eclipse, Typhon. Pyr. 61 seems also to ascribe eclipse of the moon to the activity of Set: the text speaks of Set devouring a portion of the Horus-eye, which then became "a little eye of Horus". Plutarch speaks (*Is. et O.* c. 55) of a smiting, and blinding, and swallowing of the eye of Horus by Typhon, and gives a cosmic explanation of the whole. The smiting of the eye, is, he says, a symbol of the moon's waning, and the blinding a symbol of the moon's eclipse. (3)

In the further development of the legend of Horus we hear of a bitter conflict between Horus and Set, and many

(1) The interweaving of the legends concerned with "the Eye of Horus that was far away" is discussed in Sethe's *Zur altägyptischen Sage vom Sonnenauge* (Leipzig, 1912) and Junker's *Onurislegende* (Wien, 1917). See also Spiegelberg, *Der ägyptische Mythus vom Sonnenauge* (Sitzungsber. d. k. preuß. Ak. 1915).

(2) Pyr. 575: 576: 635 speak of a repulse of the associates of Set by Thoth: but the reference in the context seems to be to enemies of Osiris. Cf. Pyr. 1979 and 651. *Totb.* 108, 7 says that Set is compelled to disgorge what he had swallowed.

(3) According to *Totb.* 116, 3, Set swallows the eye of Horus; according to c. 108, 7 he is compelled to vomit it forth again. The Pyr. text 118 refers to the swallowing, and Pyr. 39 to the vomiting forth. Pyr. 1450 refers again to the swallowing of the eye: "Pepi has not swallowed the eye: he is, therefore, not deserving of death" (*i. e.* is not Set-like).

details of the struggle have been handed down — though usually in a fragmentary, and often in an unintelligible, fashion. Horus and Set are now no longer cosmic forces, but leaders of armies, and rival kings; Horus is no longer a solar god, or a god of heaven merely: he is the son of Osiris, and the nephew of Set. The struggle is waged, not for the rule of heaven, but for the possession of Egypt. In one description of the struggle Set tears out the eye of Horus, and Horus rends away the *virilia* of Set. Thoth intervenes between the combatants, and receives a wound in the arm while doing so. He succeeds, however, in bringing the struggle to an end. He heals the wounds received by Horus, Set and himself in the conflict. All this is often spoken of in Egyptian texts. Pyr. 535 represents the dead Pharaoh as bringing back to Horus his eye, to Set his testicles, and to Thoth his arm. With this should be compared *Book of the Dead* (Nav.) c. 102, 7. 8. *Book of the Dead* 17, 30—32 gives many details of the struggle. (1)

The Ritual of Abydos (Mar. *Ab.* I, pl. 37 b) describes Thoth's activities after the close of the struggle thus:

It is obviously difficult to explain the tearing out of the eye, and the rending away of the testicles in a purely cosmic fashion. These and other details of the conflict seem to be products of popular anthropomorphic fancy. Thoth's healing of the wounds of the combatants, and of himself (as the story says, by the application of his spittle, Pyr. 2055), is clearly a

(1) There were current, it would seem, many versions of the legend dealing with the struggle. According to Berlin, Pap. 3055, col. 3, 8—9, Set blinded the eye of Horus by poking his finger into it. We hear also of a disease which befel the eye of Horus at sight of Set in the form of a swine. With this is to be connected the representation of a swine pursued by an ape (= Thoth) in *Description de l'Égypte*. Antiquités, tom. II, plate 35, 2. It was as a swine that Set, in this version of the legend, had swallowed the eye of Horus. With this we may compare Plutarch's statement (*Is. et O.*, c. 8), that the Egyptians offered a swine in sacrifice once a year at full moon (cf. Aelian, *De natura animalium*, X, 16). Cf. also Herodotus II, 47, who says that the Egyptians were wont to sacrifice swine to Dionysos and Selene. Cf. Baudissin, *Adonis und Esmun*, p. 149 f. For swine pursued by ape, see Maspero, *Études de Myth.* II, p. 175: Lefébure, *Le mythe Osirien*, p. 43—59 (esp. p. 52). The swine-hunt is often represented — for instance — in the Tomb of Seti I. Cf. Baudissin, *op. cit.*, p. 149.

secondary feature of the narrative, derived from the popular view of Thoth as magician, and, therefore, physician.

Thoth's chief activity in the struggle is mediation or reconciliation. It is noteworthy that this work of conciliation is mostly described in forensic fashion, as a sort of judging or arbitrating. Thus arose the description of Thoth which is so common: "He it is who judged the rivals and reconciled the brothers". In the Pyr. texts Thoth appears often as "he who judged the combatants" (cf. Pyr. 306). (1) The dead king becomes one with Thoth in the while he actes as judge or arbitrator "between the combatants" (Pyr. 289 c). This activity of judge or umpire between Horus and Set has won for Thoth his familiar epithet (2) or more fully, . With this function of Thoth we may connect the Pyr. texts which assign to the dead king the office of judge of the "two brothers". Thus Pyr. 712 says of the deceased ; and in Pyr. 1750 he is judge or arbitrator of the "two great gods" . In Pyr. 1963 we hear of one who "judges the two brothers and separates the two contending gods". The of Pyr. 273 seems to be intended for Thoth. (3)

(1) Cf. for Pyr. 229: 289: 304.

(2) Cf. *Book of Dead*, Nav. 169, 20: Edfu R. I. 297 etc., etc. The Delta Hermopolis is . What is the reference in Vatican 16, ? Lefébure (*Le mythe Osirien*, p. 120 f.) suggests that refers to Thoth's rôle as moon-god. When heaven and earth are mingled in one common darkness the moon-god, Thoth, comes, and separates them by his light which distinguishes things from each other. He refers to chs. 123 and 139 of *Totb.* as a support for this view.

(3) Cf. also, in connection with the "combatants" and their reconciliation, the Pyr. texts 126. 229. 311. 1899. 1913. 712. Cf. reference to , Pyr. 1724. The of Pyr. 126 need not be Thoth (see Cairo 20520 M. K.)

In the *Book of the Dead* Thoth appears again as "judge of the rivals", and as the one who restrains or brings to a close the conflict (). In ch. 123, 1—3, we read: , "I have made their struggle to cease: I have caused their complaint to end." (1) That the "Rivals" are Horus and Set appears here from the determinatives, and it is the usual theory of Egyptian theologians. It is likely that the struggle which Thoth thus undertook to bring to a close, was regarded as a political conflict for the supremacy of Egypt. (2) It is likely that we have here ideas which are present also in the Osirian legend. But the Horus of these texts is not Harsiesis, but "Haroëris"; and the inheritance for which he does battle is not that of Osiris, but that of Geb. The political aspect of the Horus-Set conflict is suggested by a number of ancient texts which speak of the "struggle" (*ḫnnw*) as ending in  (Hermopolis Magna, Eshmunein). This would mean that the war between the "rivals" was finally brought to a close in Thoth's nome in Middle Egypt. The most important of the texts in question is Pyr. 229 — 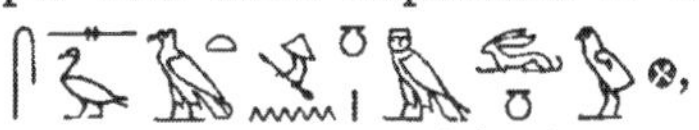, and with it should be compared, Pyr. 311 and 315. (3) Are we to infer that Her-

---

and *Book of Dead,* Nav. 178, 11—13). From Pyr. 1011 and 1379 it would seem to follow that the 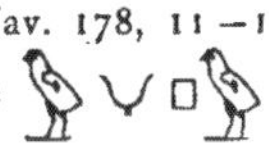 may sometimes be 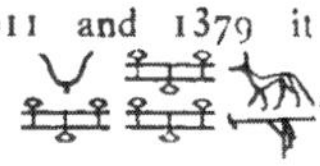.

(1) Cf. *Book of Dead,* c. 75, 5—7.

(2) Jéquier thinks (*Sphinx,* XVII, fasc. V) that the legends of Osiris-Set and of Horus-Set are to be explained partly totemistically, and partly, geographically or politically: the legends, he conjectures, reflect ancient tribal conflicts: "Une des tribus (Osiris) écrasée à un moment donné est secourue par une tribu venant d'ailleurs (Horus), qui reprend à son compte ses traditions, et finit par réduire en une certaine mesure le clan ennemi (Set) après quoi survient un compromis qui divise le pays en deux zones d'influence, l'un des deux peuples ne devant arriver que peu à peu à la suprématie absolue tout en laissant à son adversaire la satisfaction morale de la séparation politique du pays en deux parties." The political division of Egypt between Horus and Set is clearly indicated in such a Pyr. text as 204, where Set is *nb tꜣ šmꜥ* — a position held later by Horus of Ḳus.

(3) A distorted parallel to Pyr. 229 exists in a Brit. Mus. Stela-text (190) belonging to the late period:

.

mopolis Magna played a great part in the predynastic struggles of North and South? The positions of Thoth's city and nome was such that they could, if necessary, take a decisive part in the early battles. It is, however, possible that the  of the Pyr. texts referred to may be, in reality, , the northern Hermopolis of Pyr. 191. If it is, the texts which put the close of the *ḥnnw* between Horus and Set contain merely an unintelligible mythological allusion. But it is more reasonable to suppose that there is question of 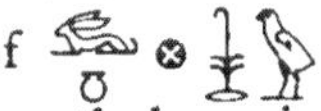 (Pyr. 190), and that something more than mere mythology is here conveyed.

It would almost seem as if the word *ḥnnw* which appears in Pyr. 229, was used as a *terminus technicus* for the conflict between Horus and Set (cf. *Book of the Dead*, 42, 17—19). The Book of the Dead gives an interesting passage in ch. 182, 19—21, in this reference:

"I am Thoth" 

"I have made Horus happy: I have appeased the 'Rivals' in the hour of their 'trouble'. I come: I have washed away the blood-stains. I have appeased the 'Rivals': I have put away every evil thing."

Schneider (*Kultur und Denken der alten Ägypter*, p. 389) thinks that the Pyr. texts 163, 173, 175 suggest the existence of an early alliance between Thoth's nome and Set. He would explain the passages in which Thoth appears as judge or arbitrator between the rivals, by postulating an activity of the 15th nome as arbitrator in the pre-dynastic conflicts (cf. *ibid.*, p. 420). If determinatives were of great importance, as they are not, in the Ptolemaic texts, we might take the Edfu script  as referring to a function of Thoth in delimiting the *territories* of Horus and Set.

(1) Cf. *Totb.* 123, 2—3. I am Thoth: 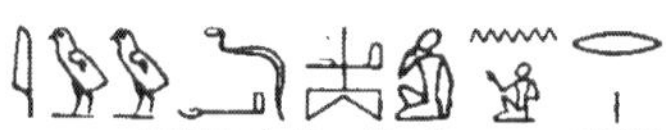

There is an equally clear instance of this technical use of *Ḥnnw* in Pyr. 1040:

"When the 'Combatants' were not yet, and the dread because of the eye of Horus had not yet arisen."

Ḥnnw seems to mean here the struggling combatants themselves, rather than their struggle. Yet, the special reference of the word is clear enough. A closely similar Pyramid text is Pyr. 1463:

(You were born) 

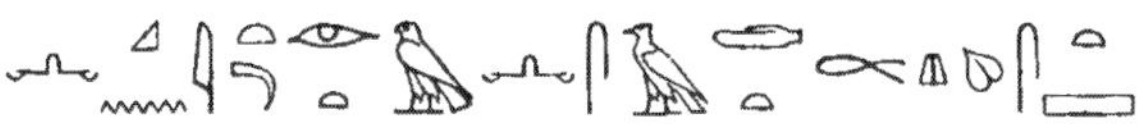

"When there was as yet no 'Conflict': when the eye of Horus was not as yet torn out (?) nor the testicles of Set wrenched away."

There are several instances of this use of *ḥnnw* in the Pyramid texts. (1) In view of what was said above about the cosmic nucleus of the Horus-legend it is interesting to note that *ḥnnw* can also mean "storm" (cf. Pyr. 304). There are several passages in which it occurs in this sense with the determinative of Set. Thus in the Turin Papyrus (23 f.) Thoth appears as he who —

There seems to be fairly definite reference to atmospheric phenomena in this text, and it is likely that something of the primitive Horus-Set legend here shimmers through. Set is here, apparently, the god of storm-clouds. We find

(1) Cf. Pyr. 289: 306: 304: 1320. How explain the place name 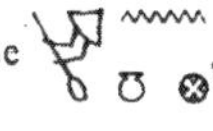, L. D. III, 8c (XVIIth Dyn.)?

(2) Read , as in Edfu R. I. 343.

ḥnnw used also for the trouble which is connected with the third epagomenal day, the birth day of Set. (1) In the Pap. Sallier IV, 13, 5  appears as a name for Set. (2)

It seems impossible, then, to evade the conclusion that the term *ḥnnw* is connected peculiarly with the story of the struggle between Horus and Set. The word has at times, at least, the meaning "storm", and is then brought into the closest relation with the person of Set. This hangs well together with the suggestion already made that Set is, perhaps, primitively a weather-god, or storm-god. The passage *Book of the Dead* 39, 14—15 gathers together a number of important features of Set thus:

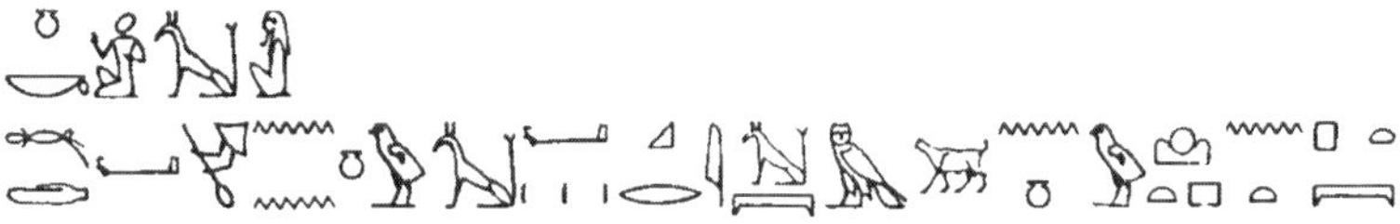

Thus the technical term *ḥnnw*, — which brings together Thoth, Horus, and Set, and is associated with a struggle that ended in Thoth's city , and suggests, at the same time, the phenomena of storm-clouds which were the foes of the sun-god, — helps to connect the various stages of the Horus-legend as it grows from cosmic myth to historical drama.

In the texts in which Thoth appears as "Judge of the Rivals, who reconciled the gods", he is represented as standing neutral between Horus and Set. But there are many texts in which Thoth can be seen to have abandoned his neutrality, and to have attached himself to Horus. In texts of this kind Set appears as a purely malicious being whose planning and actions are directed constantly against the well-being of Horus. In this stage of the legend the struggles of Set and Horus appear to be partly those of rivals on the battlefield, and partly those of opponents in a lawsuit. Set is not now so much the enemy of light, as the adversary of the All Good.

(1) Leyden I, 346, 2, 11. 12 .

(2) Again *ibid.* IV 3, 4—5. *Ḥnnw* appears determined with the Set symbol  also in Pap. Prisse, 6, 5: Ebers 56, 6. For *Ḥnnw* = "rebel", cf. Leyden I, 346, 8.

For other terms connected with the struggle between Horus and Set see Junker, *Onurislegende*, p. 136 f.

He has become more and more like the Set of the Osirian story, the enemy of the . (1) In proportion as Set became less popular in the religion of the people, he tended to become, in the same proportion, the symbol of evil. Similarly Haroëris, the ancient light-god, tends to become merged in Harsiesis, so that it is often difficult to decide whether the Horus whom Thoth supports is the Horus "who avenges his father", or the ancient god *Ḥr wr.* It is only, indeed, in passages in which Set appears as a criminal in regard to the eye of Horus, that we can be sure that we have to do with the Set of the ancient legend of Horus. It is interesting to note how the two legends — that of Osiris, and that of Horus-Set — are, at times, in the same context interwoven, and yet held apart. In the myth of Horus which Naville has published the struggles of "Horus of the Horizon" (= the ancient battle-god of Edfu), and those of Harsiesis against Set are narrated as if they were aspects of a single campaign. The battles described in this Ptolemaic text contain many echoes of pre-dynastic wars of South and North, and the Thoth of these texts is represented consistently as the friend of Horus, and not as a mediator between Horus and Set. The descriptions of Set and his companions, the leagued enemies of Horus of the Horizon, throughout the myth, suggest frequently those enemies of Re which are symbolised by the Apophis-serpent. The whole text furnishes a remarkable instance of the interweaving of legends in Egyptian speculation, and of the absence of all sharp distinctions in Egyptian thought.

Plutarch tells of a great lawsuit between Horus and Set which was conducted in presence of the gods. (2) The Horus in the case is the son of Isis. In Plutarch's story Thoth is the eloquent advocate who wins the case for Horus, the Logos whose reasoning cannot be withstood. (3) It is not easy to see how Thoth's titles 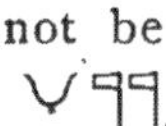, 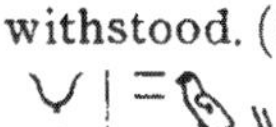 and 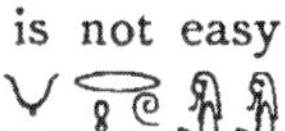 are reconcilable with this view. There is another confusion in Plutarch's story. He makes the lawsuit deal with the problem whether Harsiesis is the legitimate son, and rightful heir,

(1) Cf. Pyr. 580: 581: 587.
(2) Cf. the Pyr. texts 770: 958.
(3) Plutarch, *Is. et O.*, c. 54, 3—4: 19, 8.

of Osiris. Yet the Egyptian texts seem rather to speak of a lawsuit about the due apportioning of Egypt between Horus and Set. (1) The point of legitimacy is not raised, and the texts in question are partly, at least, echoes of the early wars. The calendar of the Papyrus Sallier (IV, 9, 5—6) tells us that the result of the lawsuit in question was, that to Horus was assigned all Egypt, and to Set the desert; Thoth, as the scribe of the gods, published the sentence. (2) It is probable, however, that the divine verdict was thought of differently in the earliest period. In the older tradition Set must have been assigned a portion of Egypt itself. In an ancient version of the legend it was Geb, and not Thoth, who reconciled Horus and Set. Egypt was indeed the "inheritance of Geb", for he was Lord of its soil, and to him, therefore, belonged the first right to assign the land of Egypt to various rulers. That Geb made the division of Egypt between Horus and Set is implied in the Shabaka text. (3) We are told in this ancient text that Geb, having brought to a close the strife between the rivals, gives the South to Set and the North to Horus. He says to them: 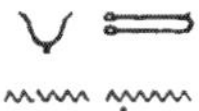 "I have judged (or sundered) you", which would seem to imply that Geb was, at one time, the . (4) Whether, however, Geb or Thoth is the original *Wp rḥwi*, this title seems to be mainly reserved to Thoth from the beginnings of the New Kingdom. Maspero is inclined to think (5) that the title had a Delta origin, and that it belonged properly to the Northern, or Delta-Thoth. The

---

(1) Pyr. 1242 refers to a lawsuit between Horus and Set concerning an injury done to the left eye of Horus (*i. e.* the moon, as above).

(2) Cf. the Hymn to Osiris. Bibl. Nat. 20, plate 27, pub. by Legrain. In *Book of the Dead*, 96, 3 f., in a reference possibly to some such lawsuit, it is said that Thoth reconciled Set "by the *nḥḥ* of the *'kn*, by the blood of the venerable ones of Geb". The passage with its unintelligibility suggests how small a fragment of Egyptian myths and legends has survived.

Amon gets the title 
in the Hymn to Amon, Cairo, 8, 5.

(3) p. 925 f.

(4) In Pyr. 957 Geb seems to act as judge in a lawsuit between Osiris and Set.

(5) *La Myth. ég.*, p. 379.

name of Thoth's city, the capital of the Ibis-nome, in the Delta is 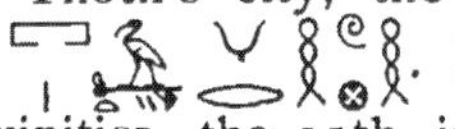. In Philae, in a procession of northern divinities, the 15th is "Thoth, the great god, 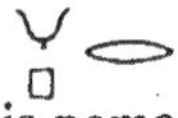 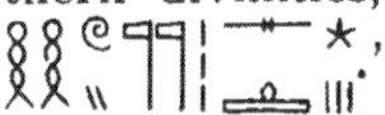." The chief priest of Thoth in the ibis-nome was also called 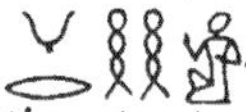. (1) Maspero's conjecture thus finds support in Egyptian texts. Yet, it is the fact that the title in question was given to Thoth not merely in the north, but throughout Egypt. If the epithet were really of Delta origin, it would probably be somehow connected with the Osirian legend, and not, as we have conjectured, with the developed form of the Horus-Set saga. If, however, as seems likely, the epithet *wp rḥwi* is practically identical with *wp ẖnnw*, it may be still regarded as arising from the legend of Horus and Set. It could, of course, easily have become connected secondarily with the name of Thoth's Delta home.

Though the ancient tradition regarded Horus and Set as the "Rivals" (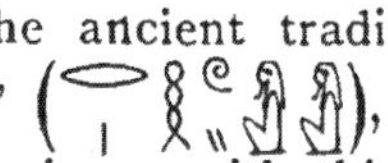), there are a few ancient texts which are at variance with this tradition: Pyr. 163 speaks of Thoth and Set as the hostile brothers, and blames them for their evil deeds, and their refusal to repent of them. Pyr. 173 and 175 threaten the same two divinities with heavy penalties. It is possible that we have here traces of an ancient legend which made Thoth and Set a pair of malignant deities, leagued in a conspiracy of evil against Horus. (2) One may have here echoes of an alliance of Thoth's nome with Set against the political power of Horus.

A remarkable Pyr. text (128) identifies Thoth and Re (i. e. moon and sun) with the *Rḥwi*, and tells how Set (here, apparently, still a venerable deity) escaped from their hostility. In the text the dead is said to have escaped certain unpleasant things  "as Set withheld himself from the *mt* (poison?) of the *Rḥwi*", who are further described 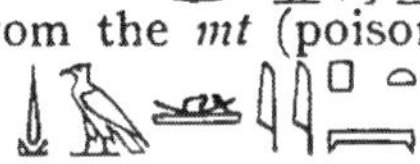 (who traverse the heavens). Then

(1) Edfu R. I., 333. Note in Edfu, R. I., 334, that  is apparently a name for the Mendes nome.

(2) Schneider, *Kultur und Denken*, p. 389, regards these Pyr. texts as pointing to a political combination of Set with Thoth.

follows the important gloss of the ancient commentator: 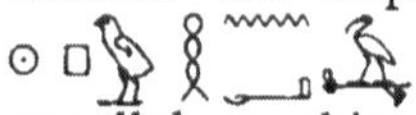 "Re, that is, and Thoth". (1) We have a parallel to this ancient text in a Cairo text of the M. K. (Cairo 20520): (2) there the gloss reads  — obviously a slight misreading. Sun and moon are here the *Rḥwi*. Since Re is, like Horus, a sun-god we might just as well have here Horus and Thoth as the *rḥwi*. (3)

In an Edfu text (4) Thoth is called 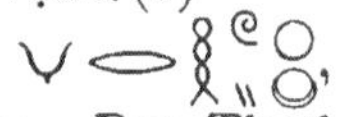, where the determinatives point to sun and moon. But Thoth could not be a "judge" of himself, and we need not concern ourselves greatly with Ptolemaic determinatives. (5)

There are not wanting in ancient Egyptian literature passages which represent Set as a beneficent and friendly deity. He is not always the enemy of Horus. This is true, for instance, in Pyr. 473, and in those ancient texts in which he cooperates with Horus for the benefit of Osiris. As god of Ombos Set is often as kind, and as helpful as any other deity. (6) He often appears as a friend of Horus. (7) It is obvious, then, that the three divinities Horus, Set and Thoth do not appear always in three distinct rôles in ancient Egyptian theology. Their characters are not always self-consistent, and, in the ancient legends they are represented as variously as the backgrounds of those legends required.

As theology developed, and political situations changed, Set came to be, less and less, the mere god of Ombos, and, more and more, the symbol of evil. He is gradually excluded from the ritual, and ritual honours and functions which had been his are gradually handed over to Thoth. Thus, for instance, in the coronation-ceremonies of ancient Egypt Set played an important part as representative of one great di-

(1) Cf. *Mission*, 14, p. 63, for parallel.

(2) The same text is found in an incorrect form *Book of the Dead* 178, 15—17.

(3) For Re = Horus, cf. Pyr. 956.

(4) Edfu R. I. 297.

(5) What is the meaning of the text, *Urgötterlied* El-Chargeh (Roeder, *Wb.*) I. 24, 25: "Horus, whom the *Rḥwi* and the Sisters raise"? Are the *Rḥwi* here Thoth and Anubis — Horus being identified with Osiris?

(6) Cf. Pyr. 370.

(7) Vid. Pyr. 141. Cf. Pyr. 1612: 1613.

vision of Egypt. When, through political and religious change, Set became "Lord of the desert" he naturally fell out of the ritual of coronation. His place was taken by Thoth. In 50 lists of divinities collected by Schenke (*Amon-Ra*, p. 124—127) Thoth appears eleven times, Set eighteen times. When we look closer at these lists we find that Set has been forced out of his place seven times by Thoth, twice by Anubis, and eight times by Horus. In the primitive forms of these lists Thoth would, then, have appeared only four times, and Set would have appeared thirty five times. Schenke thinks that the exclusion of Set began in the XVIIIth Dynasty. Doubtless, political reasons had much to do with it. Set's unpopularity seems to be connected somehow with the occupation of Northern Egypt by the Hyksos; and the great number of Thoth-names to be found among the rulers of the XVIIIth Dynasty, suggests that the cult of Thoth was important in the movement which shook off the domination of the Hyksos. Horus and Set, the gods of the "Two Lands" which made up Egypt, were necessarily the chief figures in the early ritual of coronation. When Set was excluded, his place was naturally taken by the constant companion of Horus (= Sun-god), the moon-god Thoth, the Lord of sacred ceremonial.

We may here bring together briefly the results of our inquiry into the position of Thoth in the legends of Osiris and Horus.

1. Thoth has no place in the primitive saga of the vegetation-god, Osiris.

2. In the developed, anthropomorphic, form of that saga Thoth is an important *dramatis persona.* His place in the drama is due partly to his own primitive character, and, partly, to the proximity of Thoth's shrine in the Delta to the home of the Osirian legend. The main features of Thoth's character in the legend seem to be largely individual and peculiar to him out of all relation with the Osirian religion. But there is no need to deny that the activity of Thoth in the Osirian drama may have helped to define his character more clearly for the people, and to extend his worship throughout Egypt.

3. In the older form of the legend of Horus and Set Thoth plays an essential part as guardian of the .

This office naturally belonged to him as a primitive moon-god. A deity protective of light was a necessary figure in the ancient sun-saga of Egypt.

4. In its developed form the Horus-legend has become entangled with the Osirian story. Thoth here appears either as arbitrator between two political rivals, Horus and Set, or as the active partisan and ally of one of the two. The texts which represent Thoth as an ally of Horus seem to be strongly influenced by the saga of Re and the Apophis. Features from the legend of Osiris and Set are also here present. The position of Thoth is further described in this developed and complex form of the legend of Horus as that of a judge in a suit between Horus and Set (as in the Pyramid texts), or as that of an advocate defending Horus in the case (so Plutarch), or as that of a wise friend of the contending parties who seeks to reconcile them. Here, as in the older form of the Horus-legend, Thoth still appears at times as an astral deity: and sometimes he seems to represent a political power, allied, at one time with Horus, and at another, with Set, in the pre-dynastic battles of Egypt. (1)

(1) The position of Thoth in the various legends that centre round the Eye of Horus is described and explained in a manner differing greatly from that of the text in Junker's remarkable book, *Die Onurislegende* (Wien, 1917). The text was already written when that work reached the present writer. Much, however, of the new material that Junker's work supplies has been examined for the purposes of this essay. Junker's work is so original in its method, and valuable in its results that it is sure to become an indispensable reference-book for every student.

Chapter III.

Thoth and the Enneads of Heliopolis.

The theology of the Pyramid texts is largely the product of a fusion of local cults with the theology of Osiris. Of those local cults the most important is that of the ancient solar shrine, Heliopolis. In the theology of Heliopolis itself we can trace clearly the inweaving of the Osirian saga with the local worship of Re-Atum. This inweaving appears most obviously, perhaps, in the Heliopolitan lists of the great gods, and, especially, in the list which is known as the Great Ennead of Heliopolis. In this list Osiris himself appears as a member of the family of the Heliopolitan sun-god, and Isis and Set appear with him in the same group. Further, we find that incidents of the Osirian drama have come to be localised in Heliopolis. This is true, for instance, of the great trial in which Osiris is declared victorious by the gods. (1) In Heliopolis the court is held: and it is the Heliopolitan gods who declare Osiris "triumphant". At times it would seem as if Osiris had become a sun-god at Heliopolis, just as he became 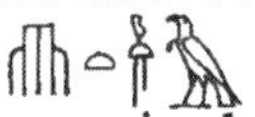 in Abydos. In the Pyramid texts the dead king, conceived as Osiris, is often represented in the guise of Osiris. It is to be noted that Haroëris has no place in the ancient Heliopolitan Ennead. (2) He was himself a sun-god, and did not need a place in the Ennead of a foreign solar shrine: In being he was really identical with Re-Atum.

(1) As suggested above, this trial is a late development of the Osirian story. For apparent references in the Pyramid texts to the trial see Pyr. 956—960, and cf. Pyr. 316—318 and Pyr. 1521—1523.

(2) Plutarch puts the birth of the "ancient Horus" before that of the gods of the Osirian cycle. Horus was a heaven-god prior to becoming a sungod. Whether the ancient war-god in falcon shape was primitively a heaven-god or sun-god is not certain: he also was called Horus. Possibly there is here the identification of a local war-god with the heaven-god or sun-god.

We have now to consider the relation of Thoth to the Heliopolitan deities.

Many attempts have been made to discover the primitive nucleus of the Heliopolitan Ennead. Schenke (1) regards that nucleus as consisting of the sun-god with Shu, Tefenet, Geb, Nut, Osiris, Isis, Nephthys, Horus. Assuming that we have in Heliopolis an Ennead resulting from a combination of Osirian and Heliopolitan theologies, the Ennead would be:

Sun-god
Shu Tefenet
Geb Nut
Osiris, Isis, Set, Nephthys.

Horus would have here no place — except, of course, in so far as he might be identical with the sun-god himself. Thoth is not included in the list. (2) His appearance in the "Little Ennead" of Heliopolis is of no great importance except as illustrating the supplementing tendencies of Egyptian theology. The deities who appear in the Ennead (apart from Re-Atum) do not appear there as local deities. They have been quite removed from the surroundings of their local cults. Osiris is here no longer the god of Dedu or Abydos; Set is no longer the local deity of Ombos. On the other hand, the ancient deities who are not included in the Great Ennead are more tenacious of their local individuality at the time when the Great Ennead was first devised. This is particularly true of Thoth. He retains his connection with a particular local shrine much longer than the Osirian gods of the older Ennead.

It is possible, and perhaps likely, that the Enneadic grouping was not a primitive feature of Heliopolitan theology. It has been maintained recently by Capart (3) that the grouping of deities in primitive Heliopolis was ogdoadic. He bases his view on the Pyramid text 317, and endeavours to show that the primitive grouping in Heliopolis was one of four

(1) *Amon-Ra*, p. 123 f.

(2) Was Thoth a figure in Osirian drama before the assimilation of Osirian cult with that of Heliopolis? It is interesting to note that Pyramid lists of the gods which begin with Osiris and Set do not, as a rule, include Thoth. Thoth goes more naturally with *Ḥr wr*. See Pyr. 826 and 832.

(3) *Recueil* 33, p. 64 f.

male deities over against four female divinities. Pyr. 317 suggests, according to Capart, this grouping:

Tefen — Tefenet
Nu — Nut
Osiris — Isis
Re — Nephthys.

Above the eight, but in a transcendence which excluded him from being grouped with them, stood the local god, Atum. We know that an arrangement of this kind existed in Thoth's city *Ḫmnw*, the "City of the Eight"; and Capart suspects that the Heliopolitan Ogdoad was formed under the influence of the ancient Eight of *Ḫmnw*. (1) If this view of Capart were to be accepted, then not merely Horus, Anubis, and Thoth, but Shu, Set, and Geb would be excluded from the most ancient Heliopolitan grouping of gods. Capart has, further, endeavoured to show how his postulated Ogdoad has developed into the Ennead of the Pyramid texts. His theory is ingenious. Re was identified, in the course of time, with Atum, and in the place of Re thus vacated was put Set (— another solar god, according to Capart). The god of heaven, Nu, was next replaced by the earth-god Geb. Shu, as the son of Re, must follow Re immediately: thus he takes the place of Tefen. The resulting Ennead would be:

Re (= Atum)
Shu (instead of Tefen) — Tefenet.
Geb (instead of Nu) — Nut.
Osiris — Isis.
Set (instead of Re) — Nephthys.

The transcendence of Atum having disappeared by his identification with Re, the Ogdoad necessarily became an Ennead. (2)

(1) There seems to have been variety of opinion in Egypt as to the first pair of emanations from the sun-god. They could be Shu-Tefenet; Tefen-Tefenet, Ḥu-Sia, or Ḥike-Sia, or Heart-Tongue (= Thoth-Horus). Cf. PSBA, vol. 38, p. 92 f. In the fusion of theologies this variety afterwards led to strange identifications. Some of these will be discussed later. The possibility that Shu, in certain aspects, might be somehow identified with Ḥu, Ḥike, and Thoth would easily lead to the passing of influences to and fro between Heliopolis and Ḫmunu. Note that in the "grosser" theories the first two emanations are male and female: in the more "intellectual" theories the two first emanations might be male (or sexless).

(2) Capart's theory rouses grave misgivings. How could Osiris and Isis be taken into an Ogdoad without Set? The colligation of Re and Nephthys (as "Lord

The contrary view, that the Ogdoad of Hermopolis is due to the influence of Heliopolis, and that the Ennead is primitive in the latter shrine, is older and more popular. Maspero has collected the evidence for it. (1) We are interested in the general question only in so far as it affects Thoth's position among the ancient gods. In the general obscurity of the problem one thing is clear — that Thoth does not stand in the ancient groupings of gods in any family relationship to the gods of Heliopolis. This supports the view already put forward that Thoth is not primitively connected with the Osirian legend. Yet, on the other hand, Thoth's relations with the Heliopolitan Great Ennead are close and that, even in very ancient texts. His relations with the chief god of Heliopolis — Re-Atum — are, as we shall see, especially intimate. It may be that the inclusion of Thoth in the Lesser Ennead, and his close connection with the gods of the Greater Ennead other than Re-Atum, are somehow conditioned by his assumption as a *persona* into the more developed form of the Osirian drama.

The Book of the Dead has made us familiar with the idea of a trial of Osiris held before the gods of Heliopolis. (2) The same trial seems to be referred to in the Pyramid texts, (3) and every student of Egyptian theology knows how the idea of this trial dominates the entire religious speculation of Egypt. The precise points at issue in the trial cannot be ascertained. In the result Osiris was declared , and was made one of the divine judges. He even became the president of the court. There is, obviously, much confusion of thought here. Possibly the whole story of the trial was elaborated to show that Osiris, as Prince, or Greatest, of the Dead, was subjected to the trial after death which every mortal must endure; in all directions Osiris should serve as the model of all men. Every man of Egypt besought for himself from the gods the verdict which Osiris had obtained. In the trial of Osiris some

of the Temple" and "Lady of the Temple") is very hypothetical. Instead of building up a new theory on Pyr. 317, it would be much more reasonable to suppose that Tefen in that text is simply an epithet of Shu, the son of Re.

(1) *Rec.*, vol. 24, p. 169 f. *La myth. ég.*, p. 244.

(2) Nav., *Totb.*, c. 1, 7—10.

(3) Pyr. 1521—1523.

charge was made against him by Set. Against this charge, apparently, Osiris was brilliantly defended by Thoth, so that the latter received for himself the title "He who made Osiris victorious against his foes."

We find Thoth active in still another great lawsuit pleaded before the Ennead in Heliopolis. The parties are here Horus and Set, and the trial is held in the Hall of the Two Maʿets. (1) It is to this lawsuit, probably, that Plutarch refers when he speaks of the successful pleading of the advocate Hermes (Thoth) on behalf of Horus against Set. The details of the divine lawsuits in which Thoth was engaged were thought out after the model of the high courts in Egypt. It has thus come about that several of Thoth's most frequently recurring epithets are connected with features of legal practice in Ancient Egypt. It will help, not merely to explain the development of Thoth's cult, but also to illustrate the methods of Egyptian speculation in religion, to indicate here some of the titles which were devised for Thoth because of his work in defence of Osiris and Horus before the Ennead of Heliopolis.

a) In the lawsuits in presence of the gods Thoth apparently acted as secretary of the court, and recorder of its verdict. This is implied in his familiar title 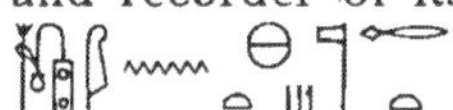, *i. e.* "Verdict-recorder for the Great Ennead". (2) Other titles betraying the same legal origin are "Verdict-recorder for the Lord of eternity", (3) "Verdict-recorder of the Lord of Maʿet." (4) "Writer of Maʿet" is a constantly recurring epithet of Thoth in the Book of the Dead. (5) In the texts of the

(1) Cf. Pyr. 770: cf. Pyr. 317. Pyr. 957 refers to a decision spoken by Geb in the *Ḥt śr* in a trial in which Set was accused of having stricken down Osiris. In Pyr. 1556 there is reference to the verdict in this, or another similar trial: Set is 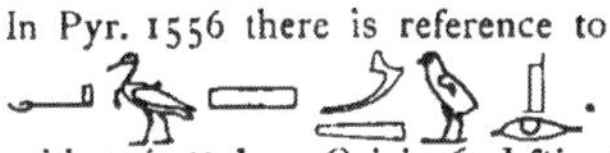. From this trial and verdict Thoth derived the epithet *śmꜣʿ ḫrw Osiris (r ḫftiw-f)*.

(2) Karnak, L. D. III, 175 c.: Turin no. 173; Edfu R. I. 297.

(3) *Ssꜣ mꜣʿ.t n nb nḥḥ*, Turin 912. Cf. the Bk. of Dd. of M. K. ch. 17 (*Mission* I, 170) where the dead describes himself as "Scribe of the Lord of All" (*i. e.* as Thoth, whose place he takes).

(4) Cat. du Musée du Caire: Daressy, *Cercueils*, Pl. XV.

(5) Cf. *Totb.* Nav. 182, 2. In Pyr. 1520—1521 he appears also as moon and as *nb mꜣʿ.t*. In Pyr. 1522/3 Thoth is the herald who announces the decision of the gods in regard to Osiris: the gods of heaven and earth, of south and north,

Graeco-Roman period he is very often referred to as "Verdict-recorder (or, 'Writer of Maʿet') for the Ennead" (*sšꜣ mꜣʿ·t n psḏ·t*). (1)

(b) A somewhat similar title of Thoth is 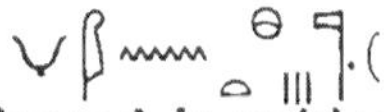. (2) Thoth puts the verdicts or decrees of the Ennead in writing:

---

of east and west rejoice, 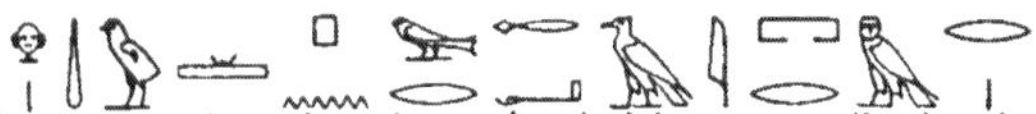  . He not merely writes down the decision or verdict but he publishes it to heaven and earth.

With *nb mꜣʿ.t* cf. the title given to Thoth in Edfu R. I. 56 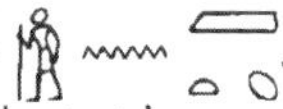. In Philae (Phot. 995) Tiberius presents *mꜣʿ.t* to Thoth, and in the text he says: "Receive *mꜣʿ.t* so as to gladden your heart, for she is the food of Your Majesty ever." *Mꜣʿ.t* in the same place is spoken of as the food which Thoth's *kꜣ* loves, and Thoth is described as *nb mꜣʿ.t ḥtp ḥr mꜣʿ.t*: 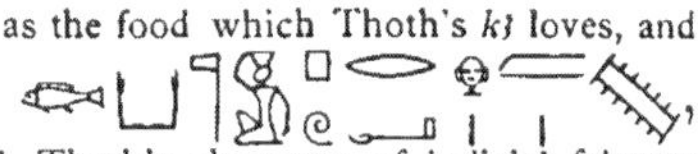, "his abomination is to be unfair (a partisan)". Thoth's character of judicial fairness is most likely a development from his rôle in the Osirian trial, and then from his rôle in the judgment-scene generally.

(1) Cf. Edfu. R. I. 297 etc., etc. In the text I have taken *sšꜣ mꜣʿ.t* as "Verdict-recorder". This sense is not certain. But it does seem clear in the titles quoted in the text that maʿet means more than "truth": the word seems to have a forensic sense, something like יָשָׁר, which itself stands close to צַדִּיק. Maʿet can be *done* as well as *spoken*. Maʿet, in the sense of "just" (τὸ δίκαιον), is an appropriate name for a fair verdict. Maʿet appears often as goddess of justice and hence the officials of Ancient Egypt often bear the title "priest of maʿet". The higher law-officers advertised their loyalty to maʿet by wearing an image or amulet of the goddess (cf. Cairo Wb. no. 73 where an official speaks of wearing on his breast a figure of maʿet). We may assume that, for the Egyptians, as for ourselves, that which is legally prescribed is, at least in theory, the just and fair. Hence to carry out what is legally prescribed is to accomplish maʿet, to fulfil all the ritual laws in the divine cult would be a particularly perfect performance of maʿet. As including what is prescribed for cult maʿet would correspond to *ritus* (*ritus sacrificiorum, ritus sacrificii*: cf. זִבְחֵי צֶדֶק) = what is of precept, and to θεσμός (particularly if determined by θεῖος or ἱερός). Maʿet can also include what is truthful in word or expression, since men can *claim* true speech from their fellows. Since the forensic reference is sufficiently clear in maʿet, it is natural that the great court in Heliopolis should stand under the patronage of the two maʿets (cf. Pyr. 317). Possibly the two maʿets symbolise the union of N. and S. Egypt under a single Supreme Court. It is possible, however, too, that the dual in the case merely symbolises the ideal fairness of the justice administered in Heliopolis. In this sense of intensified fairness the dual is used as a singular in the votive inscription of Abydos 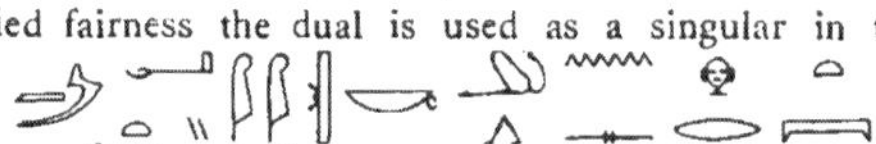 "thy justice hath reached unto heaven" (line 61/62).

(2) Cf. Thebes, Tomb of Userhat, Sethe 13, 17: Tomb of *Imn.m.ib* Champ. Not. descr. 851. Book of Dead c. 30 (Ani. 3).

but he is more than a mere recorder: he gives judgment with the court:  (Luxor: Court of Ramses II, Sethe 2, 105) — he gives his judgment along with the Ennead. This activity has given him some special names in the Graeco-Roman period: 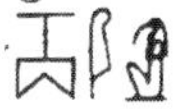 (Mar., *Dend.* II, 74 a),  (Mar., *Dend.* II, 62 b). (1)

(c) Through his activity in the court of the Ennead Thoth became the scribe of the Ennead, in general. Thus, probably, is to be explained his title in Anastasi V, 9, 2 — "the letter-writer of the Ennead (2)  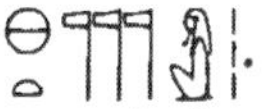.

It is to be noted that all these titles belong to the period of the New Kingdom, and to later times. As the details of the legendary trials of Osiris and Horus belong to the early period, it is likely that the legal epithets of Thoth which arose out of his connection with those trials, were drawn from the traditional legal procedure of Ancient Egypt. We find, in fact, in the texts of the Old and Middle Kingdoms abundance of legal titles analogous to those of Thoth, ascribed to important personages in the State.

We have seen that the court in which the trial of Osiris was held, and in which also, probably, the case between Horus and Set was tried, was the Great Hall of Heliopolis — probably the Supreme Court of Ancient Egypt. In the texts of the Old Kingdom the Supreme Court is called the *Ḏꜣḏꜣ·t wr·t,* (3) and the court in which Osiris was tried is called by the same name in the Book of the Dead (*Totb.* 18, 3). This shows how the general idea of the Osirian trial is dominated, from the beginning, by the thought of actual legal procedure in ancient Egypt. When we examine the titles of ancient

(1) This title may be connected, of course, with Thoth's functions as arbitrator between Horus and Set.

(2) Cf. the title in a Theban tomb (Gardiner, *Topographical Catalogue,* p. 18) 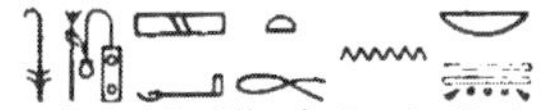 = "royal scribe of the despatches of the Lord of the 2 Lands". Thoth is similarly the despatch-writer of the Ennead. Cf. Karnak, *A text of Ramses IV,* Sethe, 22, 31—34 where Thoth is represented as appearing  "in the Hall bearing the royal document".

(3) Cairo 61, 65, 66 etc.

dignitaries, we find among them not a few which stand in the closest relation to those above identified as forensic titles of Thoth. Such title are  (Cairo, 61, 65, 66, 181, 377, Statue of O. K.).   (Cairo, 181, O. K.). The *wsḫ.t ʿȝ.t*, the Hall of the Supreme Court at Heliopolis, often appears in titles of the Old and Middle Kingdoms. In Mar., Mastabas D. 19, E a man appears as a "priest of Maʿet", and "leader of the Hall". Thoth is not leader, or president of the "Great Hall", but he is the "Scribe of Maʿet in the Hall", he is the chief scribe or recorder (the *ḫrp sšȝ*) in the Great Hall, and "Scribe of Maʿet for the Ennead". Thoth is looked on as an official of the Ennead in the same way as an ancient Egyptian dignitary would have been an official of the Pharaoh. (1)

Very probably, then, the great trial of Osiris, and the details connected with it, were modelled largely on the legal customs of ancient Egypt. Even in the later periods of Egyptian religion we find this method of constructing the divine on the analogy of every day civil life in Egypt still steadily at work. We can see this from such epithets of Thoth as 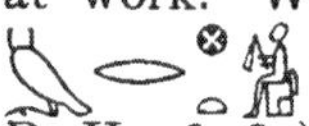 given to him in the Graeco-Roman period (Edfu R. II, 73; 80). Thus also we explain other late epithets of our god:  (Philae, Phot. 854),  (Mar., Dend. III, 55 b; Edfu R. II, 73 etc.). *Sȝb šbḫti* is, as is well known, a familiar legal title in the O. K. (2)

Through the pictorial representations of the Judgment-scene — which scene is, of course, closely connected with the Osirian legend, — Thoth has come to be associated with the weighing of the heart. Thus he has received the title 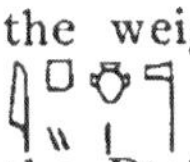 (cf. *Totb.* c. 30, Ani 3). The title is very frequent in the Ptolemaic period. It is often written with the ibis-deter-

(1) Cf. for instance the titles of a man of the XIXth Dyn. recorded in Louvre III 36, Inv. 3132: he is *sšȝ mȝʿ.t m pr mȝʿ.t*, and *sšȝ šʿt r bw ḫr niswt*. A dignitary at Gizeh (L. D. II, 34, g) is *sȝb šbḫti* and *wr dwȝ pr Ḏḥwti*.

(2) *Sȝb šbḫti* is a well-known legal title in the O. K. Cf. *Catal. gén. des antiq. ég.*, vol. LIII, no. 46. Again cf. no. 61 (*ibid.*): here the man is *sȝb imi rȝ sšȝ ḫrp sšȝ m wsḫ.t ʿȝ.t*: again, no. 65 where we read the titles *ḫrp sšȝ, sȝb imi rȝ sšȝ m ḏȝḏȝ.t wr.t.*

minative (L. D. IV, 76 e, Düm., *Baugeschichte*, 43) — appearing thus as a name of the god. (1) In the scenes of the Judgment Thoth appears in two chief rôles: on the one hand, as ibis-headed god who weighs the heart of the dead, and, on the other, as ape seated on the tongue of the balance. In this second rôle Thoth is described as (Edfu R. II, 31) "He that sits on the balance". (2) This position of Thoth, as ape on the tongue of the balance, fully explains his epithet : that epithet is on the same level as .

(1) Cf. Mar. Dend. III, 81 e, 61 a: II, 13 b: 71 b: Düm., *Histor. Inschr.* II, 57 a.

(2) Cf. Vienna, Kunsthistorisches Museum. Sarkophagus Saal I, no. XX. See also Lacau, *Text rél. Recueil*, no. 34, p. 180.

Edfu R. II. 31 calls the Pharaoh "the copy of *Ìstn* (= Thoth), who knoweth (*rḫ*) the balance". Pap. Rhind I, 7 b. 9 calls Thoth "Lord of the Scales". appears as a title of dignity, L. D. III 26, 1 c. Tomb of , Thebes. Anubis, from his activity in the judgment-scene, was called (*Catal. du Musée du Caire.* Daressy, *Cercueils*, p. 129). Since Anubis weighs the heart of Osiris along with Thoth, he is called in the Pyr. texts (Pyr. 1523, cf. Pyr. 1287). Thus, as we have already said, it is obvious that the Judgment-scene was pictorially represented at a very early period. From all this it appears how unacceptable is Loret's explanation of Thoth's epithet *tḫ*. He says (*Bulletin de l'Institut fr. d'arch. or.*, vol. 3, p. 18): "Thoth, après avoir été tout simplement «le dieu en forme d'ibis» (de = ϭⲧⲉⲱϣⲓ, ⲧⲓⲃⲓ, grue) est devenu le dieu de la justesse et de la rectitude, par suite d'un rapprochement de son nom avec celui du fil à plomb de la balance, d'où l'orthographe du nom de l'ibis." As a matter of fact has nothing to do with "ibis"; it is merely an epithet of Thoth as ape that sits on the balance. *Tḫn*, not *tḫ*, is "ibis". For the ape of the balance cf. Harris, I, 45, 11, 12: "I made for thee a balance: Thoth sits thereon — as great and venerable ape." Cf. also the Kuban Stele, 14—15, and Lexa *Totb.* XIII (Spiegelberg, *Demotische Studien*). In Lexa's text the demotic gives as the name of one of the porters "opener of hearts" (cf. Nav., *Totb.*, 125, 42—44), while the corresponding hieratic text has the "*tḫ* of Ma'et". These two epithets belong to Thoth, and the apparent want of agreement of the hieratic and demotic here is easily explained in view of what has been said above.

Chapter IV.

Thoth and Re in the Solar barque.

Thoth, as has been shown, stands with other ancient deities, such as Ptah, Min, *Ḥr wr*, Neit Anubis etc., outside the primitive Ennead of Heliopolis. Yet it cannot be denied that there are very close relationships expressed, even in very early texts, between Thoth and the Heliopolitan sun-god.

In the Book of the Dead of the N. K. period Thoth often appears as secretary of Re (or of Osiris, thought of as sun-god); and he constantly appears with the sun-god in the solar barque (1) — generally accompanied by Maʿet. Thoth is therefore a companion of the chief god of Egypt, when the latter goes on his administrative journeys. It is not unlikely that the Pyramid texts which speak of a "Scribe of the divine book at the right of Re" refer to the presence and function of Thoth in the solar barque. The Pap. Harris, I, 6—8, refers to the "writings of *Ḫmnw* the accountant of Re-Horus of the horizon". Thoth is also spoken of as "Re's scribe of Maʿet" (Thebes, Tomb of 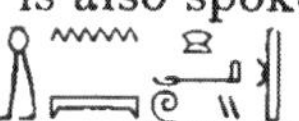 L. D. Text III, 299) = he that records the judgments of Re. We find Thoth performing a similar function for the sun-god Atum. Thus in the Votive inscription of Abydos: "Atum decreed unto thee his own length of life: Thoth wrote it (*i. e.* the decree) down, beside the Lord of All (*i. e.* Re-Atum)".

According to Pyr. 955 the Scribe of Re is dismissed in order to make way for the dead king: and Pyr. 1146 makes

(1) Cf. Nav., *Totb.*, c. 69, 11—12: Turin Pap. (P. and R.) 136 etc. In the funerary texts of the M. K. there is a formula by which the dead may become a scribe of Re (Lacau, *Text rél. Rec.* XXXI (1909), p. 10. 11). When the dead becomes, at the same time, scribe of Osiris, the identity of Osiris and Re is implied. Note the strange N. K. passage Leyden I, 346, 2, 11—12 in which Set is spoken of as being in the prow of Re's ship.

the dead Pharaoh the "Scribe of the divine book". (1) Probably the "Scribe of Re" in Pyr. 955 is identical with the "Scribe of the divine book" in Pyr. 1146; and the general sense is that the Pharaoh becomes identified with Thoth as moon-god, and assistant of Re. (2) This is implied also in Pyr. 490—491, according to which the dead king becomes the *Dḥ3i* in the prow of Re's ship who seals the decrees of Re, sends out Re's messengers, and does in general as he is ordered to do.

Pyr. 267—268 transforms the king into "Sia (the bearer of the divine book) at the right hand of Re". (3) It may, probably, be assumed that the bearer of the divine book is one with the scribe of that book. But who is Sia? In the Book of the Dead (Nav., *Totb.*, c. 174, 18. 19 [A f]) the dead speaks thus: "I am he who declares what is in the heart of the Great one on the feast of the *inś*-garment: (4) I am Sia at the right hand of Re who makes *snk* the heart of him who stands before the *tpḥ·t* of Nu." Sia is here again at the right of Re, and his functions in regard to Re are, probably, concerned with, or determined by, the "divine book". The meaning of *snk* is not clear, but the whole passage recalls Pyramid texts like 962 and 963, where Thoth beheads the king's enemies, and cuts out their hearts (cf. Pyr. 1999). In the late periods there is no doubt about the identity of Sia and Thoth — Sia being freely used in the Greek period as a name of Thoth. Further, the "Scribe of the divine book" is also clearly

(1) Cf. the prayer *Totb.* 94, 1—4 (Nav.) for ink-bottle and palette for the dead. The dead is to be equipped as a scribe.

(2) The title "Scribe of the divine book" was a title of the chief *Cher ḥeb* in the O. K. Cf. Sethe, *Imhotep*, p. 17: Erman, *Westcar* I, 21. Cf. also Davies, *Der el-Gebrawi* II, pl. XIII, XXVIII etc. We know that the "Scribes of the divine book" were wont to recite the sacred formulae of the ritual, like the *Cher ḥeb*. In Brugsch, *Drei Festkalender*, Plate VII, 7—9, 14—15, 19 it is the "Scribe of the divine book" who recites the "Praises" (the *Dua* = one of a series of ritual books). Cf. the O. K. title  (L. D. II, 97 a, IVth Dyn.).

(3) Students of the History of Religions will remember the Stoic (and the earlier Orphic-Pythagorean) idea of the moon as the abode of the blessed dead.

(4) A *nb inś* is referred to *Totb.* c. 99, 4 (Nav.). *Nb.t inś* is an epithet of Sechmet, Isis, and Hathor in the Greek period. *Nb inś* means bearer of the *inś* garment: it was some kind of garment worn (by the priests) on certain feasts. — Cf. Pyr. 268 where the same text as in *Totb.* 174, 18—19 occurs.

identified in late texts with Thoth. Pap. Salt, 825 VII, 2—4 enumerates the officials of the *Per ʿonkh* (= Library): among them is the "Scribe of the divine book" and a gloss in the text adds: "he is Thoth". Since we find that in many Pyramid texts (1) the dead is identified with Thoth, and since the identity of Sia and Thoth in the later periods makes probable their identity also in the early texts, we need scarcely hesitate to take the scribe whom the dead displaces in Pyr. 955 as Thoth.

The idea of the "divine book" seems to have been borrowed from the methods of government administration in Egypt. Just as the Pharaoh received reports from his ministers and various officials, and just as the details of all administrative work in Egypt were carefully recorded, so must the king of the world, the sun-god, have official reports, and official records. (2) Thoth, as the friend, and trustworthy minister and scribe of Re, kept for him the great book of government (the "divine book") in which every detail of Re's empire, and its administration would be carefully noted. (3) The book would not be primarily a "Doomsbook", or "Book of fate", but only an institution belonging to the practical side of Re's world-government. The presence of Thoth and Maʿet together in the solar barque is symbolical, probably, of the methods of Re's government. Maʿet denotes the justice and fairness of Re's rule; and Thoth symbolises its business-like and efficient character. (4)

---

(1) Cf. 130: 535: 709: 1233: 1237: 1305: 1507: 1725: 2150.

(2) Note the title of Thoth in Harris, I, 6—8 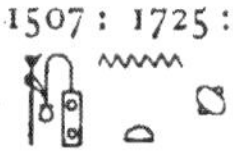 of Re — accountant of Re.

(3) Breasted (*Rel. and thought*, p. 17) notes how easily the qualities of the earthly kingship of Pharaoh were transferred to Re.

(4) For Thoth and Maʿet in the solar barque see Nav., *Totb.* c. 130, 24—26, and often elsewhere. In the Greek period Thoth's presence in the solar barque is looked upon mainly as intended for the protection of Re against his enemies. With this function of Thoth is connected his title "Great in magic in the barque of millions" (*Totb.* 182, 8). The title suggests the power of Thoth's magic as against the Apophis, and other foes of the sun-god. The Book of the Apophis (Brit. Mus. 10188, 25, 15 : 31, 20) says that it is by this *hike* (magic) that Thoth defeats the Apophis-dragon. Cf. *Horus-Myth* (Naville), Pl. VIII. In the tomb of Rameses, Thebes

It may be that Thoth's confidential position as minister and chief scribe in the government of Re, is due partly to the naive sentiment that the moon is a representative of Re, a sort of *locum tenens* for the sun-god. Thus the two great astral deities would naturally, between them, rule the world. We shall see in the following chapters how the idea of their common government of the universe led to certain interesting developments in the theological speculation of Egypt.

Ma'et is called " in the barque of millions". Piehl, *Inscr.* I, 99 η. This seems to imply that Thoth wore a figure of Ma'et as amulet in the solar barque. Cf. what was said above about the legal officials of the O. K.

Chapter V.

Thoth as lunar deity.

Plutarch represents Hermes as winning, in a game of chess, a certain amount of light, or a certain number of short periods of light, from Selene, the moon-goddess. The light or light-periods which Hermes (Thoth) thus won, he put together to form supernumary or epagomenal days of the Egyptian year. The story brings Thoth into close connection with the moon, and is probably a genuine echo of the Egyptian speculation which regarded Thoth as primarily a lunar god.

In Egyptian texts Thoth's relationship with the moon appears to be of two kinds. In a great number of texts he is represented as being practically one with the astral body — with the moon itself. In a great many other texts he appears, not as the moon itself, but as the guardian, or protector, of the moon. In our discussion of the legend of Horus and Set we have met several instances of this second kind of relationship of Thoth with the moon. It will be convenient here to examine in the first place the texts in which Thoth is treated as one with the luminary that rules the night.

a) Thoth as identical with the moon.

The later texts are quite clear as to the lunar character of Thoth, and we can work back from the clearer texts to the less obvious and suggestive texts of the older periods.

Every student of Egyptian is familiar with the constantly recurring representation of an ape bearing on his head a lunar crescent. (1) The ape is Thoth, and the crescent identifies him with the moon. The crescent-bearing ape is found

(1) Cf. Naville, *Goschen* 5, 1 : Thebes, Tomb of  Abschrift Sethe 17, 105 etc etc.

in every kind of text in periods subsequent to the N. K. He is often adressed as "Lunar-Thoth". Thus, for instance, in the Turin Pap. (P. and R. 25, 3 f.):

Hail O Lunar-Thoth who enlightenest the Duat in the necropolis!
Hail to thee Lunar-Thoth, thou self-engendered, the unknown!

Renewal of south and vigour are besought at times for the king, so that he may become like Moon-Thoth. Thus Seshat says to Sethos I: "Thou shalt renew thy youth; thou shalt flourish again like Iooḥ-Thoth when he is a child" (Mar. *Ab.* I, 51 a, 32—33: cf. Mar. *Ab.* II, 7).

We find that in the temples of Iooḥ there was usually a special cult of Thoth. To this a passage in the Book of the Dead (Nav., *Totb.*, c. 80, 8) refers: "I have made provision for Thoth in the house of Iooḥ." The identity between Thoth and the moon which is here implied is, at times, much more clearly expressed in the Book of the Dead. In ch. 131, 1—2 (Lepsius) the dead describes himself as "Re that shines in night", and the context makes it clear that the sun of the night is no other than Thoth. The idea that the dead becomes Thoth, or the moon, is often expressed. The deceased "traverses the heaven [like Re], and speeds through it like Thoth" (Nav., *Totb.*, c. 178, 20, according to A a). The same is said of the dead king in the Pyramid text 130:

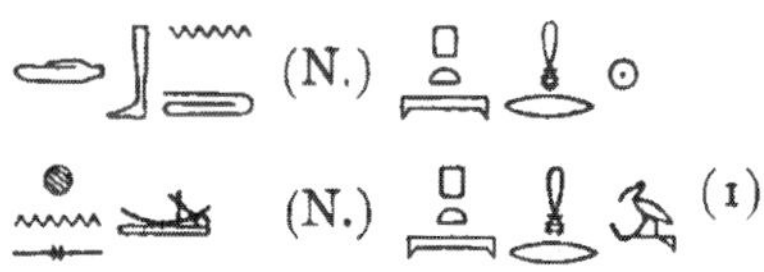

The dead Pharaoh becomes one with the sun-god Re by day, and with the moon-god Thoth by night. The verb which describes the movement of Thoth as moon underlies the

(1) Cf. the Chons-text in Edfu (R. I. 269)  . The texts vary between  and 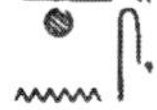. In Pyr. 920 the dead king is called  and 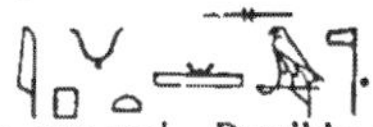. In the immediately preceding text he is identified with the sun-god. Possibly the *wni* and *wpi* here symbolise Thoth as moon-god. Thoth's chief cult-centre was *wnw*, and one of his chief positions was that of *wp nṯrwi* or *wp šnwi*.

familiar name of the Theban moon-god, Chons — "the wanderer" (the ירח of the Hebrews).

There are extant a great number of votive stelae dedicated in the N. K. to , (1) "Moon-Thoth". On one of these (Hanover no. 20) Thoth is represented as moon between two astral deities, with the legend:

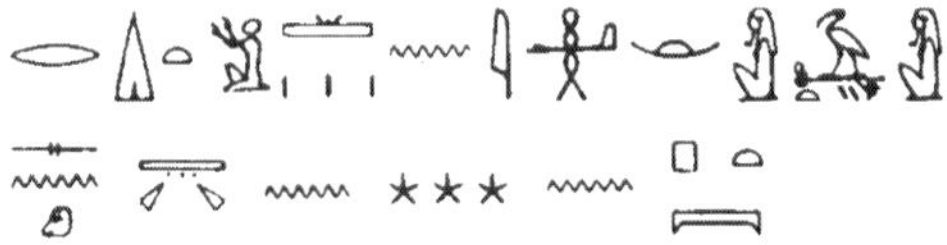

"Thanksgiving to Lunar-Thoth: veneration to the stars of heaven" — a clear recognition of Thoth's astral character. With this compare the inscription on the Turin stela no. 157: (2) over a lunar barque is the text: 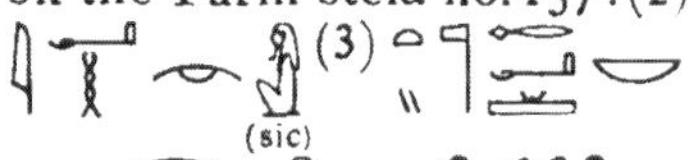 . Under the barque we read:   "Praising of Shu (= Sun-god), veneration of Iooḥ-Thoth". The rubric Brit. Mus. 933: "When Thoth and the stars are invisible" points to the same astral character of the god. A text from Karnak of the Amosis period (*Wb.*, no. 11; *Urk.* IV, 20) conveys the same conception: "Honour him like Re",  — "Revere him like Iooḥ-Thoth".

The Graeco-Roman period furnishes abundant evidence for the identification of Thoth and Iooḥ. In innumerable ritual and other scenes of the period the ibis-god (and often the ape-god) is shown wearing the lunar crescent; and the texts of the period freely identify, or confuse, the two divinities. Thoth is described, for instance, in Kasr-el-Agouz (4) as "Thoth in Hermonthis , moon resplendent in the heavens". In Dendereh (5) we find the com-

(1) Cf. Brit. Mus. 807. (2) *Rec.* 11, 168 IV.

(3) Mistake for .

(4) Mallet, *Kasr el-Agouz*, p. 82.  ought to be .

(5) Brugsch, *Thes.* I, 37, 27. "Bull of the heavens" is a well-known epithet of the moon. Osiris is called the "bull who is renewed each day in heaven" (Pierret,

posite title "Osiris-Moon-Thoth, bull of the heavens". The same composite name, a symbol of far-reaching identifications in theology, appears also in Philae. At an offering of the "Healthy Eye" to Min, the words are spoken: "Receive the Eye, that thou mayest go forth therein in thy name Osiris-Iooḥ-Thoth, that thou mayest illumine the Two Lands, and make full the Eye on the 15th [of the month]."

The Ptolemaic texts abound in epithets of Thoth considered as one with Iooḥ. In Dendereh (1) the king is called "Son of him that increaseth in size", where from the parallels obviously is Thoth.

One of the most familiar lunar epithets of Thoth which is as old as the N. K., (2) is "Lord of heaven", . Other lunar epithets given to Thoth in the later periods, are , "the Beautiful one of the night" (Metropol. Museum, New York 12, 182, 2); "the brightly shining" (cf. Pyr. 420; Mar., *Dend.* II, 58); (3) the "Silver Sun" (Mar., *Dend.* IV, 82). (4) Of the same lunar origin are Thoth's epithets

Études, p. 29: Cf. Mar., *Dend.* IV, plate 74). Thoth is also called "Bull of Ma'et" (Mar., *Ab.* I, 27). In Edfu (R. I. 56) Chons is described as *kꜣ ps* "that make pregnant the females" (thought of as moon-god). For the idea of the moon as a "mighty bull" in Babylonian theology, see Frank, *Studien zur babyl. Religion*, p. 242. On an ape-statue in Berlin (9941) Thoth is called *kꜣ m ḥ.t ꜥꜣ.t* — "bull in the Temple". Thoth is also called "Bull of the West" (Pap. Rhind). For Thoth as , see *Ä. Z.* 33 (1895, p. 125) Hymn to Thoth (Brit. Mus. 2293 statue of time of Amenhotep II). For Osiris as "Bull of the Westerners" see Pap. Brit. Mus. 10188, 3, 23.

(1) Mar., *Dend.* III 74 b. Another Dendereh moon-epithet of Thoth is .

(2) Cf. Naville, *Der el-Bahri* II, 54 = Urk. IV, 232.

(3) Cf. the reference to in Pyr. 1449. For sun and moon as , see Edfu R. I, 60. 59. 136.

(4) A Chons text in Edfu reads (Chons) . In the Book of the Dead 131, 1—2 (Lepsius). Re who "shines at night" is obviously Thoth, the .

, "Lord of time" (Brugsch, *Thes.* IV, 759), and  "Ruler of years" (*ibid.*);  "Reckoner of time" (Karnak, Bab el-Abd, Sethe);  (1) (Philae):  the "Reckoner" (Edfu R. I, 25. Cf. Nav., *Totb.* 100, 10). A very ancient lunar epithet of Thoth is "Chief of heaven", 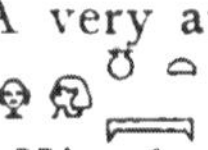 (Pyr. 2150).

It is evident now that in the New Kingdom, and subsequent periods, Thoth was commonly regarded as identical with the moon (*iooḥ*) itself. How far this identification was made in the M. K. and earlier periods it is difficult to ascertain. Certain hints of Thoth's lunar character seem to be conveyed in the texts of El-Bersheh. In Hatnub the epithet of our god "Bull of Maʿet" is fairly frequent, and one cannot help comparing this title with the lunar epithet of Thoth in the later periods "Bull of the heavens". (2) The identification of Thoth with the moon in the M. K. can be readily assumed, if it can be shown, that this identification was made already in the O. K. There are indications in O. K. texts which, though they do not, perhaps, make certain that identification, point to it, at all events, more or less clearly.

We have already discussed the Pyramid passages which speak of Sia, the bearer, and, probably, the scribe, of the divine book at the right hand of Re. It is very likely that Sia is here, as elsewhere often, identical with Thoth. The "right hand of Re" would be the natural position of honour for the second of the great astral deities, and it is reasonable, therefore, perhaps, to assume that Sia is one with the moon, as well as with Thoth. We saw above that the text of the Book of the Dead (Nav., 178, 20) which describes Thoth as the moon that traverses the sky, is directly paralleled in Pyr. 130.

In Pyr. 126, we have a ritual text which was, apparently, widely used in Ancient Egypt: "*wpw* awakes: Thoth is high". A somewhat similar text in Pyr. 1520 seems to explain the phrase "Thoth is high" in a lunar sense.

---

(1) Cf. Thoth's epithet in Philae 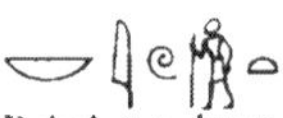 (Phot. 1011).

(2) Cf. the epithet of Nannar in Babylon: *buru iḳdu ša ḳarni kabbaru* = "powerful young bull with mighty horns" (Perry, *Hymnen und Gebete an Sin*, no. 1, l. 20); see note p. 64, (5).

"Osiris shines forth: purified is the *šḫm*: high is the Lord of Ma'et at every year's-beginning."

The "Lord of Ma'et" can scarcely be other than the Bull of Ma'et; and the reference to time-delimitation accentuates the lunar reference. (1) We find a parallel text again in the M. K. (Cairo 20520), and in the Book of the Dead (Nav. 178, 13). If Thoth is thus identified with the moon in a widely used ritual text of the O. K., his identification with the moon-god must be regarded as one of the oldest features of Egyptian theology.

The Pyr. text 130, already referred to, is the clearest ancient statement of Thoth's identity with *iooḥ*, the moon:

If Re is the sun, Thoth must be the moon. The remarkable text Pyr. 128 points in the same direction:

The "wayfarers of heaven" are Re and Thoth as sun and moon (cf. Cairo, 20520). (2)

If it must be admitted that the Pyramid texts sometimes clearly indicate the identity of the moon with Thoth, it may be shown that certain obscure Pyramid allusions become more intelligible when looked at in the light of that identity. In Pyr. 329—332 a number of beings are warned against the failure to recognise the blessed dead. They are Re, Thoth, *Ḥr špd*, and *K3 pt*. Re is, of course, the sun: *K3 pt* is Saturn: *Ḥr špd* is almost certainly an astral being of some kind. Thoth will then be here simply the moon: and we have then in this passage a list of heavenly bodies. (3) We have the same equa-

(1) Cf. Prisse, *Mon. égypt.*, pl. 31 for another echo of Pyr. 126.

(2) The whole context Pyr. 128—130 takes Re and Thoth as sun and moon. They are to take with them the Pharaoh so that he may live on that on which these gods live, so that he may rest where they rest, that he may be strong with that with which they are strong, and sail in that in which they sail (*i. e.* the barque of Re, which carries Re and Thoth). The passage Pyr. 128 appears in a very corrupt text in *Totb.* 178, 15—17 (Nav.). The gloss in the Cairo text (20520) reads .

(3) Pyr. 956, 709 seem also to identify Thoth and the moon.

tion of Thoth with *Iooḥ* in Pyr. 1153b, where Thoth and Horus with the other gods are called the children of , *i. e.* Heaven.

Just as Thoth is the "Bull of Maʿet" (Hatnub II, 7 etc.), and the "Bull of heaven" (1) (Brugsch, *Thes.* I, 37), so is he the "Strong one of the gods" (Pyr. 1237c). (2) The epithet "chief of Nut" (Pyr. 2150c) seems also to be a lunar epithet of Thoth — referring perhaps to the brilliancy and power of the luminary that ruled the skies of night. (3)

b) Thoth as protector of the moon.

Thoth, as a lunar deity, is not always identical with the moon. The theology of ancient Egypt is not a logical and self-consistent system. It frequently combines contradictory qualities in the same divinity. It is, therefore, not strange to find that, while in one set of texts Thoth is identified with the moon that traverses the skies, in another set he is represented merely as the guardian, the specially protecting deity, of the moon. (4) Here we are reminded of the Pyramid texts already discussed, in which Thoth brings back to Horus the eye of the latter. We have seen that those passages may be taken, in general, as dealing with the various perils, such as eclipse, darkness, storm etc., with which the luminaries of heaven, and particularly the moon, are frequently threatened, and with the rescue from such perils of the moon, and the other luminaries, through the power of Thoth. In all such passages Thoth appears rather as the guardian of, than as one with, the moon.

It is well known that in ancient Egypt the sun and moon were regarded as the eyes of the god whose face is heaven. Thus, in the Papyrus Ns-Chons, II, 1, it is said of the eyes of Amon:

(1) In an XVIIIth Dyn. text Brit. Mus., no. 2293 Thoth is called "the Bull among the stars". *Vid.* p. 65 *supra*. Note.

(2) Pyr. 129c speaks of the strength of Thoth.

(3) Is the title "Father of evening" *Totb.* 85, 14—15, to be referred to Thoth? In Pyr. 823 the moon is called *wr.t ḥkꜣ.w* as eye of Nut: the epithet is one of Thoth's epithets also, as will be seen below, and possibly this Pyr. text really expresses the identity of Thoth with the moon.

(4) Plutarch was familiar with this conception. Vid. *Is. et O.* 41, 4—5.

 (1)

This idea is very familiar in the Ptolemaic texts. Thus in Dendereh (Mar., *Dend.* II, 31 b): "On the 15th day of the month

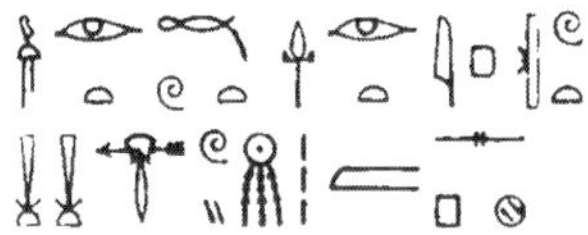

the right eye is full and the left eye is *ip*, and their rays unite." This making *ip* of the left eye, and the union of the rays from both eyes are thus referred to in another Dendereh text (Brugsch, *Thes.* I, 54): "Osiris enters into the left eye on the 15th." This entrance of Osiris (here perhaps = sun-god) into the left eye (*i. e.* union of the rays from both eyes) is again referred to in Dendereh thus:

"*Iooḥ* comes to his place — the left eye equipped with its beauty: Osiris unites himself with his left eye" (Brugsch, *Thes.* I, 30). (2)

The idea that sun and moon are the eyes of heaven is implied in the ritual text Berlin P. 3055, col. 2, 3—4 when it speaks of "the Bull that shines in his two eyes". The Bull is here Horus of the rising sun, who, like the moon-god, is a bull or mighty one among the gods. Horus is the *gmḥś* (bird) "who brilliantly shines in his two eyes" (Edfu R. I, 366). (3) That the moon, then, in certain aspects was regarded

(1) Cf. *Totb.* Nav. 151 a, 5—6 (A a). Leyden, I. 350. Hymn to Amon. That the moon is called the left eye in the O. K. appears from Pyr. 1231. On the sun and moon as the eyes of heaven see Junker, *Onurislegende*, p. 135 etc.

(2) Cf. Plut. *Is. et O.* 43, 5. At the new moon of the month Phamenoth is celebrated the feast of "Entrance" (ἔμβασις), because on that day, at the beginning of spring, Osiris enters the moon. The union of the right eye with the left means the reflection of the sun's light by the full moon. Cf. for this idea Mar. *Dend.* II 31 b. Herodotus says (II, 47) that swine were offered in sacrifice in Egypt to the moon-god at the time of full moon. This is, perhaps, an echo of the legend which spoke of Set as having swallowed the left eye of Horus while he was in the form of a swine. The swine would thus be offered to the moon-god as its defeated enemy. Cf. *Totb.*, c. 112 — for a sacrifice of swine in connection with a calamity that threatened the moon on the 15th of the month (viz. eclipse).

(3) Cf. Edfu R. I, 412. Horus is 

. Cf. the Horus Myth., XXII, 1, where it is said of Horus:

rather as the left eye of the god of heaven than as an independant deity is thus obvious. This is expressed poetically in a text of Philae (Phot. 997):

The mysterious Ba came forth from the ocean, while earth was still wrapped in darkness

Properly speaking sun and moon are the eyes of Heaven, not of the sun-god, and it is only one of the many inconsistencies of Egyptian thought when they are spoken of as the eyes of Horus of the horizon, or of any other sun-god (as, for instance, Ptah in Berlin P. 3048, col. 6, 6—8).

Considered merely as the eyes of Heaven, sun and moon were to the Egyptian of divine substance, but they were not gods. Hence they might require the help or care of some personal deity.

The two eyes of heaven are often called *wḏȝ·t*, — a term which expresses the perfection of their bright splendour. But, in the majority of texts, and practically in all the texts of the Graeco-Roman period, *wḏȝ·t* is the name of the left eye, the moon. (1) After the days of waning, disappearance, reappearance, and re-growth, the moon could well be described as the *wḏȝ·t* — the healthy, or sound, eye. After the perils of eclipse, the moon would come forth again perfect and brilliant, — "*healthy*" as before. The right eye of heaven, though it disappeared each evening in the west, showed itself again every morning in the splendours of the dawn. Its eclipse was rarer. It was exposed to fewer perils, and to lesser change,

---

. Cf. Macrobius, *Saturnalia* I, 21. *Solem Jovis oculum appellat antiquitas.* A text of Dendereh (Brugsch, *Thes.* I, 30) referring to a barque containing the *wḏȝ.t* preceded by Thoth, says: 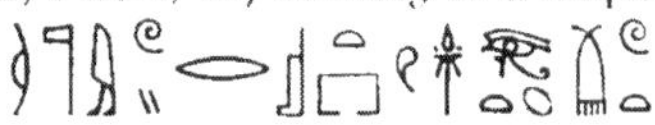 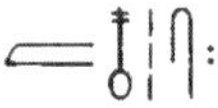: a barque containing Osiris follows. The accompanying text runs Osiris *wn nfr* .

(1) Cf. Brugsch, *Thes. I.* 34. 35. 36. 37 etc., etc.

than the left eye. And hence to the left eye, rather than to the right, was given the name *wḏ3·t*.

In the incidents of the Horus-Set legend we have seen Thoth playing the rôle of defender of light against darkness. In this rôle, as we have seen, Thoth brings back to Horus the eye of the latter, which had been injured by Set. Most of the Pyramid texts which refer to this function of Thoth, speak of the eye brought back as the left eye of Horus, *i. e.*, the moon. There are, however, a number of ancient texts in which a rescue of the right eye of Horus by Thoth, is spoken of. (1) These texts belong to the circle of thought which has produced the numerous legends of the sun-god. The 17th chapter of the Book of the Dead is the most familiar collection of such legends. In those of them in which Thoth appears, he acts, very naturally, as friend and protector of the powers of light against their foes. The right eye is not always represented as being brought back by Thoth to Horus: it seems often to return of itself and Thoth's function towards it is a some what unintelligible one of soothing it when it finds a rival established in its place, and, finally, resetting it on the face of Horus. (2)

(1) Cf. in particular the Book of the Dead of the M.·K. ch. 17. Lepsius *Älteste Texte* 31, 28—29.

(2) Cf. Nav. *Totb.* 167, 3—7. See for the whole problem of the 17 th ch. Grapow's study, *Das 17. Kapitel des äg. Totenbuches*. Berlin Diss. 1912.

Many points of Thoth's work for the right eye of Horus are reflected in the legend of the Nubian Hathor. Cf. Junker's essay: *Auszug der Hathor-Tefnut aus Nubien* (Appendix to the Abhdlgn. der Berl. Akad. 1911), and Sethe's valuable criticism of this work, and statement of the ancient legends — *Zur altäg. Sage vom Sonnenauge, das in der Fremde war* (Leipzig, 1912). The whole problem has recently been reexamined by Junker in his study, *Die Onurislegende* (Wien, 1917). In this work Junker shows convincingly that the eye with which Thoth is primarily concerned is the left eye of Horus (the moon). Apparent connection of Thoth with the right eye of Horus (the sun) is due to the interweaving of legends whose *motifs* are similar. Junker has cleared up many points which Grapow's study had left unexplained. He has also been able to take into account, and use for the further exposition and confirmation of his views Spiegelberg's recent publication of the Leyden Papyrus I, 384. Junker's *Onurislegende* is the fullest and most convincing treatment of any problem of Egyptian religion that has hitherto appeared. The present study was practically complete before the *Onurislegende* reached the author, and as pressure of other work prevented the writer from making full use of the new points of view put forward by Junker, he desires to emphasize the indispensability of the *Onurislegende* for students of Egyptian religion in general.

When Thoth brings back to its owner the left eye, or moon, he does not bring it back as a raging serpent (like the solar eye), but as a "healthy", or "convalescent" eye.

Egyptian literature delights to recur to the relations of Thoth towards the left eye of heaven. With constant repetition it tells how Thoth sought out the eye, and finding it ailing, probably, as a result of violence inflicted by Set, healed it, and then, on the day of full moon, delivered it up to it's owner in the fulness of its splendour. (1) Through his healing of the eye Thoth acquired his title "Physician of the eye of Horus" (Pap. Hearst, XIV, 5—7). We are told that the eye was cured by the application of Thoth's spittle (Book of Dead 17, 33 : 167, 3), — a detail of the legend derived, obviously, from the naïve "medicine" of the people. It is possible that Thoth's position in the later period as patron of physicians may be due to the legend of his healing of the moon-eye ; but it is equally possible that this activity of Thoth in the legend may itself be due to the general popular conception of the god.

Many of Thoth's familiar epithets are derived from his protective relation to the moon. He it is "who seeks the *wḏ3·t*-eye for its lord" (Berlin. P. 3055, col. 8, 9) : and he it is also "who makes full the eye" : he is, further, the "ba that fills the Eye" (Champollion, *Travaux sur le rituel funéraire*, p. 157). From this latter function arises his name 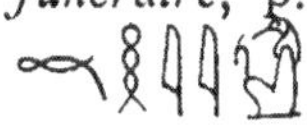 (Philae : Birth-House, Phot. 978), determined by

---

and for those in particular who would wish to supplement the information supplied by the present study on Thoth and the deities with whom he is most often associated. The angry eye which is at length pacified by Thoth, and set on the forehead of Horus is apparently the serpent of the Egyptian diadem. The angry eye which is pacified and restored to its own original place is a *motif* that belongs to the Nubian legend of Hathor (Tefenet), to the legend of Onuris who brought the goddess-lioness from the eastern desert to Egypt, and to the legend of the beautiful goddess, Hathor of Byblos, the heroine of the Papyrus d'Orbiney. Thoth's function of bringing back the moon-eye to Horus has brought him into connection with these other legends and also with the legend of Hathor as destroying Eye of the sun-god.

(1) Thoth is spoken of also as having avenged the Eye of Horus. So, Pyr. 1233. His treatment of the enemies of the Eye is perhaps described in Pyr. 575 : 635 (cf. 1336). The enemies are Set and *imiw ḥt-f*. The legends of the Eye of Horus are, of course, interwoven with those of Osiris, and also with the ritual of royal obsequies. Cf. Abydos Ritual XXXVI, Pl. 20.

the ibis-headed god. (1) Thoth it is "who makes the eye *ip* (equipped?) with all that blongs to it" (Edfu, R. I 274 etc.) He is the one too "who brings back the Eye". The text of Pyr. 58,  seems to refer to this last-mentioned function of Thoth. We have seen already that the bringing home on the wings of the ibis-god of the left eye of Horus across Lake *Nḫꜣ* is frequently referred to in the ancient ritual of the Pyramids. Egyptian ritual generally teems with reference to that same incident of the legends of Horus. Thus, for instance, in a Leyden stela-text of the N. K. (Leyden, VI, 1) Thoth is he  "who gives the Eye to its lord". Similarly, Thoth is he "who brings the Eye"  (Mar., *Ab.* I, 37, a). The same is implied in the Edfu ritual (Edfu, R. I, 25): I break the seal: I bring the Eye to its lord: I am Thoth  who bring the Eye to its lord"; and again (Edfu R. II, 16): Thoth comes  "he brings the Eye: he places it on the forehead of its creator".

This function of carrying or bearing the Eye is expressed in the ritual scenes in which Thoth is depicted as bearing in his hands an eye. It is here we must seek the origin of Thoth's title . The title may be a shortened form of the Pyramid phrase . The epithet appears in a passage of the Leyden Papyrus (347, 12, 2—4): "*Ḥu* is in my mouth: *Sia* is in my heart: praise me and honour me: 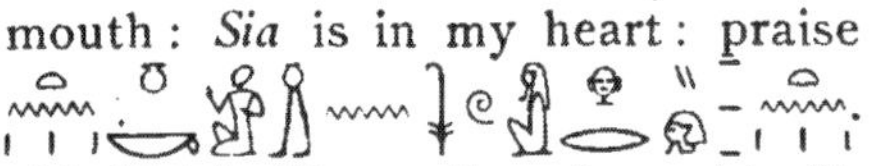. Behold, I am *'Ini św*, your chief." (2) The collocation with *Ḥu* and *Sia* makes it highly probable that the *'Ini św* of this passage is Thoth. If *ini św* is not to be understood as an abbreviation of *ini św ḥr·ś*, the *św* might be explained as due to the carelessness of a scribe who wished to write a feminine, but actually set down a masculine pronoun. However, it might be possible to explain the *św* as due to the fact that the Eye is here regarded, not as

---

(1)  is the feast of the 15th day of the month, *i. e.* full moon.

(2) For *ini św* compare *Totb.* 110, Introduction 20 (according to A a).

an eye, but rather as the astral body that the eye symbolises. Ptolemaic texts have no difficulty in referring *św* to *wḏꜣ·t* (cf. Edfu R. II, 16, *supra*: etc.), probably for the reason that *wḏꜣ·t* is equivalent to *Iooḥ*. (1) Thoth's title supplies an explanation of the fantastic script for the word "king" (Brugsch, *Thes*. V, 921: Bénédite, *Philae*, p. 145: for N. K. vid. *Rec*. 16, p. 54 Chamber of Mut in Temple of Rams. II). (2) The sign is the ape-god Thoth carrying the Eye, *i. e.* Thoth as , and the word which is thus cryptically written is , which is to be read here at least it would seem as *in św* (rather than *niśwt*).

Thoth is, then, on the one hand, the moon-god himself, and, on the other, the protector of the moon. Which of these conceptions is the more primitive? In the oldest texts both points of view are found. Both were indeed, perhaps, equally natural. The worship of moon-god was inevitable in ancient Egypt, and the identification of the moon-god with a local divinity, such as Thoth may have been, was quite parallel with what happened in the case of the sun-god. This identification, however, had the very natural result that while, on the one hand Thoth was regarded as completely one with the moon-god in heaven, his reality as a local deity living in a well-known Egyptian centre would not be forgotten. Hence the need of detaching him from the moon, so far, at least, as to make him the guardian and protector of the Sacred Eye of Horus. Logically the second point of view is corrective of the first: but which, in fact, was first in time we do not know.

---

(1) Sethe is inclined to explain *św* as an incorrect script for *si*. Vid. *Ä. Z.*, 1911, p. 24 f. *Das Wort für König in Oberägypten*. Sethe believes (*ibid.*) that the ritual phrase Thoth in Pyr. 58 proves that the use of *in św* as a name for the bearer of the eye of Horus is exceedingly ancient.

(2) This puzzle-script reminds one inevitably of the form in which Onuris' name sometimes appears, or . See Junker, *Die Onurislegende* (Wien, 1917), p. 6. Onuris = *'Ini ḥri.t*, "he who brings the One that was far away": The *ḥri.t* is the eye of the sun-god, so that there is a direct connection between *ini św* and Onuris. The writing of the name Onuris with the ape is probably due to associations with the legends of Thoth and the *wḏꜣ.t* referred to in the text.

This is not the place to discuss fully the cult of the moon-god in ancient Egypt. It may be said, however, that we have sufficient evidence to show that the moon had a formal worship of its own in the Old Kingdom. It is reasonable to assume that the worship of the moon, like solar worship, was universal in Egypt in the earliest period. It may be also assumed that, as the sun-god came to be identified with a number of local deities, — appearing thus, as Atum, Ptah, Horus, Amon etc., — without losing his own individuality as the sun-god, Re, so also the moon-god was identified with deities of local shrines at a very early period without losing his own special character of moon-god, *Iooḥ*. One such deity was the ibis-god of the 15 th. Delta nome. Another was the ancient god Chonsu of Thebes. Both the Ibis-god and Chons appear as lunar deities in the M. K., — though they have then as yet no other features in common. In the oldest texts Chons is simply the moon — the "Wanderer", as his name implies. (1) Thoth, on the other hand, though certainly a lunar deity in the older period, is also, even then, much more than merely a moon-god. His character, even in the earliest period, shows considerable complexity. The easiest explanation of the fact of Thoth's double relation to the moon is to assume that we have in his case an ancient identification of the moon-god with a local deity of pronounced individuality.

(1) It is interesting to note that Chons of Thebes in the earliest period appears always in human form, while Thoth, in the same period, is always either ibis or ape.

Chapter VI.

The symbols of Thoth.

The most familiar symbols of Thoth are the ibis and the ape. Sometimes the god appears simply as an ibis or as an ape: sometimes as an ibis-headed, or an ape-headed man. It is difficult to decide whether his ibis-symbolism or his ape-character is the more primitive. The evidence seems to point to the predominance of the ibis symbolism in the earliest period. This symbolism fits in best with the Pyramid ritual which makes the ibis-god carry the Eye of Horus, or the soul of Pharaoh over the seas of heaven. The ape-symbolism seems of itself, to have had less to do with the lunar and funerary functions of Thoth — for the ape was connected in some way, with the rising sun, and had nothing to do in Egypt with the rôle of a psychopompos. (1) The presence of an ape on the balance in the Judgment-Scene is a secondary feature. In the later periods, it is true, Thoth is often represented as a moon-god in his ape-form. But these is no trace of this kind of representation prior to the N. K. The lunar ape of the late period is, of course, a product of the identification of the ibis-god, already regarded as a moon-god, with the ape-god. It may be that the ape-symbolism gives expression to fundamental features of Thoth's character which have no relation to his rôle as moon-god. (2)

---

(1) We need not take too seriously what Horapollo says about the uneasiness and sadness of male and female apes during the time of moon's invisibility. Horapollo tells us (c. 15) that the rising of the moon was represented symbolically in Egypt by an ape raising his "hands" towards heaven. Note, however, the presence of the *kfdnw* and the *bnti* apes in the *ḥt śbḳt*: Düm. *Hist. In.* II, 57 d.

(2) One is tempted to think that Thoth's first association whith the ape-form was brought about in *Ḫmunu*, where the sacred apes were spoken of in the Hermopolitan legend of the birth of the sun-god in *Ḫmnw*. Later, the popular fancy which attributed peculiar knowledge and astuteness to the apes will have tended to invest the ibis-headed god of wisdom with the ape-symbolism. But this is little more than mere conjecture. It is to be noted that, though the ape-god is often represented as presiding, as it were, over the work of scribes, he is not usually shown as equipped with writing materials, or as himself engaged in writing.

Even if it were possible to decide whether Thoth was more primitively ibis or ape, it would still be necessary to explain how he came to be represented in these forms. In the Pyramid texts, and in all texts of the O. K., Thoth appears as an ibis. We find, however, in the O. K. period statuettes and other representations of dog-headed apes which may, possibly, symbolise Thoth. (1) If we knew the precise origin and meaning of the name , we should, perhaps, be able to decide whether ibis or ape is the more primitive as symbol of Thoth, and we might then also be able to say why Thoth was thought of under a particular form. If the name Thoth meant, as has been conjectured, "the god of ibis-form", (2) we should infer, that the ibis was the more ancient and characteristic symbol. It might then also, perhaps, be inferred that the primitive god of the 15th Delta nome was an ibis, and that a sort of crude animal worship anciently prevailed there. But if, as was conjectured above, *Ḏeḥuti* is simply = "the one from *Ḏeḥut*", the doubt must remain whether the ibis-symbol stands for a sound-value, or indicates the actual "physical" appearance of the god. In the midst of such uncertainty it is idle to set up theories of a totemistic worship of Thoth in the Delta of the prehistoric period. Neither can we say with certainty that the symbolism of the ape is secondary in regard to the nature and cult of Thoth. (3)

---

(1) See Petrie, *Researches in Sinai*, p. 123, pl. 127; *Abydos* II, pl. 9.

Cf. Bénédite, *Scribe et babouin* (Paris, 1911), p. 22 ff. Bénédite maintains that the Hermopolitan ape-god does not begin to appear in art before the Thinite period. He doubts, however, whether the early ape-figures of Hieraconpolis and Abydos are really symbols of the god Thoth: The dog-headed apes of the 3 rd Dynasty tombs at Medum and in the mastabas of the Memphite period are not, according to Bénédite, representations of the ape-god, Thoth, but rather representations of an animal which, because it was not native to Egypt, and had to be fetched from a great distance, had become a sort of exotic plaything for the members of Pharaoh's household, and for the high nobility of the early period. Bénédite is inclined to think that the splendid statue of an ape shown on p. 29 of his work, which is assigned by an inscription to the age of Snofru, really belongs to that period, and is one of the earliest representations of the sacred ape of Thoth (ibid. p. 29 f. For Bénédite's view as to the exact meaning of the ape-symbolism of Thoth see pp. 20 f.).

(2) See Brugsch, *Rel. u. Myth*, pp. 439 ff.

(3) On the ape-symbolism of Thoth should be consulted Theodor Hopfner, *Der Tierkult der alten Ägypter* (Wien, 1913), pp. 26—32. Hopfner has there

If it is to be assumed, as has been suggested, that a local deity of the 15th nome of the Delta, who was pictured as an ibis, was subsequently identified with the moon-god, we can discover various grounds for the identification of an ibis-god with the moon-god. Erman (*Rel.*, p. 10) ascribes the transformation of the moon into an ibis to popular fancy which noticed the resemblance of the curved beak of the ibis to the sickle-crescent of the moon. In the later periods of Egyptian speculation all kind of explanations of current religious symbols were devised. One of these finds an echo in Plutarch when he says (*Is. et O.* 75, 8) that the mixture of white and black in the plumage of the ibis remends one of the waning moon. (1) It may be, too, that the Egyptians saw in the dignified flight and pose of the ibis, something of the majesty of the moon as it fared across the skies, or looked down silently on men. In Haremheb's hymn (Turin) we read: "His whole attitude is like the gait of the Ibis-god 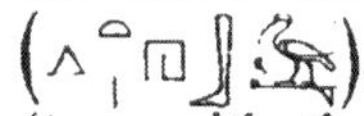, and he rejoices over Ma'et  (like the "one with the nose" [or, beak]). (2)

We find in the Book of the Heavenly Cow (very late period) elaborate attempts to explain the various symbols of Thoth based mainly on the theory of the creative efficiency of divine speech. The ibis-symbol is thus accounted for (71 f.): Re says to Thoth: "I will cause thee to send  those who are greater than thee: thereupon there came into

---

brought together the chief references to the ape-form of Thoth which are found in Greek and Latin authors.

(1) Aelian, *De natura animalium*, II, c. 38, has a similar statement. Cf. Reitzenstein, *Die hellenistischen Mysterienreligionen*, p. 94. R. quotes Aelian hist. an. X, 29, as equating the ibis with Hermes because the black of its wings corresponds to the λόγος ἐνδιάθετος, and the white to the λ. προφόρικος. The explanations of ibis-cult put forward by the non-Egyptian ancients are carefully reproduced in Hopfner, *Tierkult*, 118—119. The ibis of Thoth is the so-called "white Ibis" *(Ibis religiosa)*: it was familiar throughout the whole of Egypt. Thousands of ibis-mummies have survived from ancient Egypt. For the "white" and "black" cf. Philae, Phot. 1420: Tiberius presenting *wḏ3.t* is described: 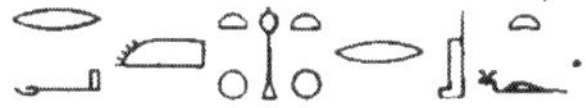

(2) Cf. Nav. *Totb.*, 125. (Confession) pl. CXXXIV 3. 

being the Ibis of Thoth" . (1) And as the ibis of Thoth was called *tḥn* as well as *hb* that special ibis-form is similarly accounted for in the same text. The text is obscure in detail but the general sense is clear: Re says:

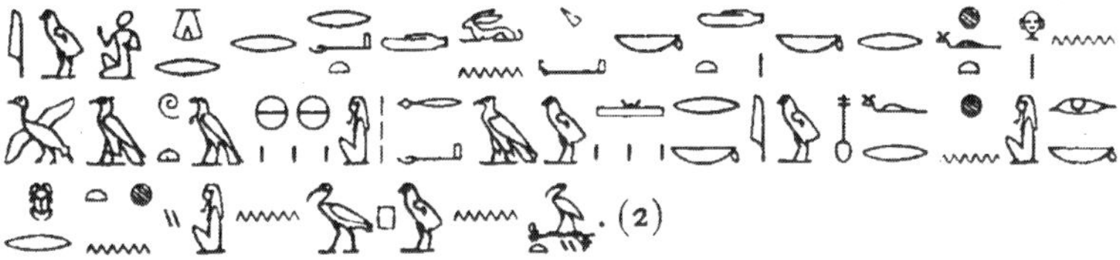 (2)

This same quaint text of the Heavenly Cow attempts in analogous fashion to explain the origin of the ape (*i. e.* the ape-form) of Thoth. (3) Re says to Thoth (73, 74): 

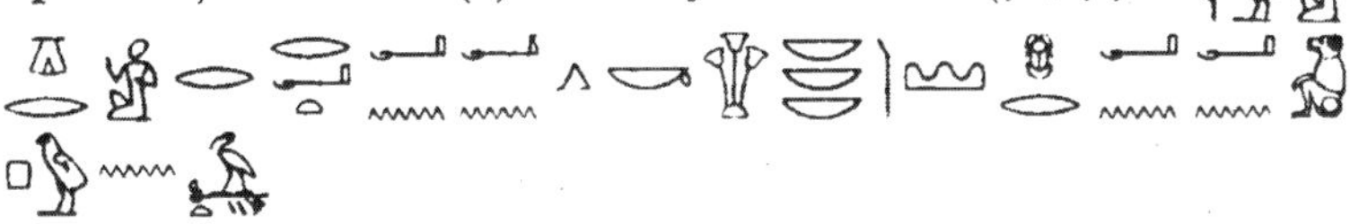

Thus the animal symbols of Thoth are due to the creative efficacy of Re's words. In the same context of this Hathor-legend the lunar character of Thoth is similarly accounted for. Re says to Thoth: 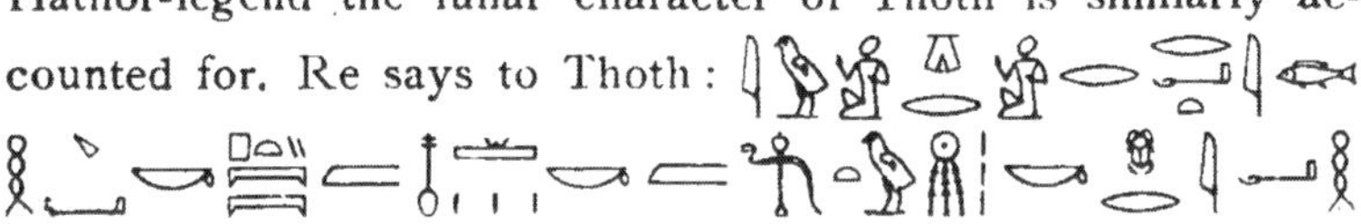

(1) Cf. Dümichen, *Histor. Inschr.*, II, 57 d (Denderch). Re *sends* his heart (*i. e.* Thoth) to Nubia to pacify Tefenet (= Hathor) "in this his name *hb* (ibis)".

(2) Cf. the Edfu text (Mammisi, p. 154): The king, the heir of  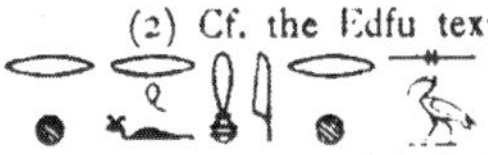 — the word *rḫs*, which may = ibis, is here connected with *rḫ*, to know.  "the knower of the Two Lands" = Thoth.

(3) The ΠΑΠΑΘΟΟΥΤ of the magical Papyrus of Paris. The ape of Thoth is the κυνοκέφαλος, the dog-headed ape (*Cynocephalus hamadryas*). The ape of Thoth is not to be confounded with the monkeys which were kept as pets in the houses of the Egyptians (κῆβοι, קוף, ), and often buried with their dead owners. At times however the ordinary house-monkeys were treated as if they shared somehow in the sacredness of the ape of Thoth. In the Demotic text of the legend of the Eye of Horus (Leyden Pap. I, 384) Thoth appears as *pꜣ šm n wnš kwf* "the little jackal-ape", *i. e.* the dog-headed ape. The sacred animal of Thoth is also called in the same text simply *pꜣ kwf* (Spiegelberg, *Der äg. Mythus vom Sonnenauge.* Berliner Akad. Sitzgber. 1915, p. 878 ff.).

 "I will cause thee to embrace the two heavens with thy beauty, and thy rays. Thereupon sprang into being the moon of Thoth". Thus Thoth's connection with the moon would be due to a chance utterance which fell from the lips of Re. All this, however, is more interesting as an illustration of Egyptian belief in the power of divine speech, than as an account of the genuine theological origins of Thoth's symbols of worship, and of his lunar character. (1)

(1) The ape-symbolism sometimes appears combined with the ibis-symbolism in a manner which, at first sight, is very disconcerting. Thus, for instance, in the Judgment-scene we sometimes see the ape-god seated on the weighing scales and the ibis-god recording the result of the weighing. Again, in *Mission* II, 4. partie, plate 39 we see represented an ape seated and holding in his hand an ibis. See also *ibid.*, plate 49. Thus the remark of Bénédite, *Scribe et Babouin*, p. 20, regarding the two symbols of Thoth: "Il est certain . . . . que tout en se rapportant à une seule divinité, ces deux formes n'arrivèrent jamais à se confondre", is not absolutely correct. Cf. Hopfner, *Tierkult*, p. 26—27 — reference to a representation in the temple of Sethos I at Bibân-el-Mulûk of Thoth as ape-headed man holding in his hand an ibis. Cf. also *Mission* II, plates 39 and 49, for representation of ape holding ibis in his right hand. See also Dümichen, *Grabpalast des Patuamenap*, 3. Abtlng., Taf. XIV. In the 6th hour of the Great Amduat is shown an ape-headed god holding an ibis who is called 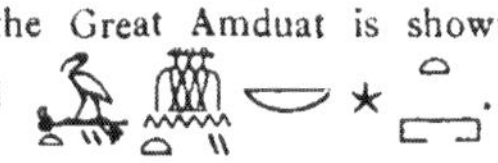. Cf. also Turayeff's work on Thoth, plate VII.

Chapter VII.

Thoth as the representative of Re.

The text quoted at the close of the last section gives expression to a familiar Egyptian idea — the idea, namely, that the moon is a representative of, or substitute for, the sun. The idea is usually expressed by calling Thoth 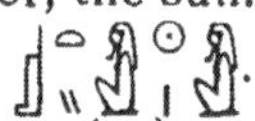. Re says to Thoth in the Book of the Heavenly Cow (74):

"Thou shalt be in my place as my *locum tenens*: thou shalt be called Thoth, the "Substitute for Re". While the sun is traversing the Duat during the night, the moon is to take his place in heaven. The legend of Re's commission to Thoth is told, of course, in this late text, merely, to explain the familiar epithet of Thoth "*'Isti* of Re". This notion of Thoth we meet in many places. The Book of the Dead (Lepsius, c. 131, 1—2) speaks of the dead as "this Re that shines in the night" (*i. e.* the dead is identified with Thoth, the *locum tenens* of Re). In the same book (Naville, c. 169, 20 accord. to Pb.) Thoth is styled . "*'Isti* of Re" as epithet of Thoth is common in the N. K. (1) There is no instance of its use in the texts of the M. K. In the O. K. the Pyramid texts speak of the dead Pharaoh as "*isti* of Re" (Pyr. 1107: 1464), and, since in other Pyramid passages the Pharaoh appears as Thoth, it is just possible that we have here an indication of the use of "*isti* of Re" as epithet of Thoth in the O. K.

The idea that the moon is a representative of the sun appears in a somewhat naturalistic form in a few texts. Thus, for instance, in the Book of the Dead (c. 130, 17), Osiris (*i. e.*

(1) Cf. Leyden V, 1: Turin 2204 etc. etc.

the dead) thought of as Re  has made brilliant the face of Thoth ; *i. e.* the light of the moon is but a reflexion of that of the sun.

We have already considered a number of texts in which Thoth is represented as a companion of Re in the solar barque, and as sharing with the sun-god in the responsibilities of world-rule. The idea of the mutual relations of Thoth and Re implied in those texts, appears, however, to be quite different from that suggested by the Thoth's epithet "*íśti* of Re". Yet in both is implied the closeness of the relation in which the two divinities stood to each other for the Egyptian mind. In the day-time Thoth journeyed with Re in the solar barque: in the night-time he travelled alone in the lunar barque as substitute for, or representative of, the sun. When the two luminaries appeared at the same time in the sky Thoth's light was but a weak reflection of the glory of Re. Thus all apparent difficulties were solved.

The Egyptian did not feel any sense of incongruity in legarding the same divinity as, at once, the lunar disc in the sky, an ibis-god or ape-god on earth, a guardian of the "Eye of Horus", a companion of Re in the "Barque of millions", and a minister and counsellor of Re in the government of the world. The tendency of Egyptian theology seems to have been rather to assign to each divinity all possible qualities and functions, than to conceive its gods as clear-cut individualities.

Chapter VIII.

The special functions of Thoth as lunar divinity.

The general aspects of Thoth's rôle as moon-god have been already considered. It now remains to show in some detail how the notion of Thoth's lunar being worked out in concrete details.

The ancient Egyptians were an agricultural people. They were interested, therefore, in setting up an exact calendar. The moon would naturally play a chief part in fixing the details of the calendar. The easily observed regularity of the moon's phases furnished a better basis for marking off periods of time than the variations of solar phenomena. Hence at a very early period in Egypt, as elsewhere, the moon was taken as the chief measurer of time. This importance of the moon is expressed very clearly in the later Egyptian texts: it is obvious enough also in the earlier texts. The Great Oasis text (Brugsch, 16, 33—34) states the time-delimiting work of the moon very clearly. Of it is said that it is:

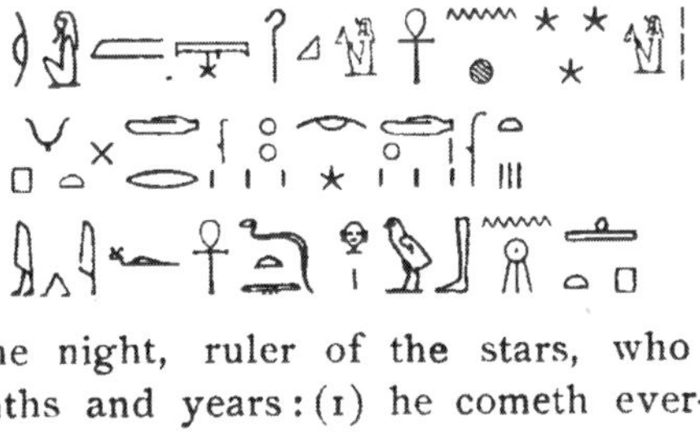

,'Moon in the night, ruler of the stars, who distinguishes seasons, months and years: (1) he cometh ever-living, rising and setting."

In the same text (l. 30 ff.) the left eye of the sun-god is said "to distinguish seasons, months, and years" (2) It is the

(1) Of Genesis I, 14. 16.

(2) Cf. the Babylonian idea of Sin — *muaddu ūme arḫi u šatti* — "who determines days, months, and years. Perry, *Hymnen und Gebete an Sin*, no. 6, l. 3.

sun that marks off day from night, but it is the moon that determines months, and seasons, and years. For the agriculturist, then, the moon was a more valuable time-measurer than the sun.

But, as we have seen, Thoth is Iooḥ, the moon. He is, therefore, the chief time-measurer. Many of his epithets express this position. He is , lord of time (Brugsch, *Thes.* IV, 759): (1) lord of old age (Philae, Phot. 1011): , reckoner of years (Edfu R. I. 297, 27): reckoner of time (Brugsch, *Thes.* IV, p. 757; Mar., *Dend.* II, 43): (2) , the Reckoner (Edfu R. I. 259): ruler of years (Brugsch, *Thes.* IV, 759): , determiner of time (Edfu R. I. 27. 291): , the scribe of time (Edfu R. I. 522): , the divider of time (Edfu R. II. 27. 31; Mar., *Dend.* II, 73 c): , he that increaseth time, and multiplieth years (Edfu R. I. 77). (3) In this last-quoted Edfu text (E. R. I. 27) many lunar activities of Thoth are brought together. He it is, according to this text, "who divides seasons, months, and years, who increaseth time and multiplieth years, who maketh record of kingship for the Ruler of the Two Lands. Thousands are at his disposal: tens of thousands in his right hand".

The most prominent function of Thoth as measurer of time in the royal annals of Egypt is his determination of the regnal years of the Pharaohs. This function is symbolised by the notched palm-branch which Thoth carries in the ceremonies of coronation. (4) It is a function which is first definitely brought before us in the New Kingdom. In the temple of Rameses II at Abydos (Mar., *Ab.* II, 2, c) Thoth is re-

---

(1) Cf. Edfu R. I. 297.

(2) A frequent epithet of the moon-god Chons: in Greek χεσεβαι, vid. *Ä. Z.*, 48, 173.

(3) As the "increaser of time and multiplier of years" Thoth was popularly invoked to grant length of days. Cf. Pap. Leyden I, 369 (Letters of XIXth Dyn.).

(4) See Karnak, L. D. III, 124 d.

presented as holding the roll and stylus: behind him stands the god  who carries the apparatus for writing, and a sort of ink-bottle (▽): Thoth says: "I write for thee years without number, and hundreds of thousands of *Ḥeb śed* feasts". Again in the Temple of Chons built by Rameses III at Karnak (Sethe 4, 25) we find Thoth in his rôle as "Scribe of Maʿet of the Ennead", saying to the Pharaoh: "I write for thee a mighty kingdom; I give thee life unending as king of the Two Lands, and everlasting life in years of peace." Sometimes Thoth records the promised years of reign by making notches in the palm-branch: sometimes he inscribes the *ḥeb śed* feasts on the *išd* tree. (1) Thoth is often assisted in this function of determining the years of royal reign by the goddess Seshat. (2)

But Thoth does not merely determine beforehand the length of Pharaonic reigns; he is "a reckoner of time for gods and men" generally. (3) Thus he becomes a god of fate foredetermining for each individual the duration of his life. The number of a man's years Thoth determines at a man's birth — or, as it is said, "on the *meskhenet*". In the time of Ptolemy IV Thoth in Edfu appears as: (4) the lord of *Ḫmnw*, the scribe of Maʿet for the Ennead, who determines time, who commands the *ḥšb* (*i. e.* fixes the length of life, fate) on the *meskhenet* (= stone or brick on which parturition took place). (5) Thoth is obviously looked on in this connection as a god of fate. (6)

(1) Vid. L. D. III, 124 and 220 d. Cf. the Hymn to Amon in the Temple of Rameses III Karnak. It is interesting to note that the god *Ḥike* (*Ḥkɜ*) appears also at times like Thoth with the notched palm-branch. See Dendereh, L. D. IV, 58 a.

(2) Cf. L. D. III, 220 d. For the Graeco-Roman period cf. Edfu, R. I, 112, 291.

(3) Edfu R. I, 112, 297: Cf. Philae Phot. 1010, where Thoth "engraves the annals for the son of Osiris".

(4) Edfu R. I, 27: .

(5) Cf. also Rhind Papyrus I, 4 b 10; a 10: 5 b 1; a 2: II, 3 b 2; a 2.

(6) Cf. Luxor, Court of Amenophis III (Mission XV, 10, 3) when the king is thus described: "Wise as Thoth on whose mouth is the breath of life, behind whom Meskhenet (here thought of as goddess) stands". For Thoth with four Meskhenets see Mar., *Dend.* II, 40 c. In the Rhind Pap. I, 1 b 7; a, 8 Thoth inscribes the day of death on the *meskhenet*. In a text of Philae (Phot. 1010) Thoth's function is  — "raises up his (the Pharaoh's) *fate*

The god who can predetermine length of life and reign must himself be raised above all limitations of time. Hence it is not strange to find Thoth described as one that looks into the future, and perceives it like the present. In the Book of the Dead, c. 182, 10 f. (Naville) it is said of Thoth   "who announceth the morrow and gazes on the future". In Deir el-Bahri (Nav. II, 47) Thoth appears also as one that knows the future. (1) Past present and future must be all the same for the "Lord of time" and the "king of eternity" (*Totb.* Nav. c. I, 3—5), for him "who guideth heaven, earth, and the nether world, and maketh life for men" (*Totb.* Nav. c. 182, 10—11 A f).

Thoth determines, not merely the bare schematism of existence: he not merely predetermines the length of men's lives, but he also fills in beforehand the details of each individual career. With this rôle of his is connected his determining of the "Annals" of the kings. (2) As he determines the "Annals" (*gnwt*) of the kings, so does he also for the Ennead. (3) Thus, as in other cases, so here, from an ordinary court-official, there has been formed a god. As the Pharaoh had his annalist, so must the Ennead also have its chronicler. But as Thoth is not a mere annalist depending on actual experience, but

on his *meskhenet*". Similarly, in Babylonian thought, Sin, the moon-god, is *nabu šarruti nadin haṭṭi ša šimti ana ume ruḳuti išimmu*, "who calleth to kingship, who giveth the sceptre, who determineth fate unto distant days". Further Sin is *paris purusse šame u irsitim ša kibitsu manman la únakkaru*, "who maketh decision for heaven and earth, whose decree no one changeth" (Perry, *Hymnen und Gebete an Sin*, no. 1, cf. Jastrow, p. 437: cf. further, Perry, *op. cit.*, no. 2, p. 12 f.). Isis appears at times as mistress of fate (so Düm., *Kal. I.*, p. 54): so also does Hathor (L. D. Text II, 209): Nephthys appears as "Meskhenet, the mistress of fate" (Mar., *Dend.* II, 43). In the Rameseum (Quibell X, 4: XIXth Dyn.) Ptah is called . The technical term for determining the fate of an individual is *ṯnn šȝi ḥr mšḫn.t šꜥi*, the god of fate appears in the Coptic forms ⲡϭⲟⲓ and ⲯⲟⲓ and in Greek personal names such as Σενψαις. *Šꜥi* is the Agathodaimon of later times (= Thoth?). *Ḥšb* = *šꜥi* in the texts quoted.

(1) Amon makes inquiry from Thoth about the future mother of Makere.

(2) Cf. Karnak, L. D. III, 15: Mar. *Ab.*, I, 34 b: Brugsch, *Thes.* IV, 735: Edfu R. I. 77.

(3) Brugsch, *Thes.* IV, 759 (Dendereh): Cf. *Mammisi*, pp. 21, 131, 140. Thoth assignes the years of rule to the sacred falcon in Philae (*vid.* Junker, *Bericht Strabos über den heiligen Falken von Philae*, p. 46 in WZKM, 26.

the "Lord of time", his rôle of annalist for the Ennead is merely his function as god of fate. When the Egyptian wished to think of Thoth as god of fate, he thought of him, on the analogy of the Pharaoh's court, as an official of the Ennead, recording the decrees which the gods issued beforehand for the life of each individual. This idea gives a still more concrete meaning to Thoth's already familiar title, "Scribe of Maʿet for the Ennead".

Thoth appears, as has been said, at the coronation-ceremonies predetermining by notches on the palm-branch the number of the Pharaoh's regnal years. It is but an enlargement of this function of his when he is said to determine the titles of the Pharaoh. We read of "the day on which the Great Name (*i. e.* the sum of the titles) of the Pharaoh was determined, the Name which Thoth made while Re was by his side". (1) To determine the "Great Name" was a very proper work of the god of fate: and it was but natural that Thoth should have associated with him in that work one or more of the great gods of Ancient Egypt.

(1) Karnak Memorial of Rams IV, Legrain's copy.

Chapter IX.

Thoth as founder of social order and of sacred ritual.

We have already examined some of the most obvious lunar functions of Thoth. A great many other activities are ascribed to him which may also — but not with equal certainty, — belong to him as moon-god. Among these may be suitably considered here his activities in the organisation of various departments of civil and religious life.

In a country in which, as in Egypt, the daily life of the people was largely ordered by reference to the phases of the moon, it was more or less inevitable that the moon-god should come to be looked on as the ordering principle of civil and religious life. The easily noted regularity of the moon's phases gave the moon a necessary predominance in fixing the date of the chief feasts in the temples, and of the chief events of the Egyptian civil year. This will have given a special importance to the early and general spread of moon-cult throughout Egypt; and with the growth of lunar cult must have gone on equally the growth of the cult of the moon-god Thoth. It is not strange, then, to find that Thoth is described, at an early period, as the founder of the cult carried on in the temples — as the originator of divine sacrificial worship, and as the author of all order in the State. Though, however, these important aspects of Thoth's activity may be largely due to his rôle as moon-god, it would be a mistake to infer that Thoth was for the Egyptian wholly or essentially a lunar divinity. The gods of Egypt can seldom, indeed, be described in a single formula. It is possible that Thoth's association with the origin of civil and religious institutions is due only by accident, or secondarily, to his lunar character.

Plutarch recognises (*Is. et O.*, c. 55) that Hermes (= Thoth) is the source of cosmic order. Hermes cut out the sinews of Typhon (= Set), and from them made the chords whence are derived, ultimately, the harmonies of world-order. This is but the mythological way of saying that Reason is the source of all order in the world. The same idea seems to find expression in Egyptian texts when Thoth is spoken of as "he whose words have established the Two Lands" (*Totb.* Nav. 182, 4). A similar idea lies behind several of Thoth's epithets: *e. g.*  — "the most ancient Legislator" (Stele of Tutankhamon l. 29, — *Rec.*, 29, 166, *cf.* Anastasi I, 9):  "Lord of laws" (*Totb.* Nav. 182, 3), , "he who gives laws, and arranges promotions" (Cairo, *Wb.* no. 116). In the Ptolemaic texts he is *śmn hpw* "he that establishes laws". "Establishing laws like the Lord of *Ḥśr·t.* (= Thoth)", is a constantly recurring epithet of the Pharaohs in the Graeco-Roman period.

From the time of the N. K., then, Thoth was regarded as the source of law, and, therefore, as the founder of the social order. (1) We are not told, as a rule, whether Thoth was regarded as the author of special classes of laws. He is simply "Lord of laws". Yet most of the legislation which is directly referred to him in the texts deals with cult.

It is as author of the institutions of temple-worship that we find Thoth engaged so often in the building and furnishing of shrines of all kinds. (2) We see him often with the architect-goddess Seshat measuring the sites of future temples. He did not content himself, however, with marking off sites: the erection, internal arrangement, and decoration of the temples were regarded as designed by him. It was usual for Egyptian shrines to boast of their complete conformity with the plans and prescriptions of Thoth. This is true particularly of the shrines of the later periods. Thus, in Dendereh (Dümichen, *Baug.* II) the inscriptions tell how the different apartments of the house of *Ḥr nb·t* correspond in structure and arrangement with the plans of *'Iśtn* (= Thoth). We are told that the length and breadth of a temple are "according to

(1) Cf. Edfu R. I, 333. Ptol. IV brings to Horus the nome of Hermopolis. Thoth is therein as 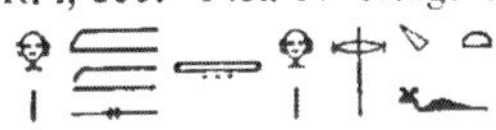 "he that establisheth order in the entire land".

(2) For M. K. see L. D. II, 150 g (XIIIth Dyn.).

the word of the knower of the Two Lands (*i. e.* Thoth), according to the arrangement of Sia (*i. e.* Thoth)". (1) The walls of temples are decorated with the designs and with the script of Thoth. Rameses built a temple for Amon whose walls of stone were 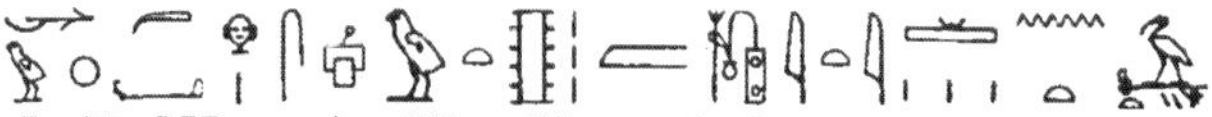 (*Ramesseum*, L. D. III, 170). The Pharaoh boasts thus of the 7th chamber of the Temple of Dendereh, which he has built for Hathor: it is like the horizon, duly constructed 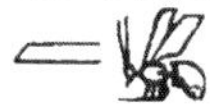 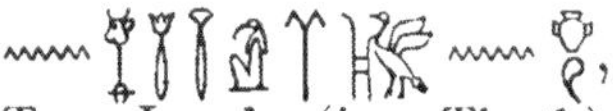, "by the work of the knower of the Two Lands (*i. e.* Thoth), by that which his heart created" (*i. e.* according to Thoth's plan). (2)

Each thing has its place assigned to it in the Temples, by the decree of Thoth. The statues of the gods are said to be set up in the shrines in their due places   "as Thoth hath decreed thereon" (Mar., *Dend.* II, 73 b). So again, according to Mar., *Dend.* II, 57 e the sacred *šḫm* are depicted on the walls of chamber 12   "splendidly executed according to the glorious words of Sia" (Thoth). The patron goddess of Dendera is sculptured in her temple  "according to the ordinances of the knower of the Two Lands" (Mar., *Dend.* I, 37 b).

The hieroglyphic inscriptions on the temple-walls which are intended not less for ornament than instruction, are according to the directions of Thoth (Mar., *Dend.* I, 39 d), and in his own script. So we are reminded in Dendereh (Mar., *Dend.* II, 13 e, etc.) that the temple-chambers are "splendidly engraved with the words of Sia". The individual temple-spaces are said to be disposed  (Edfu R. I, 23) — "as Thoth hath written thereof". In the temple of Rameses II at Abydos the Nine are said to be duly depicted 

(1) Mar., *Dend.* III, 29 a. Cf. Mar., *Ab.* II, pl. II c: Thoth with an assistant, prescribes the length and breath of Rameses' Temple.

(2) Mar., *Dend.* II, 29 d.

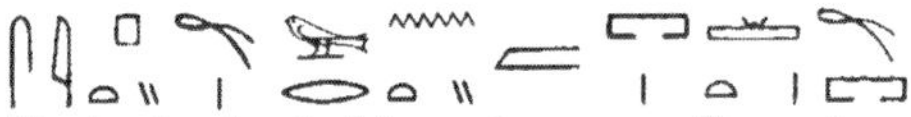 "in their shape which Ptah hath fashioned, according to that which Thoth hath written concerning their bodies in the great register (?) which is in the Library" (Mar., *Ab.* II, 9). There is here a clear reference to a set of regulations of a formal kind, in writing, dealing with the arrangement of temple-interiors; and these regulations are ascribed to Thoth as author. Thus it would seem as if Thoth were regarded as the framer of the rules of ecclesiastical architecture, and of temple-decoration in general. Thoth was the first who set down in writing the laws of sacred architecture: Ptah was the Builder who executed the plans devised by Thoth. This explains such phrases as we find in the account of the mysterious roof of the Temple of Dendereh: "it was built by Ptah and sculptured according to the writings and the beautiful words of *'Iśtn*" (Mar., *Dend.* III, 70). (1)

We know very little of the ancient official ritual literature of Egypt. But we are entitled to assume that there existed books of directions for the designers and builders of temples, and that these books were regarded as composed by Thoth. These architectural handbooks were put on a level with the books of ritual magic called "*Bau Re*" (Mar., *Dend.* III, 29 a). The various handbooks dealing with the plans of temple-structure, and the adornment of sacred shrines probably formed a substantial portion of the Egyptian temple-libraries. (2)

---

(1) Cf. Maxims of Anu (beg.): Pap. Hood, l. 1—2.

(2) It is an interesting point that Seshat, the goddess of script, is often associated with Thoth in all matters dealing with sacred architecture. This implies that there was nothing casual, nothing left to the inspiration of individual architects in the designing of Egyptian temples. It may be noted here, also, that the Egyptian was conscious of no essential distinction between the pictorial decoration of the walls of tombs and temples, and the hieroglyphic script which went along with it. The pictures had a meaning, and could be read, just like the hieroglyphs. Hence the presence and activity of Seshat in connection with the arrangement of temples.

Chapter X.

Thoth as author of the "Divine Words".

Thoth was not interested in the provision of temples for worship merely; he it was also, who devised the *minutiae* of the divine service which was carried out in the temples. Similarly the complicated ritual of the sepulchral services was traced back to his inventive and organising genius. (1)

In the M. K. the formulae of the mortuary offerings are expressly ascribed to Thoth. So we are told that the offerings for the dead were arranged 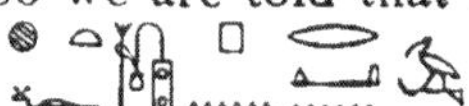 "according to this writing which Thoth hath given". (Lacau, *Sarcophages*, p. 147). Every offering for the dead should be made 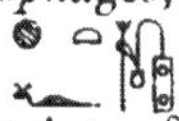 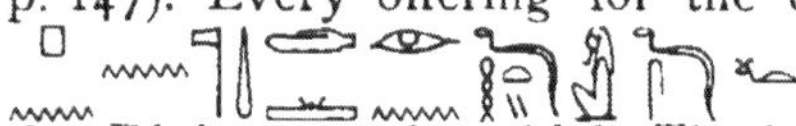 "according to this script of the Divine words which Thoth himself hath made" (Lacau, *Sarcophages*, p. 206). (2) Thoth appears, then, in the M. K. as author of the "script of the Divine words". We have the same suggestion in the texts of El-Bersheh. We read there (vol. II., p. 45) of an offering for the dead, 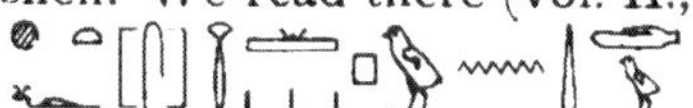 , "according to the hymn of glorification of divine words which Thoth hath made".

(1) Cf. the Babylonian title of Sin *mukin nindabie*, "he that established the sacrifices". Perry, no. 1, l. 33.

(2) There is nothing to show that "Divine words" were so called in contrast with some form of script or speech used in connection with unimportant or profane matters. Eisler (in *Die kenitischen Inschriften der Hyksoszeit*, Freiburg, 1919, p. 145, Anm. 1) has pointed out that  means "staff", "rod" as well as "word" and has inferred the possibility of such implications as "*Buchstaben*", "*Stabrunen*", "*Kerbstock*" being associated with 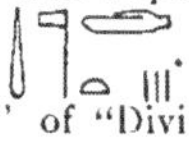. Eisler points out (*ibid.*) the existence side by side with "Divine words" of "Divine staffs" or sceptres on which were carried the heads of gods, or other divine symbols. The mysterious תְּרָפִים of the Hebrews Eisler would connect (*ibid.*) with the Egyptian *drf*. "Sollten die *Terafim* solche Stäbe, bzw. Pfähle mit "Hieroglyphen"symbolen der Götter als Knauf gewesen sein?" Eislers speculations are interesting, but they must be corrected by the facts collected in the text.

We notice here that Thoth's connection with ritual is expressed in contexts which emphasise his familiar rôle as "Lord of the Divine words". This epithet has been usually explained as "Lord (or founder) of hieroglyphics". There is, indeed, no doubt that "Divine words" often mean "hieroglyphs" in the texts of the late period. But in the texts of the M. K. quoted in the preceding paragraph the "Divine words" seem to be something other than mere script: they are carefully distinguished from the  (= the written sign, script), and seem to be what is conveyed or expressed by the written signs, rather than the signs themselves.

It is a familiar idea of ancient Egyptian literature that the mere recital of the formulae of funerary offerings was sufficient to supply the dead with all the objects named in the formulae. Thus the words of such formulae might be regarded as possessing a magical efficacy of a creative kind. They could call into being that which they signified or named. It is not unreasonable, perhaps, to conjecture that this magical or creative effect of ritual formulae is expressed by calling such formulae (as in the M. K. texts above) *mdw nṯr*. *Mdw* suggests rather the spoken word than the written symbol. (1) Hence, when Thoth is called "Lord of the *mdw nṯr*" his lordship over *spoken* words, rather than over *script*, is expressed. In his familiar epithet  (Cf. Mariette, Karnak, 16, Thutmosis III) "he who hath given word and script-sign" the word (*mdw*) is clearly distinguished from the written symbol (*drf*). (2)

Even though *mdw nṯr* does mean "hieroglyphs" in the Graeco-Roman period, it may not always have had that meaning. There is no lack of other words to express "hieroglyph" in Egyptian. The most familiar of these terms is *drf*, or better, "*drf* of Thoth". An expert in hieroglyphics is "he who knows the *drf* of Thoth" (Berlin 7316: XVIIIth Dyn.). "Hieroglyphics",

(1) *Mdw* = to speak: cf. ⲘⲞⲨⲦⲈ. There is no satisfactory proof that *mdw nṯr* ever actually means "divine staff", or "divine rod". *Per se*, of course, *mdw nṯr* could have such a meaning. Cf. the reference to חֶרֶט אֱנוֹשׁ, Is. VIII, 1.

(2) For possible connection of *drf* with חרטמים see Eisler, *Die kenitischen Inschriften der Hyksoszeit* (Freiburg, 1919), p. 145, Anm. 1.

meaning an inscription written in hieroglyphs, would be rendered *sš3 Ḏḥwti* (Leyden I, 350, recto 4, 23) or *sš3 n Ḏḥwti* (Cairo, 20539, etc.). Thus the distinction between the script and what was expressed by it could be made with sufficient clearness in Egyptian.

We hear also of "books of the Divine Words" (*Totb.*, c. 170, 5) (1) — which, obviously, cannot be "books written in hieroglyphics" merely, for in what other script could books of the time be written? The title implies rather that such books contained collections of specially effective formulae. The Book of the Dead speaks (c. 68, 9—10) of a journey which Hathor made to Heliopolis "bearing the writings of the Words (*mdw*), the Book of Thoth". This "Book" can hardly be other than a collection of sacred formulae ascribed to Thoth as author. The title "President of the mysteries of the Divine words" which we find in the early period, (2) can scarcely mean "overseer of hieroglyphs": it seems to point, as Schaefer says, (3) to the bearers' "special knowledge of script and literature, and, above all, of sacred literature". (4)

The *mdw nṯr* were, then, primarily not signs but words — words, above all, spoken by the gods (as in Pyr. 2047), but then, also, all such words or formulae as bore in themselves a divine, or creative, efficiency. Of such kind were the formulae of sacred ritual. These formulae are technically known as *mdw*. Every ritual phrase of importance is prefaced with  "Recitation of the *mdw*", as a stereotyped rubric. The Book of the Dead (c. 17, 3) puts this rubric more solemnly, *ḫpr mdw*, "the *mdw* takes place". Pyr. 333 c seems clearly to identify the "Divine words" with the effective or productive "word" of the liturgy, when it says:

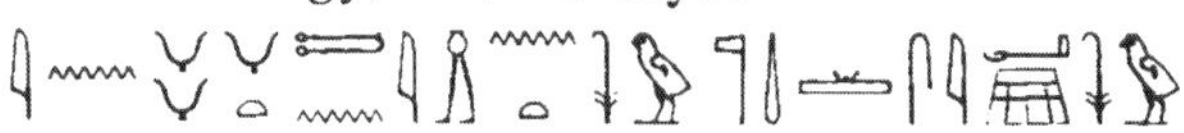

(1) "Thoth himself comes to thee with 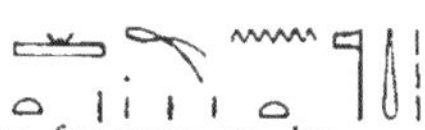" — where the "words" are, apparently, the formulae of the funerary service.

(2) Cf. Schaefer, *Mysterien*, p. 38, where I-cher-nofret appears with this title.

(3) *Ibid.*

(4) Note that the title "Scribe of the Divine Book" is given to the priest who reads the *dua* ("glorifications") in the ritual (Brugsch, *Drei Festkalender*, Pl. VII). In Pap. Salt 825, VII, 2—4 Thoth is described as the "scribe of the divine book" who glorifies Osiris every day.

"It is your messengers who bring him: it is the Divine words that cause him to ascend". The *mdw nṯr* carry the Pharaoh up to heaven. (1)

Through the close contact of ritual and magic *mdw nṯr* came to be used, not merely of ritual formulae, but of all formulae which could be regarded as having a magical value. Possibly, indeed, *mdw nṯr* may have meant "magic formulae" even before it was employed as a designation for formulae connected with divine worship. In very ancient texts we find *mdw nṯr* brought into connection both with ritual and magic. Thus in a tomb-inscription of the M. K. (Louvre C. 14) the deceased says: "I knew the mysteries of the Divine words, the celebration of the *Ḥeb-šed* feasts, and every kind of *ḥike*: no one surpassed me therein".

Hence Thoth's epithet "Lord of the Divine words" implies his lordship over the formulae of ritual and cult. That lordship implies, again, that to Thoth was assigned the duty of superintending the celebration of ritual ceremonial, and that in Thoth was found the source of all such mysterious power as was contained in charms, and spells, and all invocations of the gods.

There is abundant evidence in the texts that to Thoth was assigned the authorship of the forms of cult. Thus, in the Mendes stela (D. 10): "His majesty showed veneration to the gods of ram-form 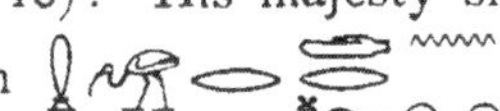 — "according to what was found in the writings of Thoth". In a hymn to Thoth published by Turayeff in *Ä. Z.* XXXIII, p. 123, it is said of the god that it is "he who has given words and script, who makes the temples to prosper, who founds shrines, and makes the gods to know what is needful (*i. e.* sacrifice and ritual)". (2) The materials to be used for the various purposes of cult had to be prepared in accordance with the directions

(1) In the Metternich Stela (107/9) we hear of the recitation of *ḥike* along with *ỉ3ḫw*, and in the same context are mentioned the *mdw* which the heart of Horus has formed. Here *mdw* (obviously *mdw nṯr*) *ḥike* and *ỉ3ḫw* are put on the same level, and all seem to refer to words of power of some kind. Cf. Westcar, VIII, 25—26, where *ḥike* = the words spoken by the magician: cf. *ibid.* VI, 12; VIII, 20—21.

(2) Cf. Diod. Sic. I, 16, who ascribes to Hermes the authorship of everything connected with liturgy.

of Thoth. The ointments, we are told in Dendereh (Mar., *Dend.* I, 72 a), have been duly prepared according to the orders of, and to the accompaniment of the recitation of the formulae of, Thoth (who is called usually in this connection , the Ibis). (1) The various oils used in the divine worship were prepared according to the directions of Thoth (Dümichen, *Rezepte* XXVI/XIII: Mar., *Dend.* I, 79. 1, 2). Even the incense was carefully prepared, we are told in the Sethos-temple in Abydos, "according to the writings of Thoth which are in the library", *i. e.*, according to the rules laid down in the rituals of the temple.

We may assume that the details of cult-ceremonial were ascribed to the authorship of Thoth, though it is only rarely that this is directly implied in the texts. (2) But it is evident that his closest connection with ritual is through his rôle as master of potent words, as "Lord of the divine words". The ordering of the details of cult will have belonged to him as the orderer of things in general, in the Temples, as well as in the State; and his function as order-bringer is, probably, to be connected with his character as moon-god. Yet, it must be noted that the ancient moon-god, Chons, was not regarded in the early period as a founder of cult or ritual. It is only later, when Chons is brought into close connection with Thoth, that he is associated with the origin and celebration of cult-ritual. It is possible, then, that Thoth's association with ritual may have been primitively due to non-lunar aspects of his character. The being of Thoth is not reducible to, or derivable from, a single formula. The double symbolism — ibis and ape — points to a fundamental complexity in his nature. It might be conjectured, perhaps, that the symbol of the ibis points

(1) Vid. Mar., *Dend.* I, 50 b; and cf. von Lemm, *Ritualbuch des Amondienstes*, p. 64.

(2) Cf., for instance, *Totb.* Nav., 44, 3 f., where the order of a divine procession is determined by Thoth. Cf. Lacau, *Textes rel.*, no. 49: 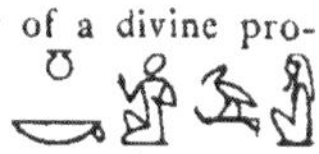
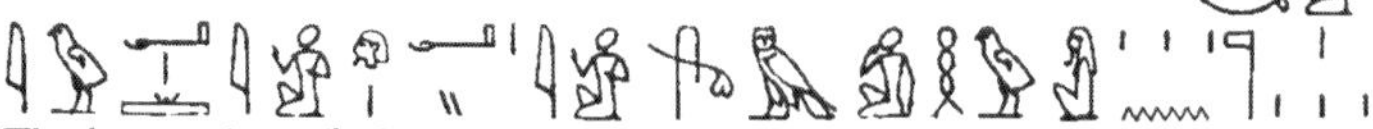 "I am Thoth; my book (?) is on my hands: I (?) guide the utterances of the gods". With the "Book" here mentioned cf. *supra* p. 94, and notice the suggestion that the contents of a ritual-book are "utterances" (*ḥw*) of the gods. Cf. with the *ḥw n nṯrw* the *mdw nṯr*.

mainly to Thoth's character as lunar deity, and that his appearance as ape suggests those aspects of his character which reveal depths of mysterious knowledge. It seems to be true, at all events, that before the N. K. Thoth is never represented as a moon-god in any variety of ape-symbolism. But, even if we were to assume that ape and ibis show us the god of wisdom and the moon-god respectively, other problems remain. How deduce, for instance, Thoth's function as funerary god from ibis-symbolism, or from ape-symbolism alone, or from both together? There is not merely a fundamental dualism in Thoth: his primitive character seems to show far more than two aspects. (1)

(1) In Babylon the moon-god, Sin, is not merely the "Lord of knowledge" [EN-ZU], as his name implies, but, also, the founder of shrines and sacrifices. *Vid.* Jastrow, *Bab. Rel.*, p. 437. Possibly the Egyptians also associated the moon with mysterious powers of knowledge, and, especially, with magic. Cf. Pyr., 823; the moon is mighty in *ḥike*. The *wḏ3.t* is used as a luck-bringing amulet. Cf. Plutarch' *Is. et O.*, 8: and Psalm 121, 6.

XI. Chapter.

Thoth the all-knowing.

The Pyramid texts, as has been seen, represent Thoth as the minister and as the scribe of Re, the sun-god. It has been conjectured above that this peculiar association of Thoth and Re may be due, in part at least, to the circumstance that the two greatest heavenly bodies, the rulers of the daily and nightly heavens, were inevitably put into a close official relationship in the primitive theologising of Egypt. In this official relationship, the moon-god would, of course, be subordinate to the sun-god, but would be immediately next to him in rank. As Re was thought of as an imperial ruler after the fashion of the Pharaoh, so the "silver sun", the substitute for, and representative of, the sun-god was naturally looked on as Re's chief minister, or vice-gerent in the government of the world. To rule the world as chief minister of Re, Thoth would require a high degree of intelligence, and a great range of knowledge. Yet the position would not demand any marvellous power of insight, or mysterious depths of knowledge. If, then, we find, as we do, in the Pyramids, that ancient texts ascribe to Thoth a peculiar power of knowledge as compared with other gods, we need not look on this as necessarily derived from his rôle as lunar vice-gerent of Re. It will be more probable that any gift or power of special gnosis which the texts ascribe to Thoth belongs to him out of all connection with the world-government of Re, — belongs to him, that is, in his own right. We have learned something already about Thoth's activity in the construction and furnishing of temples, and in the daily performance of the ritual in the shrines of Egypt. The power of Thoth as lunar deity to delimit men's lives, and to determine the course of their careers, has been also discussed. Functions such as these imply a very special endowment of mysterious knowledge, and, however the origin of that knowledge is to be explained, it is not strange to find that Thoth appears in Egyptian texts — especially in those of the later period — as the All-knowing One, as the dispenser of every kind of strange and mysterious gnosis. To him is assigned the invention of language and script. He is regarded as the patron of the sciences. He can read the secrets of men's hearts. He is the "one who knows" (1) in every direction. In the end he comes to be looked on as Understanding (or Reason) itself, personified. We shall here look rapidly through the texts for evidence on these points.

a) Invention of script, language and literature.

One of the very common epithets of Thoth is "who hath given words and script" (cf. Nav., *Totb.* c. 182, 3 f. etc.: Berlin 2293, XIXth Dyn.). The texts of the late period are particularly clear as to his invention of writing (Pap. Hearst VI, 9 f.: Ebers 1, 8—10). The script of funerary tablets is called the "*drf* of Thoth" (Berlin 7316, XVIIIth Dyn.). *Drf* means primarily legible signs, the separate characters in script: but it sometimes means "writing" in the sense of documents or texts (cf. Mar., *Dend.* III, 72 a), and, in this further sense of the word, Thoth was also regarded as lord of script. One of his most widely used epithets is *nb sš*, "Lord of writing". All kinds of texts — books, temple-inscriptions, collections of liturgical documents ("rituals"), inscriptions on stelae, and tablets were called 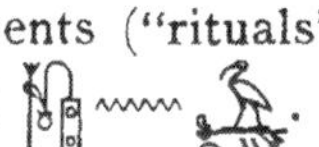.

Parallel with the title "Lord of script" goes another familiar title of Thoth 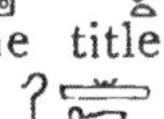 "Lord of books" (Mar., *Dend.* IV, 74 b: Urk. IV, 53 etc.). A similar title is 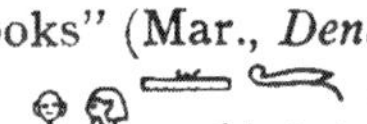 "President of books" (Philae: Phot. 1010). The Egyptian scholar or scribe was accustomed to set up in his study or library a statue of Thoth as ibis or ape. This custom, which implies Thoth's peculiar connection with script and literature explains a Ptolemaic title of the god 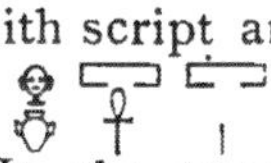 "the dweller in the library" (Louvre C. 232). (2) In the temple-archives of Den-

(1) So  in Dendereh, Mar., *Dend.* II, 35 b. For the prophetic knowledge of Thoth cf. *supra*, p. 86.

(2) Cf. Edfu R. I. 295 "Thoth of the house of books".

dereh and Philae Thoth presides in his ape-form over the niches where the documents dealing with the Temple-services were stored. (1)

As we might expect Thoth was peculiarly venerated by the scribes, and by the learned generally. Apparently it was in his ape-form mainly that he received this veneration. We have an interesting illustration of this in the fact that in the scribes' department of the Egyptian government-offices was set up a figure of the ape-god. (2) The scribal profession was, of course, one of the most highly respected of all in Egypt. It was respected, partly because of the comparative ease and pleasantness of the scribe's life, but, mainly, because the power of setting down records in script suggested to the common mind the possession by the scribe of mysterious and potent knowledge. Hence, as lord of the scribes, Thoth was regarded as the lord of all knowledge, and, peculiarly, as lord of all recondite and mysterious knowledge. He was the "knower" κατ' ἐξοχήν.

In Greek sources which are based on information acquired in Egypt we find that Thoth was regarded as the founder of human speech in its various forms. Diodorus says of Hermes: ὑπὸ γὰρ τούτου πρῶτον μὲν τήν τε κοινὴν διάλεκτον διαρθρωθῆναι καὶ πολλὰ τῶν ἀνωνύμων τυχεῖν προσηγορίας (I. 16, 1). From the same source we learn that Hermes first introduced γράμματα and that he was versed in the harmonies of the stars, and of sounds generally, and that it was he who first established the Palaestra, and laid the foundations of the sculptor's art. To him also are due, Diodorus tells us, the lyre, and discrimi-

(1) With this circumstance we must connect the texts in which we are told that important documents were found under the protection of Thoth, or in his shrine. Cf. *Totb.*, Nav., c. 137 A, 23—24; c. 148, 15—18 etc.

(2) See *Ä. Z.* 1907, p. 59 ff. Article by Borchardt on the Egyptian Foreign Office. In the tomb of 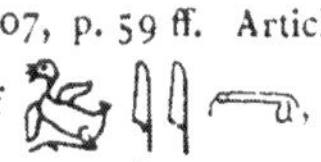, Thebes (Sethe 17, 105) is depicted an 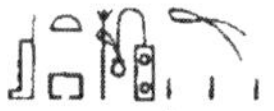 in the midst of which sits an ape wearing a lunar crescent who is called 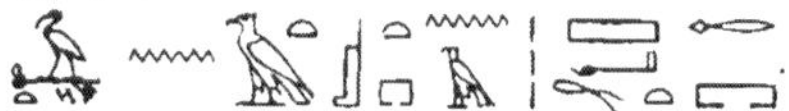. The deceased is a "royal letter-writer", and 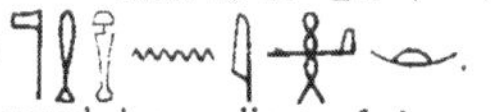. Numerous statuary groups representing the ape-god honoured by a client of the scribal profession are still exstant as a token of the veneration which the ancient Egyptian scribe paid to Thoth.

nation of musical tones, and the beginnings of the art of oratory (Diod. I, 16). In the Egyptian tradition, thus preserved by Diodorus, Thoth is the inventor of the fine arts, and to him is ascribed everything which helps to give to life civilisation and refinement. (1)

b) Searcher of hearts.

The knowledge of Thoth extended to the things hidden away in the hearts of man. "He knows what is in the heart", says a text of Karnak (Architrave of Ḥrihor, Sethe, 3, 66). "Thou art Thoth, says a Turin memorial tablet of the N. K. (Turin no. 101), who lovest Ma'et":  "thou lookest into hearts". When the eulogy of Hapi is sung (L. D. III, 175a Rams. II), it is said of him: 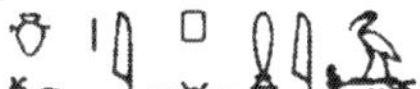 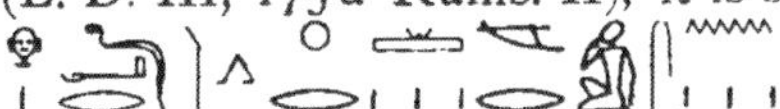 "his heart is *ip* like that of Thoth, seeking the plans (?) which they love". In Thebes (Tomb of *Nb-wnnf*; copy by Sethe) Thoth is described as "the knowing one who doth search out the hidden things of the body", and as "he that looketh through bodies, and testeth hearts". (2)

(1) It is interesting to note that in Plato (Philebus VII) θεῦθ is spoken of as he that distinguished the different letters, the vowels, the sonants, and the stops. Thus Thoth's connection with script and literature must have been known at an early period in Greece. In Hermetic texts of the Hellenistic period Hermes is the one who distinguishes languages and dialects (Reitzenstein, *Poimandres*, p. 37 note). With this we may compare Thoth's title Brit. Mus. 551  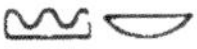 "who distinguishes the tongue of all foreign lands". For Thoth as  φαρμάκων καὶ γραμμάτων εὑρετής cf. Dieterich, *Abraxas*, p. 70. The scribe and the physician were, of course, the possessors of all knowledge that was unusual and efficacious. In the Book of the Dead, c. 125, Schlußrede 42—44 a porter who is called  "Dragoman of the Two Lands", is identified with Thoth. (For  see P.S.B.A. 1915, p. 117—125, article by Gardiner.)

(2) It is a familiar thought of the O. and N. Testaments that knowledge of mens' hearts is a prerogative of God, or of the Spirit of God which is sometimes communicated to men. Cf. Jer. 17[10]: Yahveh is חקר לב בחן כליות. Cf. the title תכן לבות Prov. 21, 2: 24, 12; and תכן רוחת Prov. 16, 2. Cf. Ps. 7, 10: Apoc. 2, 23. When the minute and all-embracing knowledge of the Pharaoh is described in Egyptian texts, we find such phrases as "who knows what is in hearts, who estimates bodies, and knows what is in them" (Luxor, Court of Amenophis III; *Mission* XV, 10, 3).

In the texts of the late period we find the epithet used as a sort of a *nomen proprium* with the ibis-determinative (Mar., *Dend.* III, 61 a : III, 81 e, etc.). This title is connected, as we have seen, with Thoth's rôle in the Judgment-scene; but it seems to convey also the divine power of Thoth to read the thoughts of men.

c) As possessor and source of every kind of knowledge.

A god whose mind is all-penetrating, and all-comprehending appears very naturally himself as "the Mysterious" (Nav., *Totb.* 116, 7) and as "the Unknown" (Turin Pap. P. and R. 25, 3—4). His gnosis which nothing could withstand, raises him above the ordinary Egyptian divinities. He cannot be classed with them, and is, therefore, the Unknown and Mysterious. (1)

Thoth's prudence is just as remarkable as his intellectual power. He is the "prudent of heart", so that a great and successful ruler is best described when he is said to be: "prudent of heart, like the Lord of Hermopolis" (Luxor, Stela of Rams. II; *Recueil,* 16, 56). With this should be compared what is said of Rams. III (Med. Hab. RIH, 142): . (2)

The prudence and the heart-searching power of Thoth are spoken of also in the M. K. À Cairo text of the XIIth Dynasty (Cairo 20538) speaks of the Pharaoh as "the god Sia who is in men's hearts: his eyes examine the hearts of all". The similarity with the later texts dealing with Thoth's knowledge, and the otherwise familiar identification of Thoth

(1) It is not surprising then that the source of apocalyptic knowledge in the Hermetic literature is Thoth, in his form as Hermes Trismegistos.

(2) Cf. with the above generally the prayer to Thoth in *Poimandres* (Reitzenstein, p. 22 f.): ἐπικαλοῦμαι σε τὸν τὰ πάντα κτίσαντα, τὸν παντὸς μείζονα, σὲ τὸν αὐτογέννητον θεόν, τὸν πάντα ὁρῶντα καὶ πάντα ἀκούοντα καὶ μὴ ὁρώμενον. In the same prayer Thoth (Hermes) is described as: οὗ οὐδεὶς θεῶν δύναται ἰδεῖν τὴν ἀληθινὴν μορφήν. The note of mysteriousness is here present, as in the epithet .

with Sia suggest that here also the reference is primarily to Thoth. (1)

Other epithets which imply the great knowledge of Thoth are not rare. This, he is  "the expert one" (Thebes, Tomb of Paser: Dümichen, *Hist. Inschr.* II, 43 a/3) and "the wise one"  (Luxor, Amenophis III, *Mission* XV, 10, 3). When the court-scribe wishes to give an adequate idea of the Pharaoh's mind and knowledge, he speaks thus: "Behold his Majesty knew all that had happened: there was nothing that he did not know: he was Thoth in all things: there was no word that he did not accomplish" (Rekhmare, 7: cf. *Ä. Z.* 1901, p. 61).

As the "All-knowing" Thoth had a particularly complete knowledge of Egypt: This is expressed in one of the most familiar of his Ptolemaic titles,  "he that knows the Two Lands". (2) Thoth, himself all-knowing, is the source of all deep knowledge and acumen which men possess. He gives to men knowledge itself and the faculties of mind. He makes men sharp-witted, and ready speakers. Haremheb calls his *šśrw* a gift of the Lord of Hermopolis. The , as Thoth is called, is the donor of all human farsightedness and astuteness. (3)

d) As Sia.

We have already discussed the problem of the identity of Sia "the bearer of the divine book at the right hand of Re". The god Sia appears in Egyptian texts as a deified personification of Reason or Understanding (4) — not at all primarily as a personal Logos, but simply as the faculty of Under-

(1) Cf. Moret, *Mystères*, p. 171, who seems to take the same view. See, in particular, his note 2, *ibid.*

(2) Often written with the ibis-determinative  (Mar., *Dend.* II, 29 d etc.). The reading is indicated in Dendereh (Dümichen, *Baugeschichte*, 42/6) as .

(3) Note that in Babylon Sin, the moon-god, is "the wise one of the gods" (Perry, no. 8). Possibly his Sumeran name EN-ZU is to be explained as = "Lord of knowledge".

(4) Possibly Sia = Perception. For a valuable study of Sia and Ḥu by Gardiner see *P. S. B. A.*, vol. 38, p. 43—54.

standing personified, and treated as a god. It is a deification parallel to that of Seeing, and Hearing, (1) and Utterance (= *Ḥu*). It may be said here, in general, that Sia is in no sense a Logos or Nous thought of as an emanation from, or as a self-manifestation of, a primitive divinity. This is indeed simply to say that Egyptian ideas must not be misrepresented in a Greek, or other non-Egyptian, method of exposition. The very existence, however, of a god of Understanding in Egyptian theology inevitably raises questions of parallelism and dependence as between Egypt and the Hellenistic world in matters of philosophical theology. Some of these questions will suggest themselves in the course of this study: but here already the general principle must be laid down that Egyptian conceptions must be studied as exclusively as possible from the native Egyptian point of view.

That Sia is, at times, identical with Thoth we have seen. Yet the latter is often enumerated along with Sia as a distinct divinity. To Sia and to Ḥu is assigned a special manner of origin which marks both of them off from Thoth. The 17th ch. of the Book of the Dead (Nav. 17, 28 ff.) represents them as sprung from a drop of blood which issued from the phallus of Re. This legend of their origin reminds one of the materialistic creation-story connected with Shu and Tefenet. And there are indications that the story is but a crass form of a myth which represented Understanding and Utterance as the first potencies which sprang from Re, by the help of which Re then proceeded to build up the world. (2) As we shall see later, Thoth and Horus were regarded, at least in one important ancient school of Egyptian philosophy, as the two first creations of Re; so that there is good reason in Egyptian texts for bringing Thoth into close connection with Sia and Ḥu. The distinction of Thoth from both Sia and Ḥu, and the close relation in which he stands with them are illustrated by the frequent appearances of the three divinities together n the same context. At times it seems as if the three divi-

(1) Cf. the hymns of Isis and Nephthys, Pap. Brit. Museum 10188, where Thoth is associated with "Hearing" and "Seeing" (or, possibly, where Thoth = *Iśtn*, is called the Hearer and Seer). On a Turin altar (*Transactions*, III, 110 f.) Thoth appears as "the seeing and hearing one" in the *Ḥt-ibt*.

(2) See Gardiner's articles, *P. S. B. A.*, vol. 38, p. 92 f.

nities are felt to be three phases of a single deity, or three aspects, so to speak, of a single concept (cf. Urk. IV, 49/18: Mar., *Dend.* III, 32 k—l). Ḥu and Sia appear frequently in the solar barque. (1) It is only reasonable that Re, the ruler of the world, should have with him in his royal barque, as his counsellors and as the symbols of his rule, Understanding and Command.

There can be no doubt that the Egyptians looked on Sia as a separate and independent deity, but it is, by no means easy to determine how clearly his individuality was realised. He seems to have had a character easily identified with that of other deities. Whenever it was necessary to emphasise the special wisdom of any god, it could be done most simply by identifying that god with Sia. Thus, of Amon it is said in the Leyden hymn (Leyden I, 350; 6 [= R s.], 1—2): "All countenances are turned towards him: men and gods say , he is Sia". Similarly it is said of Horus (Edfu R. II, 15) 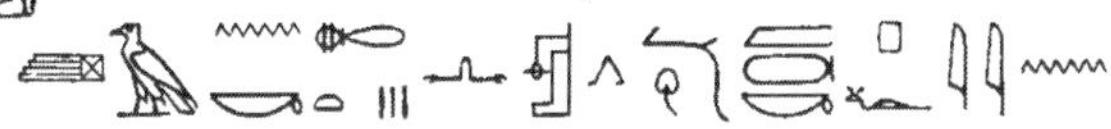  "thou knowest bodies even when no tongue doth move, in this thy name Sia". (2) Sia was, indeed, so abstract a divinity that he could be thus easily assimilated to other divinities — and to none more easily than to Thoth, the most mysteriously wise and prudent of the gods. Though Sia is at different times, identified with very various gods, he is identified far more frequently with Thoth than with any other. Throughout the huge body of texts of the Graeco-Roman period the identification of Thoth with Sia is so frequent that Sia is simply a second name of Thoth. Particularly is this the case in the ritual scenes in which the figure of Maʿet is presented by the Pharaoh to the deity who is being honoured. In nearly all these scenes Thoth is called Sia, and the king who presents Maʿet is styled "son of Sia", or "likeness of Sia" — apparently because he takes the place of Thoth in the ritual action. In the Ptolemaic texts Sia is very frequently determined with the ibis-headed god, thus,  (Mar., *Dend.* II,

---

(1) *Totb.* M. K. 17. Lepsius, *A. T.*, I, 16—2, 17. Cf. *Mission*, I, 168.

(2) Cf. Ps. 139, 4.

52 b, 71 b). Sometimes the identity of Sia with Thoth is expressed in an epithet, as, 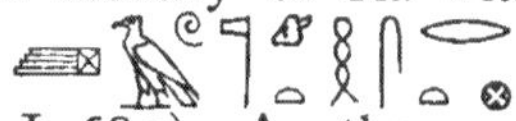 "Sia Lord of Hermopolis" (Mar., *Dend.* I, 68 a). As the presence of Ma'et in the barque of Re symbolises the fairness and justice of the sun-god's rule, so also, in the ritual scenes in which the Pharaoh offers to the god an image of Ma'et, it is implied that the rule of the Pharaoh is just and fair, like that of Re. When the king offers Maʿet as if he were Thoth, and is called Sia, or "Likeness of Sia", it is claimed implicitly by him that he is, in his life generally, and in the due performance of ritual particularly, a veritable Thoth, whose every action is an expression of Sia or Reason.

It must not be supposed, however, that in the deification of Sia, and in his identification with Thoth, there is any subtle metaphysics. Sia is merely a personification of understanding or perception: he is not a Logos in the sense of a self-revelation of a primitive deity. The reason, or perception, or understanding of any god might be thus personified, — and not merely the understanding of a primitive deity. It was natural, and indeed inevitable, that the intelligence of Thoth, the wisest of the gods, should be more frequently personified than the understanding of other divinities. (1) As god of literature, and of science, of theology, and of ritual, as the fountain and source of all knowledge and wisdom, Thoth, "the knowing one", would, most easily of the gods, come to be fused with Sia. But there is no deep methaphysics in the fusion. Thoth, simply as Sia, is not to be regarded as a world-ruling Nous in the Stoic sense. How far a conception analogous to the Stoic Logos was possible to Egyptian thought will be seen in the following chapter.

(1) How simply other divinities could be identified with Sia may be gathered, for instance, from the Edfu text quoted above, p. 105, R. II, 15, where it is said of Horus: "Thou knowest bodies without the movement of a tongue, in thy name Sia."

Chapter XII.

Thoth as Creator.

Egyptian theology does not show, in general, any clear tendency towards system. The great mass of religious texts in Egypt is marked by vagueness and even inconsistency. Individual gods are very rarely clear and well-defined personalities. Indeed, it is a feature of Egyptian theology that nearly every one of its gods is capable, in one way or another, of being fused with others. This fusion takes place, usually, as a result of the popularising of cults over wide areas. (1) In the earliest period each district was under the almost exclusive patronage of the local deity: but, as the intercommunications of the various districts became in course of time more intense, and as one or other dynasty or district became specially powerful in the political life of Egypt, or, as certain cults, of their nature universal, or, at least, national, became more prominent, fusions of all kinds took place among the Egyptian gods. The local cult of each district generally showed itself ready to identify its god with the more powerful and popular god of a wider area. Thus, it might happen that a god like Re, or Atum, or Ptah could be identified with practically every divinity in Egypt. And when fusion of local deities with gods of wider influence had taken place all over the country, it was easy, as a next step, to interfuse the local divinities with each other.

We must not, therefore, be surprised to find that local gods of apparently slight importance, often appear decorated with the titles of the great cosmic deities, or that these great cosmic deities often appear to be particularly related to some local cult. The case of Set, who, from being a local god — probably a storm-god — was raised to the rank of enemy-

(1) Such popularising was, in many cases, the direct or indirect result of political movements.

in-chief of the powers of light, has been already mentioned. The existence of solar divinities with varying attributes in different, and often widely separated districts of Ancient Egypt, is, probably, due also to the fusion of local cults with cults of their nature more widely known. The policy of identifying the divinities of local cults with the greater gods of Egypt, led to this, also, as suggested above, that each local god could assume the qualities, and activities of any or all of the great cosmic creative divinities. In this way any local god might become, through the ambition or zeal of his priests and worshippers, the primitive god, the creator of the world.

Not only was there much fusion in Egypt of local gods with the cosmic deities, but the latter also tended to become interfused with each other. It is not strange, therefore, to find that Thoth, who stands forth among the great ancient gods as the wise and learned one, should appear as a wise creator, or as a sort of demiurgic Reason, or Logos. This may be due to the familiar tendency, just mentioned, to attribute to the god of a local shrine the activities of a primitive divinity. It might, of course, on the other hand, be the product of a genuinely speculative turn of ancient thought, taking Thoth, or Reason, as a creatively active mode of appearance of the primitive deity — a turn of thought similar to that which excogitated the Demiurgic Nous of Greek speculation.

It is well known that the solar theology of Heliopolis, and the religion of Osiris dominated the theological speculations of Egyptian priests at all periods familiar to us through texts and monuments. The Osirian cult and the Heliopolitan theology appear, in most of our texts, as inseparably connected. The main speculative and systematic elements which appear in their fusion, are due, probably, to the solar theology. The dramatic factors are supplied by the cult of Osiris.

Solar theology secured, at an early period, predominance in Egyptian thought, and retained it throughout the whole course of Egyptian history. (1) Each of the ancient centres of

(1) The fact that it was the solar theology of Heliopolis, rather than that of any other ancient solar centre, that secured predominance in Ancient Egypt is most probably to be accounted for by the political preponderance of Heliopolis at a very early period.

sun-worship had, however, its own peculiar system of theology. This was probably due, as has been suggested above, to the presence in each shrine of features derived from local (possibly non-solar) cults. But there was, of course, something common in all the local theories of solar theology. In all of them, so far as we can see, the speculation of the great primitive shrine and centre of sun-worship at Heliopolis made itself strongly felt at an early period. In each centre of sun-worship, the deity of the place, transformed into a copy of the Heliopolitan Re or Atum, appeared as the primitive deity, as creator; and in each centre there was a special local theory of creation. Yet, so influential throughout the land was the theology of Heliopolis, that the creation-legends of Atum's shrine are reflected in most of the local cosmogonic systems. And this is true, not merely of local cults of which the sun-god was the deity, but also even of districts where a moon-god appears as chief divinity — as, for instance, *Ḫmnw*, the "City of the Eight". Even in this lunar centre we find traces of a solar theology, particularly in connection with creation. Indeed there is much evidence to show that some of the most important details of the Heliopolitan story of creation were localised in *Ḫmnw*. (1) It cannot surprise us, therefore, if we find in Egyptian theology, not merely a close connection between the speculations of Heliopolis and those of *Ḫmnw*, but even an attempt to fuse them systematically.

In the theology of Heliopolis the "great gods" were the offspring of the primitive god. The gods of heaven and earth and air and water, the Nile-god who made Egypt fertile, and the unfriendly divinities who devastated the land with drought, and burning glow, and storm — all should be, at Heliopolis, the children of the local god Re-Atum. This is so far true

(1) Cf. Nav., *Book of Dead*, c. 17, 4—5 : c. 64, 8—9 : c. 5. In the text of the Great Oasis (Brugsch, 26, 22—23) the scene of Amon's becoming is the "Height', of *Ḫmnw*. So in the Ptolemaic inscriptions of Bab el-Abd, Karnak, there is a reference to the Eight "who created light in the "Height" [of *Ḫmnw*] and took their place in Hermopolis with their father, the venerable one [*Špśi* = Thoth]". If the oldest creation-legends connected with the sun-god, are associated with Thoth's city, we must not be surprised to find that Thoth is identified, in some forms of speculation, with the first creation of Re (see below, p. 115 ff.). In certain forms of the creation-legend it would seem as if the *ḳ3i* of Hermopolis was the place where Shu made distinction between earth and heaven. Cf. *Totb.*, c. 17.

that the Ennead of Heliopolis presents a sort of summary of cosmological teaching. The gods of the Ennead are the gods of earth and heaven, and their grouping is indicative, to some extent, of the Heliopolitan view of creation.

In the first great group of Nine Thoth does not find a place, and it is clear that his presence in the second Nine is due merely to systematisation. Excluded, then, from the first Ennead Thoth is excluded from the old Heliopolitan theogony and cosmogony. Other ancient gods are also omitted from the great Ennead of Heliopolis. One of these is Ptah. And yet it is to be noted that Ptah himself at a very early period, if not primitively, was a solar deity at Memphis. It is clear, then, that some of the most important of the older gods of Egypt were not included among the gods honoured in the shrine of Re-Atum. Yet we find that attempts were made at a very early period to bring both Thoth and Ptah into connection with the creation-theories of Heliopolis. One of the most interesting documents of Egyptian theology deals directly with the problem of reconciling and interweaving the creation-theologies of Heliopolis and Memphis, and incidentally also with the relations between Thoth and the Heliopolitan Ennead.

The document in question is the so-called Shabaka text. (1) It is so important for the study of Thoth's cult that it must be here summarised and discussed.

The chief aim of the text is to depict Ptah, the local god of Memphis who presided over the guilds of stone-cutters and sculptors of ancient days in Memphis, as the first of the gods, and the creator of all things. In order to find a place for other gods and other theologies, while still asserting the preeminence of Ptah, the other important gods of Egypt, including Thoth and the Heliopolitan deities, are explained to be mere manifestations of Ptah. From the primitive god Ptah there issued eight emanations. These are so many different forms of Ptah, and constitute with him a Memphitic Ennead. In the next place we are told that Ptah and the Heliopolitan god Atum, are one, or, more precisely, that the creative activity of Atum is really a function of Ptah. Since the whole

---

(1) Published in a critical ed. by Erman, *Ein Denkmal memphitischer Theologie*, Sitzungsb. d. P. Akad. 1911.

creative activity of Atum is but a function, or energy, of Ptah, each creative aspect or element of Atum must be, in some way, a form or manifestation of Ptah. Now all the members of Atum are to be regarded as creative. Among the organs of Atum his heart and his tongue are the most important, for it was by these that the gods were created. Atum is Ptah, and Ptah must create, like the sculptor that he is, by drawing forth plans from the treasure-house of his heart, and giving them effect by the command of his tongue. Thus the heart and tongue of Atum become, in the Memphitic theology, forms of the artist-god, Ptah. With the heart and tongue of Atum the text identifies the gods Thoth and Horus respectively. These two gods constitute together one of the eight primitive forms, or emanations of Memphitic Ptah. The other seven forms are then shown to be identical with other organs of Atum. Whatever, then, the Heliopolitan god Atum, the world-creator, thinks, speaks, or executes, is thought, spoken and accomplished by one or more of the eight primitive forms or manifestations of Ptah. It follows that the gods who, in Heliopolitan belief, sprang from the mouth of Atum, viz. Shu and Tefenet, in reality sprang from Ptah. The old Heliopolitan legend told how certain gods were brought into being from the glands and hands of Atum; (1) but, since the various members and organs of Atum are really forms of Ptah, it follows that the Heliopolitan gods, generally, have taken their being, in truth, not from Atum, but from Ptah of Memphis.

As in Heliopolis, so in Memphis, the primitive god is thought of as creating first of all other divinities, who then, in turn, create all other beings in the universe. The divinities first created here are Thoth and Horus, the heart and tongue of Ptah. (2) By the thought of Ptah's heart, and the utterance of his word were called into being Atum and his Ennead (Horus and Thoth standing, therefore, here also, outside the

(1) Cf. Pyr. 1248. Cf. Pyr. 1652 and 1871.

(2) Cf. the manner in which Ḥu and Sia spring from the god Re. Cf. *Totb.* 17, 28 ff. It is important to note the various pairs of divinities which spring from the primitive deity — Shu-Tefenet: Tefen and Tefenet: Ḥu-Sia (= Utterance-Intelligence): Horus-Thoth. Perhaps we ought to find here an explanation of the frequent association of Thoth with Ḥu and Sia. Cf. *supra*, p. 104.

primitive Heliopolitan group). The next product of the heart and tongue of Ptah is the  — so that, not only the gods, but the "divine words" were created by Thoth and Horus. (1)

It is to be noted that the heart (= Thoth), and the tongue (= Horus) are not here conceived as two independent deities, but as a single form or emanation of Ptah. It is only in Atum that they are sundered — as separate organs of that god. It is obvious that the creative activity of Ptah, exercised, as here described, through thought and command (= Thoth-Horus: Sia-Ḥu), is just such activity as would befit the head of a school of sculpture.

In the ancient commentary which is attached to the text (2) Thoth recognises that Ptah, the "creator of the gods", is "greater in power than the gods". It was Ptah who founded every city and nome: it was he who built the temples, and set up the statues of the gods therein. The text assigns the earliest stages of the Osirian legend to Memphis — possibly in order to claim for Memphis the beginnings of ritual, or possibly, because Horus appears in this theology as a form of Ptah. The whole aim of the quaint text seems to be to set forth the theology of Heliopolis in a Memphitic form, and it serves well, therefore, to illustrate the tendency, already described, to assimilate the theologies of different shrines. For our purpose it has the special value that it helps us to give a reasonably full answer to the question raised in the preceding chapter as to the possibility of conceiving the Egyptian Thoth as a sort of demiurgic Nous in the Hellenistic sense. (3)

The text obviously represents Thoth as an organ, or faculty, of Atum — not as a manifestation of that god. He is a form of Ptah, also, but only in the same sense in which Horus and the other deities are forms of the god — viz. as a member or organ of Atum. Thoth is not set apart from the other deities in such a way as would imply a special philo-

(1) It is right to call attention here to the statement of Philo of Byblos (recorded in Eusebius, *Praep. ev.* I, 10, 390) that Τάαυτος created the hieroglyphic signs as so many images of the gods, and that these images of the gods were then hidden away in the innermost shrines of temples built to receive them.

(2) P. 941. Cr.

(3) See Bousset, *Kyrios Christos*, pp. 381 ff. for an attempt to explain the demiurgic function of Hermes by the latter's identification with Thoth.

sophy, or Logos-theory dealing with him. When Thoth is described as the heart of Atum, the outlook implied is like that of the Hymn to Amon of Leyden (I, 350. Recto 5, 15—17): "His heart is Sia: his lips are Ḥu: all that exists is what is in his mouth". (1) The style of the Memphitic text is normally Egyptian. Ptah is the primitive deity: the other gods are, therefore, his members and organs. Thoth is simply the thinking heart, just as Horus is the commanding tongue of Ptah. Of Ptah, as of Amon, an Egyptian poet might have said: "His heart is Sia (= Thoth): his lips (= tongue) are Ḥu (= Horus)".

In making Thoth the thinking faculty of the primitive deity the Memphitic text does not, therefore, necessarily speak of a creative Logos or Nous. The text, indeed, does not make Thoth the heart of Ptah, but only the heart of Atum, and Thoth is connected with the heart of Atum just as the other gods are associated with the less noble organs of that deity. The identification of Thoth and Horus, as the first creative form of Ptah, with the thinking and commanding faculties of Atum obviously implies the theory of a creation by command; but there is just as clearly implied in the text the more crude and materialistic kind of creation which was carried out by the glands and hands of Atum. It would be a mistake, therefore, to look for a genuine anticipation of Stoicism, or for any form of systematic philosophical thinking in the Shabaka text.

Since the text is as ancient as the Old Kingdom, the idea of Thoth as the heart of the solar deity must belong to a very early period of speculation. The idea occurs with striking frequency in the later literature of Egypt. Though in the Shabaka text Horus appears as the tongue of Atum, in the course of time he gives up this honour to Thoth, so that the latter appears both as heart and as tongue of the

(1) Cf. same hymn I, 350, recto 4, where it is said: "Amon arose from the ocean. Another form of him is the Ogdoad: he is the begetter of the primitive gods: he completed (*tm*) himself as Atum: he is the universal lord, the first who existed."

In the same document (recto 3, 22f.) it is said of Amon: "The Ogdoad was thy first form, so that thou mightest complete them into an Ennead". Again (*ibid.* I, 350, recto 4), the fingers of Amon are identified with the Ogdoad.

sun-god. (1) In Abydos (Mar., *Abyd.* I, 52) Thoth the Great is called the "Tongue of Re, and Lord of divine words". Possibly the same idea is partially suggested in the Turin Papyrus (P. and R. 23, 5) in the titles "Thoth the Great, the Bau of Re, the representative of Atum".

Identification of Thoth with the organs of the sun-god is very frequent in the texts of the Graeco-Roman period. Thus we find him called "heart of Re, tongue of Atum, throat of *Imn-rnf*" (Brugsch, *Thes.* IV, 759. Cf. Brugsch, *Religion*, p. 50 ff.). In Edfu (R. I, 269) Chons (= Thoth) is called "throat of *Imn-rnf*". The designation "Heart of Re" is applied to Thoth with striking frequency in the Ptolemaic texts. An echo of the Shabaka text is to be found perhaps in Dümichen, *Geogr. Inschriften* II, 42 where Thoth is called "Heart of Re, mighty in his words" — where the reference to creation by command seems to be fairly evident. So often does Thoth appear as "Heart of Re" in the Ptolemaic texts, that the title comes to be used as a personal name of the god. This is seen in the script 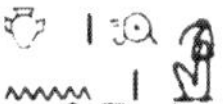 or  (Mar., *Dend.* II, 62, 65 a, 9 a etc. etc.). "Heart of Re" is thus simply an equivalent of "Thoth". (2) Possibly this explains why Thoth is occasionally called "Heart" simply,  (Mar., *Dend.* II, 9), and, possibly again, this throws some light on the saying of Horapollo (I, 36) καρδίαν βουλόμενοι γράφειν ἶβιν ζωγραφοῦσι, τὸ γὰρ ζῶον Ἑρμῇ ᾠκείωται πάσης καρδίας καὶ

(1) Reitzenstein (*Poimandres*, p. 237) cites a passage from the Papyrus Insinger according to which Thoth (?) is heart and tongue of the wise man. This means, according to R., that the thoughts and words of the wise man are the thoughts and words of the god himself. Hence the wise and pious would be in the god, and *vice versa*!

(2) Cf. the Dendereh text in Düm., *Hist. Inschr.* II, 57 d. Re wishing to soothe his angry daughter Tefenet sends to her his heart

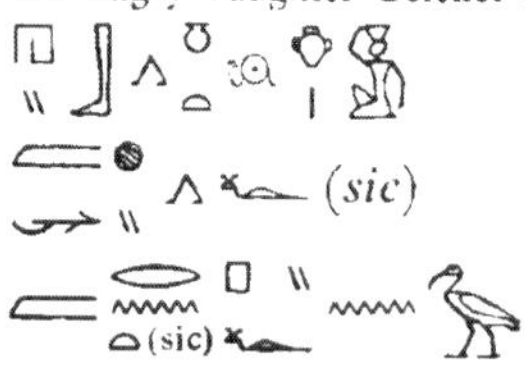

The heart and the Ibis (= Thoth) are here connected, not however, directly through the identification of Re's heart with Thoth, but through the assonance of 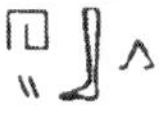 and .

λογισμοῦ δεσπότῃ, (1) In Edfu (R. I, 274) Chons (= Thoth) appears as heart of Atum, and (*ibid.* 273) as "heart of Re, which knows all things". One can scarcely refuse to see here a reminiscence of the theology of the Shabaka text.

There are some indications that the epithet "Heart of Re", so often assigned to Thoth, gave rise to much speculation in the Greek period. (2) The most interesting indication of such speculation is, probably, an Edfu text dating from the time of the fourth Ptolemy (Edfu R. I, 289). The text deals primarily with the origin of the Ogdoad of *Ḫmnw*. It locates their birth in Thebes — betraying, thus, the spirit of the solar theology of that centre, and furnishing another instance of the fusion of systems above referred to. But, though, the text is chiefly concerned with the "Eight" of the "City of the Eight", it is interested also in Thoth, the Lord of the "City of the Eight", and tries, obviously, to explain his title "Heart of Re".

The text begins with a reference to "the Eight great and mighty ones of the beginning, (3) the venerable gods who came into being at the beginning of all things, the gods who were begotten by *Tnn*, and who sprang from him . . . . who were brought forth (*mś*) in Thebes, and sculptured ( = "Ptah-formed") in Memphis. All things came into being subsequently to them." Then the text (4) goes on:

(1) In Mar., *Dend.* III, 15 c d  is written for *ib* (heart) in a puzzle-script. Cf. Düm., *Geogr. Inschr.*, 2. *Abtlg.*, Taf. 80.

(2) For an echo of the Shabaka text in Horapollo, see Erman, *Beiträge zur äg. Religion* (Sitzber. d. preuß. Ak. 1916, p. 1151 ff.). 4. *Herz und Zunge.* The passage is Horap. I, 21: it speaks of the heart as the leading or ruling principle of the body and the tongue as that which produces everything that is.

(3) They are called here 

(4) Professor Junker has suggested the following emendations (with translation) of portions of the passage:

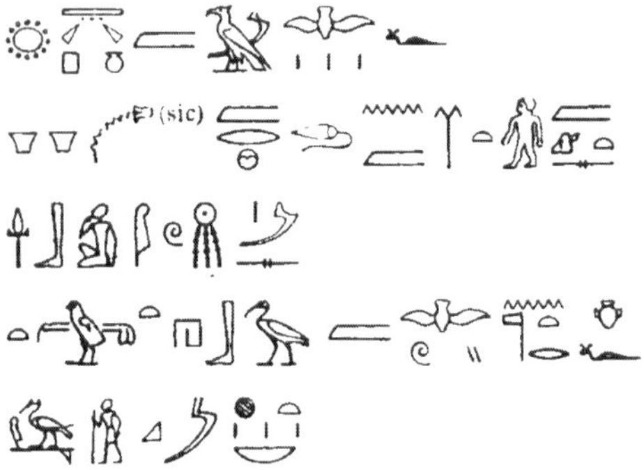

(a) 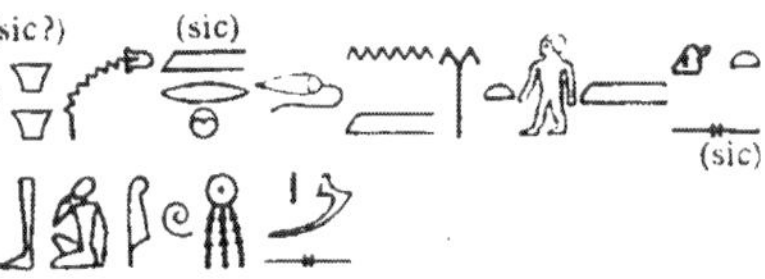

The lotus-bud spewed forth from within it a dwarf-maiden

whom "the Shining One" (= Re) loves to gaze on.

. . . .

(b) 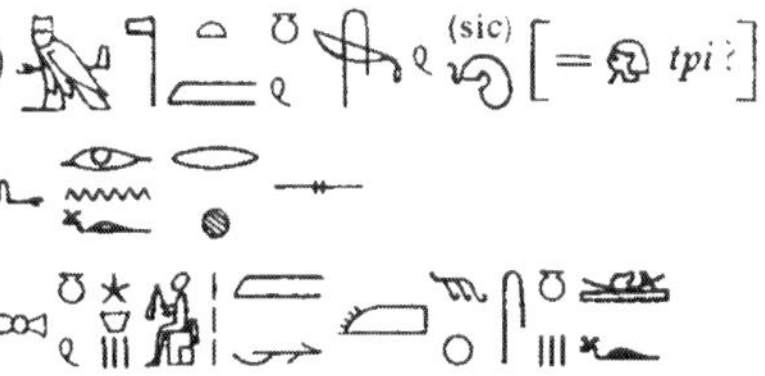

Behold, the god completed his first (?) plan,

and did not make it known.

He interred the ancient venerable ones when their time was completed.

For a parallel Prof. Junker has referred me to the Edfu text, Roch. II, 51. "The living gods who came forth from Re . . . . who repose at the west of Thebes"

Since the god, in order to seal their plans . . . .

Their time on earth was completed,

and their Ba flew heavenwards.

. . . .

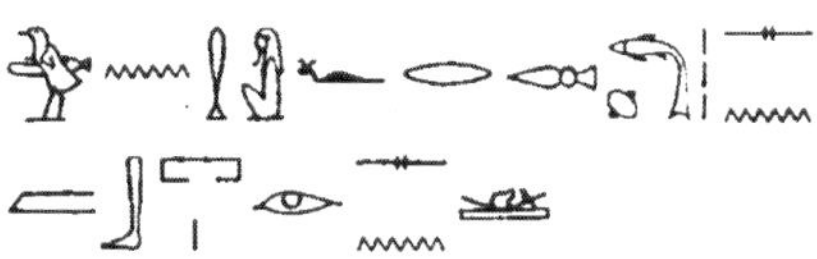

His Majesty (Re) gave command that their bodies should be interred

in the place where they were.

In Edfu II, 51 the venerable dead are called  and . Hence the  above are the *tpiw-ᶜ*.

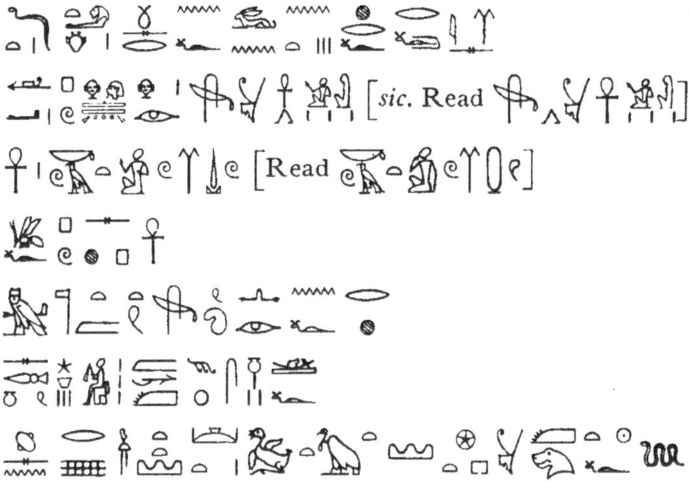

"Conceived in the ocean, born in the flood, a lotus came forth in which was a beautiful child who illumines this land with his rays; cast forth (reading = vomit: cf.) [from the lotus] was a bud (), in which was a dwarf-maiden whom Shu delights to look on. An ibis was begotten of the thought of his (*i. e.* Shu's) heart — Thoth, the great one, who created all things, the tongue (1) and heart that knows everything which is with him (*i. e.* Re) . . . . (2) This unique one, the governor of the Two Lands, who guides the living. "The Living One" his name is called.

(1) Cf. parallel Edfu I, 273, Chons, heart of Re, who knows all things according to which we can readily correct into .

(2) Possibly ought to be . Should we read instead of referring it to Re? Cf. Edfu, R. I, 296 . Cf. the description of Horus in Edfu (Piehl, *Inscr.* II, 78. Time of Ptol. IX):

His task is the creation of life . . . . He assigned (or buried?) them (i. e. the Eight) to the western nome of ⲬⲎⲘⲎ. the Duat of the *Km-ꜣtf.*"

The text is obscure in detail, but its general meaning is clear. It contains an attempt, obviously, to explain the importance of the ibis-god by a reference to his origin. That origin is shown to be closely connected with the origin of the sun-god himself. This is not strange, since, as is well known, the scene of several Egyptian creation-legends was laid in or near the "City of the Eight". But the point of special interest peculiar to this text is its preoccupation with the familiar epithet of the ibis-god — "Heart of Re". Here again we have clear echoes of the theology of the Shabaka text, for here *Ṯnn* (= Ptah) is again chief creator, and the Eight are described as "sculptured" (= "Ptah-formed") in Memphis; and here again, the heart and tongue of the chief god are the instrument of creation generally. It looks almost as if we had in this text a fragment of theological speculation explaining Thoth's epithet "Heart of Re", and giving grounds for his authority over the Eight of *Ḫmnw*. The spirit of the text connects it more closely with Thebes than with Heliopolis, but, after all, Amon of Thebes is a form of Re.

In this legend Thoth appears as the first-begotten of Re. This relation of Thoth to the sun-god is suggested also by a number of familiar epithets of our god, such as, "eldest child of Re" (Metternich Stela 244), "the great one, the eldest child of Re" (Edfu R. I, 266), "the most ancient one begotten at the beginning" (Dendereh : Düm., *Geogr. Inschr.* III, 57). The primordial character of Thoth, as eldest child of Re, is thus fully expressed in a Dendereh text (Brugsch, *Thes.* IV, 760): "Thoth, thrice great, Lord of Hermopolis, the glorious ibis (*tḫn*), presiding over Egypt 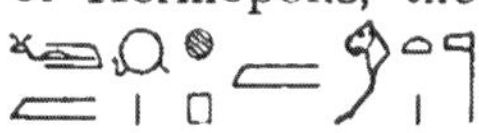, sprung from Re, born at the beginning." (1) The Thoth-epithet "sprung from Re" is not confined to Ptolemaic texts. In a text of the time of Queen Hatshepsowet in Speos Artemidos Thoth is

---

(1) Cf. Düm., *Geogr. Inschr.* III, 49 Dendereh. Thoth is 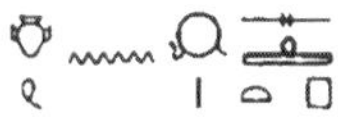
.

described as "the great one, sprung from Re". (1) "Eldest" comes, thus, to serve as a standing epithet, or personal name of Thoth (cf. Edfu, Mammisi, p. 14: Düm., *Baugeschichte*, XXV). (2) This fact explains the circumstance that in the Rhind Papyrus the Demotic script *Ḏḥwti* corresponds to the hieratic *Śmśw* (Brugsch, *Wörterbuch*, p. 1233). With Thoth's epithet *Śmśw*, and with the equivalent epithet may be paralleled another of his titles, (Dendereh L. D. IV, 76 e). (3) It is the fact, of course, that other gods, as well as Thoth, are sometimes described as "born at the beginning", but in every case in which an epithet like this is applied to a god, it is claimed for, the deity in question that he is, at least one of the great primeval gods.

As first-born of the gods Thoth came to be regarded as creator of all that became subsequently to himself. A very natural extension of this creative activity made him creator of himself, so that he is sometimes called "self-caused" or "self-begotten" (Turin Pap. P. and R. 25, 3—6). (4) In the Shabaka text we have already seen him functioning as a creator, but there he functions as creator only as a form of Ptah, and not, as it were, in his own right. But, just as many of the local deities of Ancient Egypt were revered as creators, and were not regarded as being sufficiently dignified without that activity, Thoth of Hermopolis also became a world-fashioner on his own account, and a rival of Atum, Chnum, Ptah, and others. Each of the creative gods of Egypt fashioned the universe after his own manner. Ptah formed the

(1) *Urkunden*. IV, 387 .

(2) *Śmśw Rʿ* is properly speaking an epithet of Re's son, Shu.

(3) With these epithets of Thoth may be usefully compared certain Babylonian titles of the moon-god Sin. He is called *tumu sag Enlillá*, "chief son of Enlil" (Perry, no. 3, l. 5). He is also often called *mar restu sa Bel*, "eldest son of Bel" (Combe, *Culte de Sin*, p. 17). *Aplu gitmalu* "the perfect son" is another of his titles (Perry, no. 7, l. 9). It is to be noted that in Babylon Shamash, the sun-god, sometimes appears as son of the moon-god (cf. Combe, *l. c.*, p. 18).

(4) The Turin text adds . As he has no cause of his being outside himself, so there is no higher reality through which he can be known.

gods as a sculptor. Amon begot (*ms*) them: Chnum formed gods and men on his potter's wheel, and so "built up the world". Thoth also is "the maker of all that is" (Edfu, R. I, 164): he is "the heart of Re which hath made the Ennead as well as himself" (Edfu, *ibid.*): he is "the Great one who hath created all things" (Edfu, R. I, 289): he is "the heart of Atum which hath fashioned all things" (Edfu, R. I, 274). He is obviously regarded as a creator in his own right. But Thoth was neither ram, nor sculptor, nor potter, and could not create like any of these. The Shabaka text, and the many other texts above referred to, give us an idea of the peculiar kind of creation which was carried out by Thoth. He created as the heart of Atum, or of Re, and as the tongue of the sun-god which commanded thoughts into being. His special mode of creative work is creation by utterance. In the Thoth of later Egyptian speculation the aspects of thought and utterance which appear sundered in the Shabaka text are brought together into their natural unity. For the Egyptian the knowledge and power of the scribe were mysterious, for the scribe, like a god, "brought into being what was not" (as Pyr. 1146 a, c says of the scribe of the divine book): hence of Thoth, the chief scribe, it is said:  "what comes from his heart, at once takes place" (Brugsch, *Thes.* IV, 760). (1) The word of the thinker gives being to his throught, and, hence, the creative power of Thoth is exercised in the utterance of command. Whatever exists, then, is a creation of Thoth's heart projected by utterance into the physical reality of experience. The oldest Egyptian texts are familiar with the productive and creative power of certain spoken words. That idea underlies the magical formulae of the Pyramids. It gives a very real meaning to the votive tablets, and to the stelae of the Old and Middle Kingdoms. It is an idea which comes to expression frequently in Egyptian

---

(1) Cf. prayer to Thoth Poimandres, p. 22: "I invoke thee ἐκ μὴ ὄντων εἶναι ποιήσαντα καὶ ἐξ ὄντων μὴ εἶναι. Cf. Edfu, R. II, 16: "Whatever is began through his [Thoth's] command"; and "little is there which hath come to be without his words". Note the epithet of Chons (= Thoth) in an inscription on the statue of *Ḏd-Ḫnsw-iwf-ʿnḫ* (Cairo, *Wb.*, no. 45) 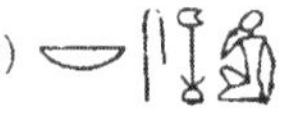 "lord of thought".

funerary literature. (1) The creative power of utterance is implied in all passages which speak of magical and mysterious names of kings and gods. (2) That speech possesses creative efficiency is a genuinely oriental notion. Among the Semites the far-reaching power of the formula of blessing or of cursing, and the deep importance of the name, are well-known. It is therefore quite oriental and Egyptian to suppose that a word can summon a thing into being, or banish it into nothingness. The writer of the Shabaka text gives us clearly enough to understand how he conceives of creation through speech or utterance. He says: "When the eyes see, the ears hear, and the nose inspires breath, they convey that to the heart: that (viz. the heart) it is which causes every decision to go forth, and the tongue it is which pronounces what the heart has thought. It (the tongue) fashioned (thus) all the gods, and the Ennead: (3) and every divine word also came into being through what the heart conceived, and the tongue commanded" (*op. cit.* p. 939 f.). Thus, even the ancient period associated with Thoth's creative action the idea of a production by thought and utterance, — by Sia, if we wish to express it so, and Ḥu. It is important to note how, in the Shabaka text, the gods are first produced in this way, and then the "divine words", *i. e.* probably all such formulae as were themselves endowed with a productive or creative power.

Thoth, then, created by thought and utterance. So it is said of him Edfu, R. I. 267: "Thou art the god sprung from the god (*i. e.* the sun-god) himself, for whom the gates of the horizon opened on the day of his birth: every god came forth at his command: his word passes into being: thou art Chons-Thoth." (4)

(1) Cf. Nav. *Totb.*, c. 17, 5—7.

(2) Cf. *Totb.*, c. 17, 5—7. When Re devised the names of his members, his retinue (*imiw ḫt-f*) were created. In the Book of Dead of M. K. c. 17 (Lepsius, *Älteste Texte*) when *Si*} used the word *miw* in reference to Re the sun-god came to be known as (and therefore to be) a cat (*miw*). Similarly Thoth appears often (especially in the Horus-myth of Edfu) as a name-giver.

(3) Cf. Edfu, Mammisi, p. 14. "Thoth .... Heart of Re, who made the Ennead after himself."

(4) The epithets of Thoth as creator are often transferred to Chons. Thus, in Edfu (R. II, 68) Chons is "the heart of Re which knoweth all that hath happened in heaven; tongue of *Tṯn* which knows what is, and commands all that

If Thoth is a creator, like other deities, in his own right, and after his own fashion, why is he so constantly spoken of as creating in his rôle of "Heart of Re"? This seems to make him subordinate, as a creator, to the sun-god. It is possible, however, that this is due chiefly, or solely, to an attempt to fuse the theologies of Heliopolis and Hermopolis, to an attempt, that is, to equate the god of Hermopolis with the sun-god Re. Thoth himself as creator, out of all contact with Re, was a creator who worked like the scribe and philosopher, by thought, and by the power of productive speech. If, then, the attempt were made by a priest of Hermopolis to show that Thoth and Re are but different forms of a single deity, either deity must become a form or manifestation of the other. Obviously the thinker, Thoth, could more easily become a manifestation of Re than manifest himself through Re. Besides, Thoth, as moon-god, was already a substitute for, or representative of Re. Yet in the fusion of the gods Thoth must not be made inferior to Re. The problem was solved, on the one hand, by transferring Thoth's creation-activity to Re, and, on the other, by identifying the thought-principle of Re, the root-principle of creation, with Thoth. This is what we actually find in the strange Edfu text quoted above: it is also what is implied in calling Thoth "Heart of Re". Thoth is conceived as the first product of Re's thought, but he is also, the thinking faculty itself of Re. Further, the thought-act of Re's heart by which Thoth is produced, is, at the same time, an act of the god who is the "Heart of Re". Thus Thoth is, in every sense, self-begotten.

It would be wrong, however, to see here any deep metaphysics. There is really nothing here of a Stoic, or Philonic Logos. There is nothing more here, in fact, than the natural result of an Egyptian tendency to equate or fuse the theological theories of different cult-centres. Apart from Re, Thoth

takes place on earth. He is the throat of *Imn-rnf*, Chons, the great god in Edfu." Again (R. I, 273) Chons is "the heart of Re which knows all things, the tongue of *Tm* which understands every thing."

The theory of creation by utterance, as held in Egypt, has often been discussed. See Maspero, *Études*, II, p. 259; Moret, *Le Verbe créateur et révélateur en Egypte* (*Rev. d. l'h. des Rel.*, 1909, p. 279 ff.); Reitzenstein, *Zwei religionsgeschichtliche Fragen*, p. 83.

is himself a creator, a primitive god, not a creative Logos sprung from another deity. But, like most other Egyptian gods, he comes to be forced into the system of Heliopolitan speculation; he has to come to terms, as it were, with solar theology, and then he becomes the first-born of Re, the "Heart of Re", and "tongue of Atum", and "throat of *Imn-rnf*". Reitzenstein appears to err, therefore, in suspecting a Greek, and, in particular, a Stoic influence as showing itself in Thoth's title Heart of Re. (1) Egyptian tendencies, obviously already at work in the Shabaka text, fully account for the epithet.

It still must remain, of course, an unsolved problem to determine whether Stoic influence may be traced anywhere in the hieroglyphic texts of the Ptolemaic period. The problem will remain unsolved until some scholar fully familiar with the thought and language of the Egyptian texts of the Ptolemaic period, and fully familiar, also, with the documents of Stoic philosophy, devotes himself to its solution.

(1) *Zwei religionsgeschichtliche Fragen*, p. 73.

Chapter XIII.

Thoth in magic.

Thoth is a moon-god. He is god of wisdom, and orderer of the cosmos. His word has power to call things into being. It is little wonder, then, to find him endowed with great magical powers. Magic presupposes always a special Gnosis. The magician claims to possess a higher and deeper knowledge than others, a knowledge of the secret nature of things, and of the hidden connections which hold things together. He is the wise one who knows the real names of things, the one whose words have power to control mysterious forces, and to ward off invisible perils. And the magician does all this by the power of his special gnosis, and without any appeal to physical strength.

Thoth, as the wisest of the gods, became for the Egyptian, of necessity, a magician. We saw above that Thoth stands in closest relation with temples and cult. Between the prayer of worship, and the formula of the magician there was a striking similarity. Ritual and magic stood near each other in the ancient religions. Thoth, therefore, as lord of ritual, became also inevitably, lord of magic. Again, we have seen that Thoth was the skilled physician who healed the damaged eye of Horus, and that he was the patron of physicians generally. Magic and medicine were, at one time, but different names for the same science. Thoth, as physician, was thus, already skilled in magic. Finally, the priests and physicians were of the learned professions, of "those wo know", and Thoth, as the knowing one *par excellence,* could not fail to become the patron of both professions, and, therefore, a magician equipped with all possible knowledge of the worlds of gods, demons, and men.

The pyramid texts make it quite clear that magic played a great part in the life of ancient Egypt. The funerary ceremonies for the dead king, which occupy the major part of these texts, consist largely of descriptions of magical acts, and the formulae which accompany them. The magic formulae of the Pyramid texts are already so ancient as to be stereotyped, and it is clear that the scribes who have handed on the Pyramid texts often had no clear idea of the sense of the ceremonial formulae which these texts contain. Some of the formulae transmitted in the Pyramid texts had, already in the Old Kingdom, become so unintelligible, that the scribes, in certain cases, add to them a commentary. It is clear, therefore, that a tradition of magic rites and formulae had already become fixed in the Old Kingdom. The question arises, then, whether we can find traces of Thoth's connection with magic in the earliest period of Egyptian literature. In the later periods this connection is clear. We can, therefore, most conveniently begin with the later period in order then to reach back, if possible, to the oldest texts.

In the Ritual of Amon (Formula 41; Berlin, P. 3055, 24, 5—7) Thoth is called "the great in magic". He gets the same title in the Book of the Dead (Nav. 182, 8. Af.). In Edfu he is called "learned in magic". In the Ptolemaic period "great in magic" has become, like "Heart of Re", a personal name of Thoth, and is written with the Thoth-determinative — (Mar., *Dend.* III, 67a). We find Thoth also designated simply "the Magician" (Düm., *Baugesch.* 50). (1) There are traces of a god Ḥike as far back as the O. K. (Cf. Mariette, *Mastabas* B. 4), and he appears occasionally at other times (Cf. Lacau, *Text. rel.* 78, Rec. 31, 164 ff. Metternich Stela, 43: Dendereh, L. D. IV, 58a). It is, therefore, possible that the name (2) might be intended to identify Thoth with the ancient god Ḥike. It is also, of course, possible, in the abstract, to regard the god Ḥike of the O. K. as a form of Thoth.

(1) The "Great one" and the "Magician" of the Amduat (7th hour, according to Sethos IV, 43) is, probably, Thoth.

(2) Thoth is described Edfu, R. I. 164 as "he who wrote magic-books".

To make clear the function of Thoth as a magician we must here examine briefly the applications of the term *ḥike* as a substantive in Egyptian.

In the Pyr. texts, and in the oldest texts of the Book of the Dead *ḥike* appears as a power (or quality) which is possessed by the gods, and by all the deified dead. (1) It is something which is needed to make divinity complete — a necessary item, so to speak, of a god's equipment. It is represented (Pyr. 397) as a quality of the gods which the king assimilates by devouring the substance of the gods. (2) It is, further, set forth as a power or equipment of the Dead of which they may be robbed by various enemies in the Underworld. (3) It seems, thus, to resemble, somehow, other qualities, or endowments needed for the full perfection of the glorified Dead — something, that is, on the same plane as the so-called Kas of Re. It deifies to some extent. Again, it is clear from a number of passages that *ḥike* implies power over things demonic and evil. It is used, for instance, against the foes of the sun-god, (4) or against sickness — particularly against various forms of poisoning. (5) The power thus employed against evil is often described as if it were something carried in the mouth, and put into action by utterance. (6) In a few isolated passages *ḥike* seems to mean — strangely enough, at first sight, an evil thing or influence which is to be expelled. (Ebers, 34, 7 etc.)

Looking at the use of the word *ḥike* generally, we find that it seems to include the whole field of what might be called magical. It is a sort of mysterious power which can produce effects beyond the sphere of man's achievement: (7) it is a something before which demons of sickness, and of poison — evil demons in general, must give way. Hence the

---

(1) Pyr. 397 : 250 : 924 : 1318 : 1472.

(2) Cf. Pyr. 403 : 410 : 411.

(3) Book of Dead, 32, 1 : 31, 4 : 90, 7—10.

(4) Cf. Pap. Brit. Mus. 10188, 25, 15 : 31, 20. Thoth comes with *ḥike* to destroy the Apophis.

(5) In the Metternich Stela Thoth comes with *ḥike* to expel poison.

(6) Cf. Book of Dead, 31, 4 : 108, 8: Naville, *Myth of Horus*, plate XXII.

(7) In the Westcar Papyrus *ḥike* = the charms of the magician (VI, 12 VIII, 25—26 : VIII, 20—21 etc.). It is by *ḥike* that, according to the Pap. Sallier (IV, 3—4), Thoth transforms the severed head of Isis into the head of a cow. Cf. Pyr. 855 : Book of Dead, 24, 1—4 : 23, 7—8.

uraeus serpents, the deities who guard the king, are "great in *ḥike*" (Pyr. 1832. Cf. Erman, *Hymnen an das Diadem der Pharaonen*, pp. 13, 24, 35, 48, 50). Isis and Nephthis, as protectors of Osiris, are also "Great in *ḥike*". Thus *ḥike* seems to include the whole sphere of magic, and to extend beyond it. Erman says of it rightly (*ibid.* p. 13, note 2): It is *„die übernatürliche Kraft, die auch außerhalb des Zaubers wirkt"*.

Thoth then, when he is called *„Great in ḥike"*, or "Ḥike", appears as a god of magic. As "Lord of divine formulae" he was in a specially favourable position to use his *ḥike*. No evil thing, whether foe of Osiris, or spirit of disease, could withstand the power of his words. He was in this sense truly 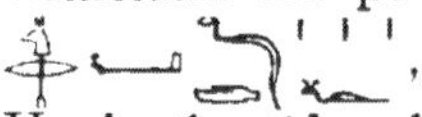 „Mighty in his formulae" (Dend. L. D. IV, 58a). He is the "dreaded of demons" and the "Lord of dread" to evildoers. (1) Great in power of charms Thoth protects Osiris, and wards off the enemies of that god by his  and his . (2) The effect of his "Glorifications" would be to intensify the divinity of the being whom he guarded, and to deprive of all strength the foes of the latter. The  of texts of the late periods, which meant at first to "glorify" or "deify", comes, finally, to have magical associations — somewhat like δοξάζειν in the literature of the Hellenistic period. (3)

The important part played by Thoth in the legends of the Eye of Horus has been explained already as due mainly to his lunar character. The peculiar aspects of his activity in certain forms of that legend, however, which seem to lay stress on his powers of eloquence and persuasion, and on his capacity to speak words of wondrously soothing and pacifying influence can scarcely be detached from his rôle as a god of magic. Between the ritual formula which produces the effects it describes and the words which calm and soothe the anger of the Eye of Horus (or of Hathor-Tefenet) there is in common an element which might be called magically productive or

(1) Cf. Book of Dead, 134, 8 f. (where *Ištn* = Thoth). For  see Pyr. 2110c.

(2) Cf. Book of Dead, 182, 8—11 : Mar. Dendereh III, 77 a/b, 3 : Florence, *Cat. gen.*, Schiaparelli, no. 1603.

(3) Cf. Reitzenstein, *Hellenistische Mysterienreligionen*, p. 142.

creative. Hence the strength or excellence of Thoth's speech is partly at least, magical, and his predicates "excellent in speech", (1) "soother of the gods", (2) "pacifier of *Nsr. t*", (3) "cool of mouth", (4) "the peaceful one that knows how to repel evil", (5) "the sweet of tongue", (6) etc. etc. should all be connected somehow with his skill in magic.

It is by his "Glorifications" especially that Thoth not only protects, but also soothes the gods. This effect of his words is conveyed most commonly in his epithet (Edfu, R. I, 297, and often). (7) It is said of him in Philae, (Phot. 15) "who soothes the heart of the gods by his words". In this Thoth is like Sin the moon-god of Babylon, who is described as *muniḫ libbi ilāni.* (8) The words or formulae of Thoth seem to drive

---

(1) *iḳr ḏd,* Horus-Myth, Nav. Pl. I.

(2) Śḥtp *nṯrw,* passim.

(3) Śḥtp *Nsr.t,* frequent in the Onuris-legend.

(4) , Turin Pap. P. and R. 24, 1—4. In the same text Thoth is described as .

(5) , Erman, *Denksteine aus der theb. Gräberstadt,* p. 1103 f.

(6) , Horus-Myth, Nav. Pl. I. The folk tale of the Leyden Papyrus (I, 384) published by Spiegelberg gives a description of some of the oratorical powers of Thoth, and of his skill as a *raconteur* and of his persuasiveness as a pleader. Junker quotes in this reference an interesting text from Ombo (I, 122): Tiberius presents a moon-eye to Chons: in the text Chons is called "Chons-Thoth, the great *šḫm* who brought from *Bwgm* the Great One who had been far away". Chons-Thoth is here styled: — "The Prince who judged the gods, who soothed the *rḥwi* with his honeyed tongue" (See *Onurislegende,* p. 163), Thoth's appeasement of the *Nsr.t* was achieved we are told by his *si3ḫw*. Cf. Philae Phot. 1643: Thoth, (Junker, *Auszug* p. 48).

(7) The magical value of Thoth's appears already in the Pyr. texts: they have power to open the gates of (Pyr. 1713: Cf. Pyr. 706, where Anubis, rather than Thoth, seems to effect the "glorification": but even here it is as Thoth that the King is "glorified". Cf. Berlin 1188 for parallel).

(8) Perry, *Sin,* no. 6, l. 6: "who soothes the heart of the gods".

away from the hearts of the gods the gloom and depression caused by the presence of powers of evil.

We have here the genuine oriental idea that certain formulae have a potency to resist or expel the influence of malicious spirits. There are indications that the magical formulae of Thoth existed in special collections. A statue in Cairo (No. 583, XVIIIth Dyn.) says: "I was initiated into the divine book: I saw the glorifications of Thoth". Probably the contents of the "divine book" were mainly made up of the protecting, and deifying charms, or "glorifications" of Thoth the "Scribe of the divine book", "who wrote the books of *ḥike*".

The magician is necessarily a being of great power, since even the strongest antagonists — even demons, are compelled to submit to him. It is not improbable, therefore, that a number of epithets implying the possession of great power and strength which are often given to Thoth, are connected with his rôle as magician. Such are, perhaps, "Lord of strength" (Book of Dead 182, 8), the "strong one" (Book of Dead, Lepsius c. 11, 4),  (Pyr. 1725 b), (1) 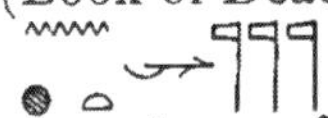 (Pyr. 1237 c). The power and strength of Thoth are shown forth in his magic formulae. His frequent designation in the later texts — "Thrice Great", may well point to the god's position as Lord of *ḥike,* and, hence, the Coptic magical Papyrus of Paris, when it calls Thoth ⲠⲚⲞ ⲠⲚⲞ ⲠⲤⲀⲂⲈ may be regarded as referring to his magical influence, and to his peculiar wisdom by which he acquired that influence. (2)

---

(1) Cf. Dendereh, L. D. IV 76 c , Philae, Phot. 1448. 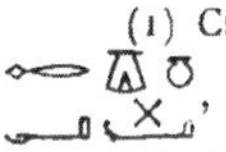, Philae, Phot. 1434.

(2) "Thrice Greatest" must be ultimately traced to the frequent designation of Thoth as ꜥꜣ ꜥꜣ wr. For Thoth as "eight times great" cf. Reitzenstein, *Poimandres*, p. 118 (note), and Griffith, *High Priests*, p. 58. Griffith finding in his text the epithet "Eight times great" applied to Thoth, explains it thus: ꜥꜣ = μέγας : ꜥꜣ ꜥꜣ = "twice great" : "twice μέγας" (Rosetta stone μέγας καὶ μέγας) = μέγιστος. Now 8 = 2^3. Hence since ꜥꜣ ꜥꜣ (2) = μέγιστος "eight times ꜥꜣ" must = τρισμέγιστος. However τρισμέγας occurs as an epithet of Hermes, and possibly τρισμέγας and τρισμέγιστος were really felt to be identical: in that case τρισμέγιστος would be simply a rendering of ꜥꜣ ꜥꜣ wr. "Many times", says Plutarch (I. O. 36, 4), "we are wont to call *thrice*". Maspero reading in his text of *Satni-Khamois* (*Contes pop. de l'Eg. anc.*, p. 171) "Thoth the nine times great" explains that ꜥꜣ ꜥꜣ is a comparative, and ꜥꜣ ꜥꜣ ꜥꜣ (or ꜥꜣ ꜥꜣ wr) a superlative (and therefore = μέγιστος). Hence when Thoth is called

By his charms or "glorifications" () Thoth protects the gods and deifies the dead: by them also he delivers men from the perils that threaten them from the evil demons that surround them. (1) To be delivered from those threatening dangers, a man needs only to invoke Thoth's name on himself, for he becomes thereby, for the moment, identical with the god. This is the thought of the formula in the Turin Papyrus (P. and R., 125): "No sickness alighteth on him: he is Thoth the Great, the son of Re on the throne of Atum". Another way of insuring oneself against sickness is to identify oneself by potent words with Horus, for Thoth will then hasten to protect the new Horus as he once protected the child Horus from the scorpion's sting. (2) The protection of Thoth seems to have been peculiarly efficacious against scorpion-attacks. The aid of the god is sometimes invoked in sickness by reminding Thoth of his own physical troubles, and his own successful treatment of them. "O Thoth heal me as thou didst

---

"nine times great" we have a superlative of a superlative, *i. e.* "thrice greatest" τρισμέγιστος. It has been suggested that Thoth's title "eight times great" is to be explained as a reference to the fact that eight dog-headed apes were his δορυφόροι in *Ḫmnw*. It is to be noted that the title of Thoth's High Priest at *Ḫmnw*, *Wr dỉw* "the Great of the Five", has been similarly explained as referring to the four deities who were worshipped at an early period along with Thoth in *Ḫmnw*. The four primitive divine beings afterwards became, by the addition of four female deities, the eight δορυφόροι of Thoth and thus arose the name of their city *Ḫmnw*. "The Great of the Five", as a title of Thoth (as well as of his high priest), is related to the title "five times great" which Thoth receives (cf. Griffith, *Demotic Pap.* col. II, l. 26 ff.) in exactly the same way as "eight times great" would be to the epithet (which Thoth does not, apparently, actually receive), "the Great of the Eight". Note that  is written for "eight" in the late period (Dümichen, *Geogr. Inschr.*, 2te Abt., Taf. 80). Meade argues (*Thrice Greatest Hermes*, p. 104 ff.) that the epithet τρισμέγιστος was applied to Hermes as early as 250 B. C. The evidence, however, for this view is slight. Champollion says (Panth. Ég., Plate 30) that "Thoth twice-great" is the ibis-headed Thoth, and that "Thoth thrice-great" is the hawk-headed Thoth. He gives, however, no proof of this assertion.

(1) Cf. Dend. Düm. *Baug.* XXV. "Thoth, the great, the eldest son of Re comes  and puts to flight the dread of Hathor." The divine words here are the . The  which Thoth brings to give strength and wide scope of movement to the dead (*Totb.* Nav. 170, 5) are also, clearly, a collection of magical formulae.

(2) Metternich Stela 136—140.

heal thyself", is a prayer of the Book of the Dead (71, 6), which reminds Thoth of the arm-wound he received when he intervened in the struggle between Horus and Set. The powerful protection of Thoth's magic is alluded to in the saying in Anastasi, "My god Thoth is a shield round about me" (Anast. I, 8, 3).(1)

As magician Thoth is powerful patron of physicians, and so, he is asked to give skill to "those who know things", and "to the physicians who are in his train" (Pap. Hearst VI, 10).(2) We have seen that, in the older texts Thoth acted as physician of the eye of Horus. From the Ebers Papyrus (90, 16) we learn that he once cured Horus from something like an unpleasant cold. For the ancients magic and medicine were so closely related that we cannot always mark them off clearly from each other in Egyptian texts. Medicine was the science which dealt with the rites and formulae by which the unseen malicious spirits which caused disease could be expelled from the bodies of men. Its sphere was, therefore, largely coextensive with that of Magic.

The functions of Thoth as physician and magician help to explain the existence of enormous numbers of amulets in the form of figurines of Thoth which have been found in all parts of Egypt. Possibly also this side of the god's activity had much to do with the swift growth of his popularity in the Graeco-Roman period. In this period he appears clearly as an Egyptian Aesculapius. Thoth of Pnubs is represented in Philae in a temple-decoration of the time of Tiberius as Aesculapius, holding in his hand a staff round which a serpent winds itself.(3) In the Nubian temple of Dendûr Thoth of Pnubs is shown in human form crowned with the diadem of Shu: he is seated and holds in his left hand the symbol of

(1) Ps. 3[4] אַתָּה יהוה מָגֵן בַּעֲדִי.

(2) Cf. Ebers 1, 8—10. "Thoth gives words and script: he makes the books,

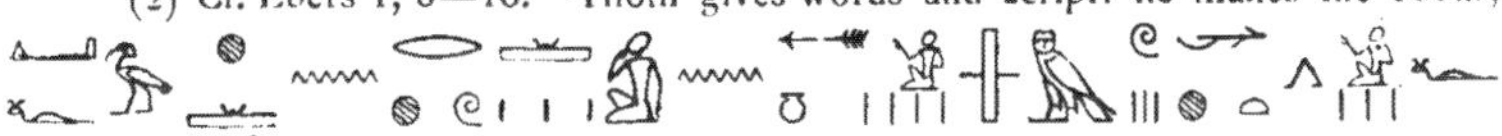

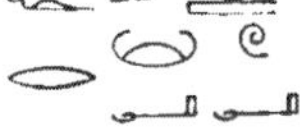 — he gives success to the learned and to the physicians in his train, to diagnose" (?).

(3) Rosellini, *Monumenti del culto*, Pl. XVIII, 3.

life, and in his right a serpent-encircled staff, or wand. (1) The symbolism clearly associates Thoth of Pnubs with Aesculapius. With this rôle of the god is connected his epithet 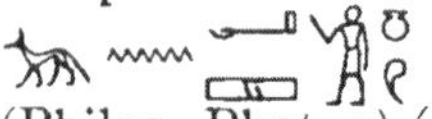 "He who comes to him that calls him" (Philae, Phot. 2). (2) It is an epithet which belongs to Thoth in a special way in his form of Iśtn. The title given to the god in Kasr-el-Agouz *Śtm* = "the Hearer", has been brought into connection with the Aesculapian character of Thoth, — possibly with good reason, since the real Egyptian Aesculapius — Imhotep, is prominent in the temple of Kasr-el-Agouz. In Daressy's *"Textes et dessins magiques"*, p. 15 (*Cat. du Mus. du Caire*, 9405) is a reference to the need of invoking Thoth in time of peril, and to the haste with which the god brings help: "Thou grantest that Thoth comes to me when I call, and that he rescues me from the "".

At least in the late texts, therefore, Thoth appears as a *Heilgott*, as a saviour, and protector from evil — especially the evil of sickness. As the saviour who comes when he is invoked Thoth was one of the most popular of all the gods, and many hymns and prayers addressed to him by individuals of all classes have come down to us. It is to be noted that the form of Thoth in which he is thus popularly invoked, is most frequently his lunar, or ibis form; Thoth, as an Edfu text has it, is 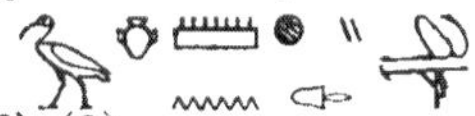 "the Ibis splendid in *ḥike*" (Edfu, R, II, 16). (3)

---

(1) Blackman, *Dendûr*, Pl. XLII. For a similar symbolism in Philae, see L. D. IV. Pl. 75 b. Cf. Champollion, *Lettres écrites d'Égypte*, p. 123. For a description of Aesculapius see Pausanias, Cor. 27: κάθηται δ' ἐπὶ θρόνου βακτηρίαν κρατῶν, τήν τε ἑτέραν τῶν χειρῶν ὑπὲρ κεφαλῆς ἔχει τοῦ δράκοντος.

(2) Cf. Dendereh, Mar. III, 67 a. Baudissin, *Adonis und Esmun*, p. 337, note 2. Junker maintains (*Die Onurislegende*, Wien, 1917, p. 9) that the representations of the sceptre with scorpions and serpents is a *"spätere Zutat"* of the post-Ptolemaic period. Yet, even though the Aesculapian *insignia* of Thoth of Pnubs may be of later (Roman) date, they fit in, nevertheless, with more anciently recognised features of the divine physician, who healed the Eye of Horus. For Junker Thoth of Pnubs is but an *Erscheinungsform* of Shu (= Onuris).

(3) Cf. the text Anastasi III, 5, 4 where Thoth is spoken of as protector against the evil eye: 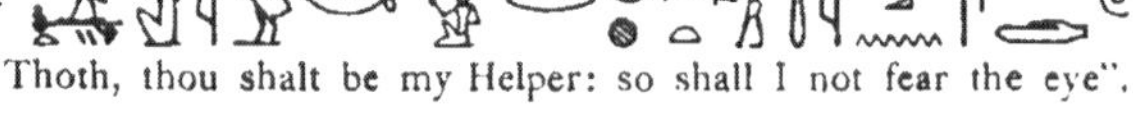 "O Thoth, thou shalt be my Helper: so shall I not fear the eye".

The texts so far considered make it clear that Thoth was a god of magic in the New Kingdom, and troughout the later period. It is not true, of course, that Thoth is the only great magician among the gods — even in the later periods. Every god possessed something of the peculiar quality, or power which is called *ḥike* — some gods having more of it, others less. Thoth, probably on account of his special gnosis, and his connection with ritual formulae, was regarded as having a very special equipment of *ḥike*. It now remains to be seen whether he was also in the Middle, and Old, Kingdoms regarded as a god of magic.

Thoth appears with considerable prominence in the funerary texts of the earlier periods. This, of itself, would suggest that his connection with magic is very ancient. The early recognition of Thoth as author of sacred ritual would point in the same direction. Yet the textual evidence in the Middle Kingdom is otherwise almost nul. In the Old Kingdom there are traces of a special magical gnosis being assigned to Thoth. The remarkable reference in Westcar to the 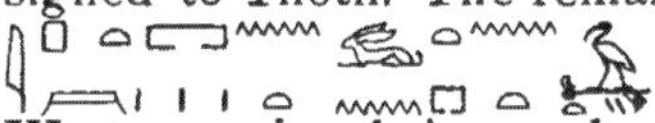 seems to connect the magic of the Westcar wizard in a close, though somewhat unintelligible, fashion with the god. In the Pyramid texts the moon as eye of Nut is called 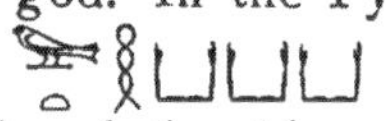 (Pyr. 823), and it is not unlikely that Thoth's relationship with the moon in the Pyramid texts implied a share of the god in the *ḥike* of the moon. The moon was associated with magic in the thought of several ancient peoples, (1) and it would seem at times as if that association caused the moon to be invested occasionally with a malicious and sinister character. This may, perhaps, throw some light on the strange circumstance that Thoth appears at times in the Pyramid texts as hostile to the dead king (see Pyr. 954; 955). In certain texts of the Pyramids Thoth is described as a being of dread aspect who slaughters the enemies of Osiris (Pyr. 635; 962). A similar idea seems to be conveyed in the Book of the Dead (134, 10—11) where *Iśtn* (= Thoth) is spoken of as the " 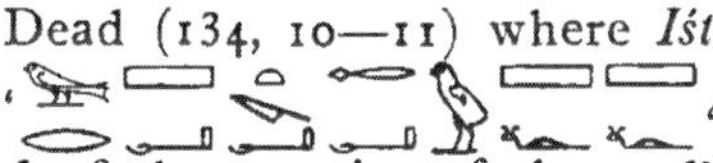  who bathes in the blood of the enemies of the god".

(1) Cf. Psalm 121, 6.

This being, "great in slaughter and mighty in dread", seems to bear little resemblance to the mild and benevolent ibis-god. There is something uncouth and barbarous in this description of Thoth; but it is at least possible that we have here a trace of an ancient view which ascribed to Thoth such malicious and dangerous power as the thought of the old world sometimes associated with the moon. Thoth's title 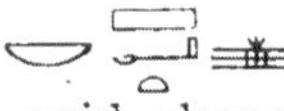 "Lord of terror" in Pyr. 2110c may also, as we said above, refer to his function as magical protector of Osiris. (1)

The prominent part assigned to Thoth by the Pyr. texts in the ceremonies of preparing the royal dead for burial suggests, almost inevitably, his possession of magical powers. His position as "Scribe of Re" and "Bearer of the Divine Book" points in the same direction. "Scribe of the Divine Book" was a familiar title of the priest who is called *Her-ḥeb, ḥer d3d3* in the Old Kingdom. (2) In the later periods certainly, and, therefore, probably in the earlier also, the *Herḥeb* was regarded as peculiarly equipped with magical power. This power, then, must also have belonged to Thoth, the Scribe of the Divine Book *par excellence*. When in Edfu Thoth is called the great *Herḥeb* it is but another instance of the presence in Ptolemaic texts of ancient religious thought. The idea of Thoth as a god of magic in a special way may be regarded then, as an ancient possession of Egyptian speculation. (3)

---

(1) Cf. Plutarch, *Is. et O.*, ch. 8. The Babylonians often ascribed to the influence of Sin such diseases as were known to pass through definite and regular phases. Vid. Combe, *Sin*, p. 36 f.

(2) Cf. Erman, *Pap. Westcar* I, 21: Erman, *Religion*, p. 178 f. The book containing the formulae to be recited in funeral services was called the "Book of the craft of the Her-ḥeb". L. D. II, 71 b—72 a. The effect of these formulae was to "glorify" the dead (cf. Berlin, 7796).

(3) Several of Thoth's epithets not referred to in the text are clearly to be explained from Thoth's connection with magic. One of these is 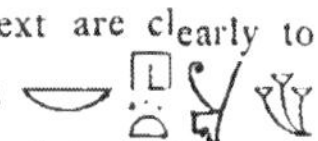 (Dümichen, *Baugeschichte* XXV: Edfu, Mammisi, p. 76): At the close of ritual functions when offerings had been presented to a divinity there took place the ceremony of 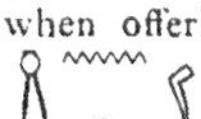 *int rd* (= "withdrawal"). Part of the "withdrawal" consisted in sweeping the floor of the shrine with a besom consisting of a bundle of shrubs, or something similar. This besom was the *hdn*, and because it was supposed to remove uncleanness and other hostile influences from the shrine of the god, it was invested with magical qualities and entrusted to the care of Thoth, who thus became *nb hdn*.

So familiar was Thoth's association with the *ḥdn* that he acquired as a sort of *nomen proprium* the title "He of the *ḥdn*", 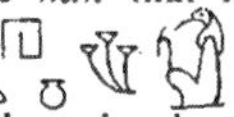 (Mar. *Dend.* III, 53 r). The formula to be spoken during the *int rd* is given in the Ritual of Abydos, ch. 36 (Mariette, Tabl. 20): 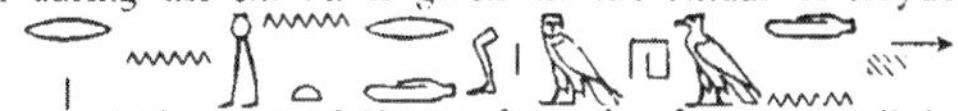: „Thoth comes after having rescued the eye of Horus from its foes: no evil being male or female doth enter into this house". Thus the *ḥdn* is (or represents) Thoth. Note how in Dendereh (*Baug.* XXV) the epithets *nb ḥdn*, *śmśw*, "Lord of script", "ruler of books", "Heart of Re" are grouped together in the same passage. For the *int rd* see Davies and Gardiner, *Tomb of Amenemhet*, p. 93 f. and *Tomb of Antefoker*, p. 25. Just as Thoth could thus become the *ḥdn* so also, perhaps, in somewhat analogous fashion did he become the  "*śḫm* of the gods". The *śḫm* was a staff provided with eyes through which the indwelling god could see and with which the god could be eventually identified (see article by Spiegelberg, *Recueil* 28, p. 163 ff.). A staff (or sceptre) of Thoth called  is mentioned in Pap. Bologna 1086. A sceptre of Chons is frequently spoken of in the texts of Edfu — but it may be the falcon-headed sceptre of Horus. The staff or sceptre of Thoth was, most probably, regarded as possessing magical qualities.

Chapter XIV.

Thoth as god of the dead.

In the Pyramid texts Thoth is associated with the ancient god of the dead, Anubis, in reconstructing the body of the dead king (or, Osiris), (1) and in the removal from it of the traces of burial (Pyr. 1247 : 519). It is Thoth also who pronounces the formulae of "glorification" (Pyr. 796) (2) — though Anubis seems to recite them sometimes, as if he were taking the place of Thoth (Pyr. 796). We have to picture to ourselves Thoth's functions in the mortuary ritual of the Pyramid period, in general after the manner of the *Ḫer-ḥeb*'s activity in the ritual of later times. (3)

The Pyramid text speak of the dead king as being borne on the wings of the ibis-god, either up to heaven, or across the celestial oceans. (4) Again, we find that the Feast of Thoth was one of the chief memorial days of the dead. Pyr. 2118 says: "My heart is not weary to perform for thee the service for the dead every day, — on the Feast of the month and half-month, on the feast of the laying down of the candlestick, on the Feast of Thoth, and on the 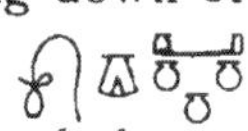 (*W3g*-feast), throughout the duration of thy years, and thy months which thou livest as god." (5) This Feast of Thoth (or "Feast of

(1) Pyr. 10: 830: 639.

(2) For this ritual in the late period cf. Pap. Boulaq, no. 3, pl. 11, 5. "Anubis-Horus accomplishes the embalming: Thoth makes thy members whole (*wḏ3*) by the charms of his mouth."

(3) For the *Ḫer-ḥeb*'s functions see Erman, *Religion*, 68 f., 151.

(4) Pyr. 387 : 596 : 1176 : 1377 b : 1429.

(5) Cf. Pyr. 820 f., where the *w3g*-feast is clearly a day of the dead; cf. 811, 861. For the Feast of Thoth in the Old Kingdom see L. D. II, 56, 85 b, 86 a b, 88 a b, 89 a b. The Calendar of Rams. II in Medinet Habu puts the *w3g*-feast in the 18th Thoth, and the Feast of Thoth on the 19th Thoth. Vid. Brugsch, *Thes.*, p. 364. There is mention of the Feast of Thoth in the tomb of Meten, *IVth Dyn.* (L. D. II, 5). The Thoth-feast continued to be closely connected with the ritual of

w3w't, and to gaze on the beauty of Thoth (Cairo, 20473 M. K.).(1) A funerary text of the M. K. published by Lacau (*Sarcophages*, p. 161) represents Thoth as a Psychopompos. He stretches out his hand from heaven to grasp the arm of the dead in order to lead him up to the kingdom of the gods (cf. *ibid.*, p. 201 and Pyr. 1247 d).

In the New Kingdom and later periods the rôle of Thoth in the Judgment of the dead becomes more and more important. In these later periods the ceremonies which Thoth, Anubis, and Horus anciently performed for the dead Osiris are still performed by them for the dead worshippers of Osiris. Mortals were still subjected to the same dread Trial through which their great patron and model, Osiris, had so triumphantly passed. The priests who take part in funeral services of the late period call themselves by the names of Horus, Anubis and Thoth.(2) The ceremonies of reanimation of the dead were carried out even in the latest period of Egyptian culture, and the priests who perform them appear as Horus, Anubis and Thoth.(3) Similarly, in the ceremony of "Opening the mouth" the *Ḫer-ḥeb* priest appears as Thoth.

To Thoth, as patron of the dead, prayers for a pleasant burial are addressed in the later periods. A Turin Stela of the New Kingdom (Turin, 1031) prays to Thoth for a "beautiful burial after a great old age". Similarly in the tomb of 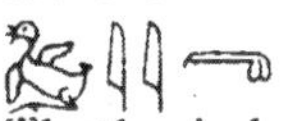 in Thebes (Sethe, 17, 105) to the prayer: "O Thoth, judge of Ma'et, give me the west of old age after 110 years". Thoth was also invoked by the people as a protector in the underworld: "Come to me", says a worshipper of Thoth in Pap. Sallier I, 8, 4, "when I go into the presence of the Lords of Ma'et".

---

(1) The Thoth-epithet *ipi ib* connects Thoth with Anubis who, as god of the dead, was also *ipi ib*.

(2) Cf. Berlin P. 3055, Col. I, 6—7: "My arms are for thee the arms of Horus; my hands are for thee as those of Thoth; my fingers are for thee as hose of Anubis, the Lord of the divine Hall". This text is taken from the ritual of Amon; but the cult of Amon is an echo of the funerary ritual of Osiris, (and, therefore, of the funerary liturgy of Egyptians generally).

(3) For a good representation of this ceremony in the late period see Sieglin und Schreiber, *Die Nekropole von Kom-esch--Schukâfa*, Tafelband, Tafel 27. For the ritual of the ceremony see, Pap. Boulaq, no. 3: *Rituel de l'embaumement*.

Thoth as above stated, functions as Psychopompos in the Pyr. texts. The same function is often assigned to him in documents of later periods. Even in the Greek period, the idea is as general as in the O. K. that the dead fly to heaven on the wings of Thoth (*tpi dnḥ Dḥwti*). (1) As the earth opened for the dead at the words of Thoth in the Old K., so in the Graeco-Roman period, the doors of the earth are opened by Thoth for the dead; and by him also the gates of heaven (*ḳbḥw*) are thrown open. (2) As Psychopompos Thoth sometimes carries with him the symbol of the west (vid. Daressy, *Cercueils*, p. 99 and the representation, plate XLIV). In the temple of Rams. II at Abydos (Borchardt, p. 13) Thoth is called "Thoth of the westerners". With this may be compared his epithet in the tomb of  in Thebes (Champ. *Not.* I, 161): "Lord of *Ḥśr·t*, he who is in the west".

Thoth's rôle as Psychopomp may, perhaps, have contributed to his early identification with the Greek Hermes — whose rôle as guide of the dead is familiar. (3) Like Thoth, Hermes was also regarded as εὐταφιαστής (vid. Eitrem, *Hermes und die Toten*, p. 46). As the days of rejoicing with the dead fell together with the feasts of the moon's phases in Egypt, so also sacrifices were offered to Hermes on every νουμηνία (Eitrem, *ibid.*, p. 41). At the New Moon, and on the 7th day of the month,

---

(1) Maspero, *Catal. général. Sarcophages des époques persanes et ptolémaiques*, p. 29.

(2) Maspero, *ibid.* p. 48. In Pyr. 658 we see how, by the words of the ritual, the dead is delivered from *ȝkrw* (*i. e.* the earth-god) and the resistance of the *śḥdw* is broken down, so that the king is enabled to enter through the door of heaven. Cf. Pyr. 796 : 1713.

Horus and Thoth sometimes act together as guides of the dead. Cf. Ostracon, Queen's College, Oxford. M. K. (a duplicate to Anastasi I, 3, 5): "Mayest thou be pure, and may thy limbs become divine with the brothers, while Thoth and Harachtes make thy soul to ascend". Note Thoth's title, *Śšmw* = Leader (Pap. Hearst, VI, 9—10) and his epithet in *Totenbuch*, Nav. 182, 10 (Af): 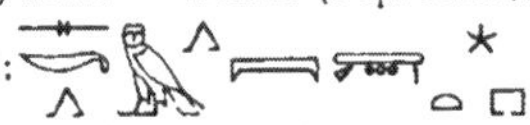.

(3) Thoth's relation to literature and speech, and his rôle of secretary to the Ennead, and to the sun-god, would, of course, also tend to connect him with Hermes. Plutarch speaks freely of Thoth as Hermes. For Hermes as moon-god see Siecke, *Hermes der Mondgott*, Leipzig, 1908. For Hermes as Psychopomp cf. Roscher, *Lexikon*, p. 2374 f.

the dead were honoured by special ceremonies in Delphi; and in Argos the thirty days of mourning for the dead ended with a sacrifice to Hermes.

Possibly the special favour which Thoth enjoyed among the people in Egypt, as shown by the enormous number of statuettes of ibises and apes that have survived, was largely due to his rôle as protector of the dead. (1) The innumerable statues and amulets of Hermes still extant seem also to be due mainly to the work of Hermes among the dead, and, especially, to his protecting influence as guide of the dead.

---

(1) It might be urged here also that the pictorial representations of the Judgment, which were so universally familiar in Egypt, in which Thoth appeared so prominently as advocate of the dead, as weigher of the heart, as recorder of the verdict etc., must have helped greatly to make Thoth popular as a god of the dead. *Cf.* p. 142 *infra*.

Chapter XV.

Thoth in Egyptian Ritual.

We have already seen that Thoth was honoured in Egypt as the Founder of ritual. But his connection with ritual was not merely that of a founder or inventor. In the innumerable representations of temple-liturgy, court-ceremonial, and funerary ritual which can be seen everywhere in Egypt Thoth appears not merely as the Lord of sacred formulae, but as the leader in the actual sacred ceremonial itself — as a sort of official master of liturgical ceremonies. This is obvious in the case of Osirian cult. The Pyr. texts seem to imply this liturgical activity of Thoth also. They represent Thoth as acting with Anubis in preparing for burial the corpse of Osiris (Pyr. 830, 639): (1) as purifying with Horus the body of the god (or king) (Pyr. 519b, 639); as pronouncing the deifying formulae over the body (Pyr. 1713). Thoth it is who equips the dead with efficacious means of protection against the dangers of the Beyond. When the dead has to enter into the presence of the Great Tribunal of the gods Thoth leads him in, makes pleading for him with the Judges, weighs his heart in the scales against the feather of Maʿet, and, in the end, records the verdict. The details of all this ritual and ceremonial are familiar in the literature of the Book of the Dead: What Thoth once did for Osiris, the same must he do for every dead Egyptian — since the Osirian ritual was the standard and guide for all funerary ritual in Egypt. Hence, as has been already noted, the priests who took part in funerary celebrations regarded themselves as incorporations of the Osirian gods. It will be true, of course, that the Osirian liturgy was, in its

(1) For a late illustration of the cooperation of Horus and Thoth in the embalming of the dead see Möller, *Die beiden Rhindpapyrus*, I, p. 31 ff.

turn, largely determined by ancient customs connected with the burial and veneration of the dead. Possibly it may be held that the gods of the old Osirian drama reflect, to some extent, the priests and magicians who, in the primitive period, provided all that was necessary for the dead. When Thoth was given a place in the Osirian ritual, it was a place determined partly by his personal qualities, and, partly, by the associations of ancient custom. Thus his rôle in funerary ritual was imagined as that of a primitive *Ḫer-ḥeb* of Osirian liturgy. In the later thought of Egypt the *Ḫer-ḥeb* was himself regarded as some sort of incorporation of Thoth. Throughout the whole speculative and religious development of the Egyptian mind there are many traces of this quaint kind of action and re-action between traditional custom and artificial speculation.

It has been shown already that Thoth played a great part in Egyptian court-ceremonial. The fixing of the royal names, the determining of the years of reign, the foretelling of royal feasts and victories -- all these are functions assigned to Thoth in the coronation-ceremonies. They are all fully illustrated on the monuments. In the actual coronation-ceremonies a priest, of course, took the part of Thoth. Even in the joyful liturgy of coronation there are echoes of the funerary, or Osirian, ritual. One of these is the purification of the king. This is very often represented. Sometimes it is performed by Horus and Set, sometimes by Horus and Thoth.(1) A very interesting feature of the coronation-ceremonial was the symbolical uniting of the Two Lands — represented by the rush and the papyrus. The ceremony was called *Smȝ tȝwi.* Properly speaking this ceremony belonged to the two gods who represented the two great divisions of Egypt — Horus and Set. It is, however, a remarkable fact that Set disappeared at an early date from the representations of this ceremonial. His place was taken by Thoth. This circumstance is to be associated with the substitution of the name of Thoth for that of Set in the lists of gods. In the purification-ceremony at the coronation Set also tends to disappear, leaving his place to Thoth. All this, of course, is somehow to be connected with the gradual

(1) For rôle of Thoth and Horus in the ablutions of the king before he takes part in the temple-ritual see Blackman, *Temple of Deir*, plate 42.

degradation of Set to the level of a Typhonic being.(1) In several representations of ritual the figure of Set has been replaced by that of Thoth, but the accompanying legends containing the name of Set, have been left unchanged (cf. LD. III, 37b; III, 65d; III, 238a).(2)

The substitution of Thoth for Set is to be explained partly by the rôle of Thoth as Lord of ritual, and partly by the circumstance that Horus and Thoth appear together in many other familiar ceremonies of court-procedure, and temple-cult, and thus, would be regarded as suitable companions in the coronation functions.

In the temple-cult, as has been said, many features of funerary ritual were reproduced — as a result of the dominating influence of Osirian religion in the temples. If we look closely at any particular temple-liturgy, that of Amon for instance, we find in it numerous points of contact with the Osirian drama. Thus in the temple-worship of Egypt Thoth appears active almost in the same fashion in which he functions in Osirian worship.

It is true that the ritual of Egyptian temples was not quite taken up with the religion of Osiris. Other ancient myths and legends, over and above those of the Osirian cycle, are echoed and reflected in the temple cults. Thus, for instance, many legends of the sun-god (such as the legend of Hathor-Tefenet), and many cosmogonical legends find expression occasionally in the worship of the temples. In the ritual texts which refer to such legends Thoth appears in the fashion proper to him in the legend in question. Junker, in his excellent treatise, *Der Auszug der Hathor-Tefnut aus Nubien,* has shown how from the pictorial representation of ritual actions an important legend in which Thoth plays a prominent part, can be actually, in large measure, reconstructed (cf. also his *Onurislegende*).

It must be admitted, however, that we cannot discover in every ritual act the legendary elements which be behind it. This is true, for instance, of a ritual action which is very

(1) Cf. Lepsius, *Abhandlung über den ersten ägyptischen Götterkreis*, p. 183. Meyer, *Set-Typhon*, p. 51 f., cf. p. 40 f., 61 f.

(2) For this question in general see Roeder's article "*Set*" in Roscher's Lexikon, p. 770.

generally assigned to Thoth in the later texts — the presentation of the *wnšb* (mostly to Hathor). (1) It has been conjectured that the *wnšb* is a water-clock, and that Thoth is associated with it as lord and measurer of time. But the *wnšb* (or *wtṯ*) is, apparently, most frequently used in the ceremony of the pacification of Hathor (as the angry Horus-eye) by Thoth, and it is difficult to see how a water-clock could serve such a purpose. In the Nubian legend of Hathor Thoth is sent as an ape-god to calm the angry Hathor and induce her to come to Egypt. It is possible that the ape which appears as part of the object called *wnšb* was regarded as symbolical of the god who was sent to pacify Hathor, and that, thus, the *wnšb* came to be a recognised feature in the ceremony of pacifying the angry Horus-eye. It is to be noted that the ape-god who calms Hathor, and induces her to leave *Bwgm* for Egypt in the form of the Nubian legend contained in the folk-tale published by Spiegelberg, (2) is called *wnš* (the dog-headed ape, apparently) and there may be some kind of morphological connection between *wnš* and *wnšb*. As the Hathor of the Nubian legend is the lunar eye of Horus, there is a close connection between the *wnšb* and lunar cult. If *wnš* and *wnšb* are morphologically related (the *b* of *wnšb* being a formative element) the lunar implications of the *wnšb* could be explained from the moon-legend of the angry Hathor. (3)

A very prominent feature of ritual functions throughout the later periods is the presentation of the figure of Maʿet. In most instances of this ceremony Thoth is present, either in person, or as represented by the king (or priest). We have already discussed some of Thoth's associations with Maʿet.

---

(1) Cf. Dendereh, M. D. III, 22 a — according to which the  has been made after the directions of Thoth.

(2) Leyden I, 384.

(3) On all this cf. Junker, *Onurislegende*, p. 147. 163 and passim. See also his *Der Auszug der Hathor-Tefnut aus Nubien*, p. 22 f. For the *wnšb* as a protection of Hathor see Mar., *Dend.* III, 73 e: Düm., *Baug.* XVIII, 14. In Mar., *Dend.* III, 22 a Thoth appears himself as the *wnšb*: he comes as *wnsb* in order to protect Hathor. In the Nubian legend the *wnšb* is generally employed rather to distract and amuse Hathor than to protect her.

Junker (*Onurislegende*, p. 163, Anm. 2) notes the possibility that *wnšb* may be an enlargement of *wnš* and points out the apparent interchangeableness in Philae texts of *wtṯ* and *wtb*.

We have seen the two together in the barque of the sun-god — Thoth as chief minister of the Ruler of the universe, Ma'et as symbol of Re's methods of government. In somewhat similar fashion the two come to be associated in ritual. Thoth is the Lord of ritual: Maʿet is the symbol of conformity to law, and, especially, of conformity to ritual law. Thus when Thoth presents Maʿet to a divinity, his action symbolises the perfection of the ritual service which is offered to the divinity in question. When, as sometimes happens, Ma'et is presented to Thoth himself, this is partly due to Thoth's relation to justice, and partly to the symbolism of Maʿet just described, *i. e.*, the offering of Maʿet to Thoth implies the perfection of the cult which is intended to be offered to him.

Another function at which Thoth is constantly present is the offering of the *wḏ3·t*. Since the *wḏ3·t* is the lunar eye of Horus, it is, obviously, the duty of Thoth, the guardian of the moon-eye, to be present when that eye is brought back to its lord. Thoth, as has been shown, is the *ʾIni św*.

Chapter XVI.

The chief temples and shrines of Thoth.

It has been shown above that Thoth anciently stood outside the Heliopolitan group of gods, and that he was not one of the actors in the primitive Osirian drama, but was brought into it in a more or less secondary fashion. Hence it is reasonable to infer that the cult of Thoth was known in Egypt previously to the Pyramid age and previously even to the growth and spread of Osirian religion. It is not possible, however, to determine where Thoth had his most ancient shrine. The "Place of Thoth" (1) referred to in Pyr. 1271 cannot be located by any other Pyramid reference. It is probable that in the early dynastic period — possibly even in the pre-dynastic period — Thoth had already several cult-centres. The standards of Hierakonpolis (I, pl. 29) show the sacred ibis of Thoth, and in Hierakonpolis, too, we find a representation of a primitive shrine of Thoth which seems to point to the existence of a cult of the ibis-god in Hierakonpolis in the days of Narmer. (2) With the shrine depicted in Hierakonpolis should be compared the representation of a shrine, or other enclosure, in the midst of which stands an ibis, in Royal Tombs, II, pl. X, 2. Here an ox is being offered in sacrifice to the Ibis-god, who is shown standing on a pedestal; and it would seem as if the ceremony takes place on the "festival of the pilgrimage to Hermopolis". Possibly the enclosure within which the ibis stands represents Hermopolis.

"Royal Tombs" I, pl. 1, speaks of a Feast of Thoth "in the great houses", or, "in the House of the Great Ones".

(1) . This is not to be translated, "Throne of Thoth" as Turayeff thinks (p. 24).

(2) The "shrine" of Thoth consists of an ibis standing on a pedestal, before which is set an altar for sacrifice (Hierak. I, pl. XXVI B).

Plate XII (*ibid.*) shows an ivory tablet from the tomb of Semempses on which the ape-god appears perhaps as an object of worship (cf. sketch on pl. XVII, *ibid.*). (1)

The frequent references to the "Feast of Thoth" in the O. K. testify to the antiquity of the public worship of the god. (2) Hence we are probably justified in finding in a "House of Thoth" mentioned in L. D. II, 17 (IVth Dyn.) an indication of the existence of an independent temple-worship of Thoth in the earliest dynastic period. Such a cult would imply the existence also of a definite priesthood ministering to the god. We are not surprised, therefore, to hear in the IIIrd (?) Dynasty of a priest "of the Temple of Thoth" called  (*Le Musée égyptien,* p. 13). (3) We hear also, of a priestess of Thoth in the O. K. (4) "The House" (or Temple) "of Thoth" is frequently spoken of in the O. K. (5), and we find in that period the priestly title, or title of dignity, which is later so familiar — "the Great of the five of the temple of Thoth" (L. D. II, 15: IVth Dyn. Gizeh). (6) This title , as we shall see, had a special connection with the worship of Thoth in Hermopolis Magna (*Ḫmnw*).

(1) The statuettes of apes found in graves of the O. K. (Petrie, *Abydos* II, pl. 6, 9, 10, 11) need not be regarded as representations of Thoth. Possibly they represent merely the pet monkeys which were popular in Egyptian homes of the time. Cf. Capart, *Débuts* (Eng. trans., p. 220): Bénédite, *Scribe et babouin* (Paris 1911), p. 28.

(2) Pyr. 2118. L. D. II, 5, 18, 26 (IVth Dyn.): Cairo 1304 (O. K.): Mar., *Mast.* D. 60: Cairo, 1485: Mar., *Mast.* D. 16 etc. etc. Possibly we should translate "Feast of Hermopolis", rather than "Feast of Thoth". But, in any case, the public worship of the ibis-god seems to be implied.

(3) For the title 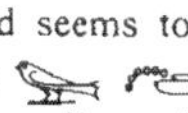 cf. Gizeh, L. D. II, 89 c: Newberry, *Beni-Hassan* II, pl. 1, p. 11. Vid. *Recueil,* 1903, p. 210, article by Naville; also, *Recueil,* I, p. 26. For a "prophet" of Thoth, see Mar., *Mast.* D. 5.

(4) See *Transactions of Congress for Hist. of Rel.* 1908, Vol. I, p. 223; a paper by Miss Murray on Priesthoods of women.

(5) Cf. Mar., *Mast.* D. 67. Here should be recalled, also, perhaps the reference in Westcar 7, 5—8 to the 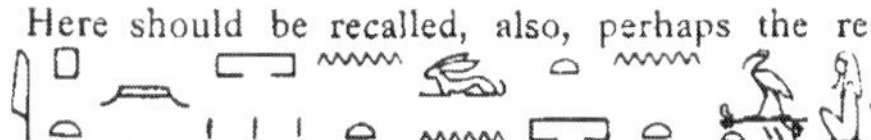.

(6) In this text the title in question belongs to the son of a king who is also a "Judge" (*s3b*), and a *Ḥer-ḥeb.* For the title see also L. D. II, 34, g: Petrie, *Medum. Tomb of Nefermat,* pl. XX. *Ḥm-Iwn* of the Hildesheim collection is a 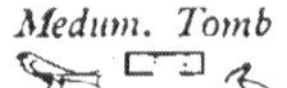.

If the scene in the Royal Tombs just referred to represents a feast of Thoth in Hermopolis, we have in it the first trace of a definite cult-centre of the god. It cannot be said with complete security that the Hermopolis in question is the Hermopolis Magna of Upper Egypt, rather than Hermopolis Parva of the Delta. Both towns are mentioned in an ancient list of centres of worship in Pyr. 191, (1) as *Wnw* of the South and *Wnw* of the North. It is known that the two *Wnw* were important centres of Thoth's worship in the M. K. It is very difficult, however, to decide which of them is the more primitive home of Thoth's worship. Since, however, the nome of the Ibis (no. 15) is in the Delta, and the nome of which Hermopolis Magna was the capital is called the nome of the Hare, it has been conjectured that the Ibis-god, Thoth, was first worshipped in the Delta, and that his cult in Hermopolis Magna (*Ḫmnw*) developed later. (2) Such a view is based on the assumption that the nome-standards or nome-symbols represent the primitive objects of worship of the nomes. This is, however, a mere hypothesis. Where can one find a trace of the worship of a hare in the 15th nome of Upper Egypt? Again, how, on this view, could we explain the designation of the northern Hermopolis in the Pyramids as "*Wnw* (*i. e.* the Hare-nome) of the North"? It would, indeed, be very satisfactory if we could show that Thoth, the ibis-god and moon-god, was primitively worshipped in the Delta, and that at some later, indeterminable, date he was somehow assimilated to an ape-god revered as a god of wisdom in *Ḫmnw*. This hypothesis would explain the combined rôles of Thoth as, on the one hand, lord of time and order, and, on the other, lord of wisdom and literature. Unfortunately, however, it must remain a hypothesis, for we know nothing definite about the beginnings of Thoth's worship either in the Delta, or in Hermopolis Magna.

The representations in Hierakonpolis and the Royal Tombs point, perhaps, to a fairly general worship of Thoth in the O. K. The existence of a special priesthood of Thoth

---

(1) Cf. Pyr. 167, 229, 314: Petrie — Kahun, 18, 40—42.

(2) So, Newberry, *Transactions of the 3rd International Congress of Rel.*, vol. I, p. 211 f.

in the O. K., points in the same direction. The popularity of Thoth as god in the O. K. is also suggested by the Snofru texts (1) of Wadi Maghara in Sinai in which Thoth appears beside Hathor, as an important divinity. Thoth's title in Sinai is *nb ḫȝśwt.* (2) This is, properly speaking, an epithet of Min : (3) it shows, however, that for the Egyptian miners in Sinai, Thoth's influence was not to be restricted to a single centre, or even to the soil of Egypt itself. (4)

We have seen above that Thoth holds an important place in the funerary texts of the Middle Kingdom. Throughout this period he stands in the closest connection with *Ḫmnw*, the "City of the Eight", the metropolis of the Hare-nome in Upper Egypt. From this connection arises his frequent title 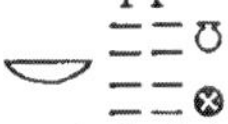 "Lord of the city of the Eight" (— the modern Eshmunein). (5)

---

(1) *Urkunden*, I, 54 : L. D. II, 152 a : *Thesaurus* 1495.

(2) With this compare Thoth's designation on the tail of the lion in Abukir  "Lord of the Trogodytes". For Thoth as *nb ḫȝśwt* in Sinai, see Gardiner and Peet, Plate VI. Cf. Plate III.

(3) Sethe, *Zur Sage vom Sonnenauge*, p. 30, thinks that Hathor, from the great number of her shrines outside Egypt, had the best title to be regarded as the "Mistress of foreign lands".

(4) Students of the history of religions will probably be familiar with Voelter's attempt to argue from the presence of Thoth-worship in Sinai to a connection between the Hebrew leader Moses and Thoth. In his book on the Hebrew Patriarchs (*Die Patriarchen Israels.* Leyden, 1912), and in his recent pamphlets, *Wer war Mose?*, and *Jahve und Mose* (both published by Brill, Leyden) Voelter has brought together a great mass of arguments to show that the Hebrew God Yahweh is really a form of the Egyptian god Ḥar-Sopd, and that Moses is a form of Thoth. The presence of Hathor in Sinai Voelter associates with the legends of the Eye of the sun-god (Horus) which was brought back to Egypt by Thoth. The stòry of Moses and Sippora is but an attempt, according to Voelter, to give a historical form to the legend of Thoth and Hathor. The speculations of Voelter are often highly ingenious, but they are, for the most part, quite out of all relation with facts, and do not deserve to be seriously discussed.

Eisler (*Die kenitischen Weihinschriften der Hyksoszeit,* Freibg. 1919, p. 154) thinks that Thoth is in place in Sinai because, 'Der Herr der Offenbarungen und Geheimnisse gilt offenbar auch als Herr der unerforschten Länder". He says further: "Vielleicht ist Thoth auch als Gott, der die Brunnen in der Wüste kennt und offenbart (Pap. Sallier, I, 82 ff. . . . 'Thoth ein Süßwasserbrunnen für den Dürstenden in der Wüste') hier verehrt worden." A stone figure of a baboon found by Petrie in Serabîṭ, Eisler supposes to be a representation of the ape-god Thoth. This, however, is by no means certain.

(5) Cf. Cairo, 20025.

The texts of Hatnub and El Bersheh are the fullest and most familiar evidence for the association of Thoth with *Ḫmnw* in the Middle Kingdom. (1) From this time forward is the most frequently used of all Thoth's epithets. (A practically equivalent epithet, , "he that is in *Ḫmnw*", occurs also from time to time. See *Book of the Dead*, c. 17, 5.)

It is reasonable to suppose that the political influence of the nomarchs of El Bersheh must have helped to spread and popularise the cult of Thoth in the Middle Kingdom. The nomarchs show their interest in that cult by giving themselves the titles of Thoth's priests. Often they call themselves (2) which was apparently the title of the chief priest of the City of the Eight (cf. Edfu Rochm. I, 129).

The temple of Thoth in *Ḫmnw* is frequently mentioned in the texts of Hatnub and El Bersheh, and on the basis of these texts we can form some notion of the organisation of Thoth-cult in the god's chief shrine.

It may be assumed that the City of the Eight as a whole was under the patronage of Thoth. The city contained, it would seem, numerous shrines and sacred places. The quarter of the city which is known as stands in the closest relation with Thoth, (3) and he is, therefore, frequently styled he that presides over (Leyden V, 1. Funerary stele of

---

(1) See El Bersheh and Hatnub (Blackden and Fraser), passim.

(2) "Great of the five in the House of Thoth", or (Petrie, Medum, pl. 20). For a variation of this title see El Bersheh I, p. 16 "Great of the Five in Thoth's temples of North and South" — a title which suggests the extension and importance of Thoth's cult in the Middle Kingdom. At times the epithet "great of the Five in the House of the Eight" is given either to Thoth or one of his priests. See Leyden V, 46. Stele of early New Kingdom. The personal name *Portis* which is found in the Greek period (cf. Rylands, *Demotic Pap.*, p. 256, 283 etc.) is obviously identical with .

(3) The name appears also in the form (Thebes, Tomb of Champ., *Not.* I, 860): again, as (Turin, 912) and (Harris, I, 58, 1. Is it here supposed to be equivalent to *ḥsi* + *rꜣ*?).

N. K.). (1) Other very special Thoth-shrines in Eshmunein are the  (Davies, *Sheikh Saïd*, pl. XXVIII, cf. *ibid.*, p. 32, note 2) and the necropolis which is called the "Island of flame" (). Even in the Middle Kingdom we find Thoth describe das  (Cairo, 20025). Apparently the district known as  was what might be called the ecclesiastical district of Eshmunein: it contained the chief shrines and other sacred buildings of the city, and stood in a relation to the "City of the Eight" like that in which Karnak stood to Thebes. (2)

The meaning of the 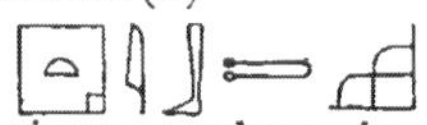 is not certain. (3) It appears in Deir el Bahri as a place in which Thoth and *Śfḫ·t-ʿbwi* make a register of the products of Punt. (4) *Śfḫ·t-ʿbwi* is familiar as an associate of Thoth, (5) and, possibly, the two deities are brought into relation with the products of Punt because of the use of these latter in the cult of the temples: but why they should appear as working together in the *Ḥ·t ib·t* is not clear — though it might be conjectured, perhaps, that it is due to nothing more profound than a confusion between 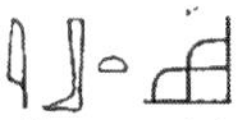 (net) and  ("measure"). The "Counting-house" would be the most suitable place for registering the products of Punt. It is not possible, however, to suppose that the "Temple of the Net" has arisen from any primitive confusion between the words for "counting", or

---

(1) Cf. Piehl, *Inscr.* I, 98. Cf. the personal name 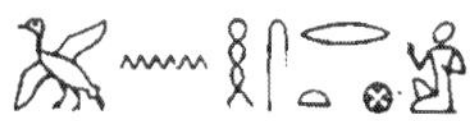 from Eshmunein, *Annales du Service*, 10, p. 101.

(2) See Turayeff, p. 119. In a Ptolemaic text (Mallet, *Kasr el Agouz*, p. 45) we see the Ptolemy presenting to Thoth an object which is called a "Great *Ḥśr.t*"; it is probably a copy or model of a shrine in Eshmunein.

(3) It is written variously: 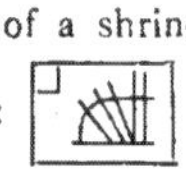 (Champ., *Not.* II, 42); 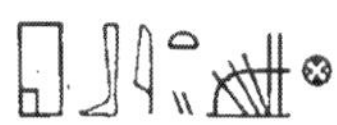 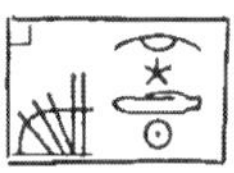 (Piehl, *Inscr.* I, 98): 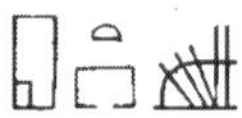 (Leyden V, 1).

(4) Naville III, 79.

(5) Cf. Mariette, *Abyd.* I, pl. 51 a.

"measuring", (1) and "net". The "Temple of the net" has associations which have nothing to do with counting. The Eight gods of Hermopolis are located there (Leyden, V. 1. N. K.) and the temple seems to belong, in a special way, to the Eight and to *Nḥm·t-ʿwꜣi* (Davies, *Sheikh Saïd*, p. 32). An Edfu text says that the heart of Re, as identified with Thoth, is in Hermopolis, 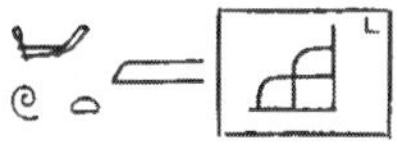 glorious in the "Temple of the Net."

The designation "Temple (or House) of the Net" was, it would seem, a puzzle even to the Egyptians themselves. Attempts were made by the priests to find for it a suitable mythological explanation. In a text published by Champollion (*Not.* II, 42) Ramses II is represented between Horus and Amon as catching birds in a net. Thoth, who stands by, and gives the sign for the pulling together of the net, is designated "Lord of *Ḫmnw*, President of *Ḥśr·t*", and, "He that is in the Temple of the Net". It is clear that the catching of the birds, under the direction of Thoth, is suggestive of some mythological incident which was supposed to have given its name to the House of the Net. (2) There are, here and there, obscure references to a capturing of Set by Horus in a net which took place in the *Ḥt-ibt.* Thus in Dendereh (Mar. IV, 73, l. 21) we read: . Possibly the reference here is to a detail of the legend of Horus and Set, according to which Set, in the form of a crocodile, was captured in a net (cf. Brugsch-Dümichen, *Rec. de mon. ég.*, III, 96, 21). (3) One is here reminded of the obscure text in the Book of the Dead (Nav.), c. 20, 1—3, in which Thoth is directed to capture the enemies of Osiris in a net (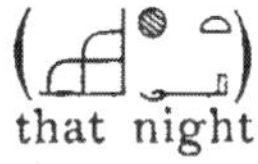) "before the *ḏꜣḏꜣ·t* of all the gods and goddesses in that night

---

(1) The script 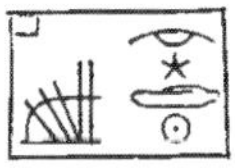 suggests the explanation "Temple of the month". This suggestion would be due, of course, to the idea of Thoth as moon. But it is, obviously, forced and secondary.

(2) Cf. Turayeff, p. 121.

(3) See Turayeff, p. 121. Cf. the text in Pierret, *Études égyptol.* (première livraison, p. 23): ; cf. L. D. IV, 88 b.

of the struggle". Whatever the origin of the name "Temple of the Net" may be, it is certain that the building or shrine so designated was intimately related with the cult of Thoth. It may, indeed, have been a part of his chief temple at Hermopolis Magna.

That the "Island of Flame" is also connected with Thoth's city and cult is clearly implied in texts of the later period. In the Geographical Papyrus of Tanis (Pl. X, *Two Papyri*, Abydos), the necropolis of *Ḫmnw* is called . The place is mentioned along with Hermopolis in the lists of the nomes in Edfu. (1) In Dendereh (Mar., *Dend.* II, 78 a) the king, when he presents a figure of Ma'et, is called "Son of the Lord of *Ḫmnw*", , "child of Sia in the Island of Flame". (2)

The "Island of Flame" is often alluded to in the funerary texts of the New and Middle Kingdoms. But the older the texts in which it is mentioned, the more difficult is its identification. Yet, even in the older texts it is always associated, at least indirectly, with Thoth and his worship. In a hymn

---

What is the meaning of , Mariette, *Mastabas*, p. 317? Junker points out (*Onurislegende*, p. 151) how the representation in Mar., *Dend.* II, 44, which shows Thoth and Shu holding a net in which an *wḏ3.t* is enclosed, is connected with an old legend telling of the capture of the Eye of Horus by Thoth and Shu. The wandering Eye was caught in a net and brought back to its owner by Thoth and Shu (or one of these gods). The net in question was the — the net of the fisherman or hunter. Possibly this capturing of the Eye by means of a hunter's net may underly the name "Temple of the Net". Cf. Brugsch, *Thes.* I, 36, 5, 6 . In Mar., *Dend.* III, 19 n, during the offering of the *wḏ3.t* to Hathor, the formula is recited: "The *wḏ3.t* is free from *nśn* , "Thoth, the Great, carries it in the net; (its) pupil is healthy". A net was used also to capture the foes of the *Nśm.t*-boat of Re (Junker *ibid.*).

(1) Edfu, R. I, 341. Brugsch, *Dict. géogr.* 1362. In Edfu R. I. 341 is the necropolis of the capital of the Hare-nome.

(2) In Edfu R. I. 129 the sacred tree of the Hermopolitan nome is spoken of as growing in the "Island of Flame" — and the sacred trees are associated with the burial-centres. It is interesting to note that Thoth's female associate *Nḥm.t* ʿ*w3i* is called in the text, Brugsch, *Thes.* 760.

to Thoth in the British Museum (no. 5656) (1) it is said of him that he made shrines for the gods and goddesses (2) in the Island of Flame. In another hymn to Thoth composed in the time of Rameses IV (pub. by Piehl, *Ä. Z.* 1884, p. 38 ff.) the "Island of Flame" is spoken of as the birthplace of Thoth.

In the Pyramid texts the Isle of Flame is either an island in the lake or ocean which the dead have to cross, or a place where the dead have to give an exhibition of their power before they are admitted to the land of the gods. In the Pyramids the name of the island is written . (3) The exhibition of might to be given by the dead in the Isle of Flame is, apparently, a struggle against lying and injustice. (4) Here again there may be some remote suggestion of Thoth's position as "Lord of Maʿet". In the Book of the Dead (A. a. Nav,) 71, 16—18, we hear of seven words which caused a slaughter on the "Island of Flame"; and ch. 15 of the Book of the Dead (Naville, c. 15 B. I. [B. a.], l. 13—14) speaks of the great god who lives on the Island, the golden youth who came forth from the lotus-flower. It is said also (Lacau, *Textes rél.* XIX, *Rec.* 27, p. 217) that *Ḫprr* was born on the Isle of Flame.

It is not obvious how the heavenly Isle of Flame corresponds to the necropolis of *Ḫmnw*. The name "Isle of Flame" is certainly very ancient. It has been noted already that the tendency of Egyptian speculation was rather to elevate things earthly into things heavenly, than to bring heavenly things down to earth, and give them a dwelling there. The reference to the birth of the solar deity on the Isle of Flame suggests, perhaps, a means of connecting the Hermopolitan necropolis with the Isle of Flame in heaven. It is well known that in Hermopolis was laid the scene of a number of cosmogonies; and according to one of those cosmogonies the sun-god appeared in Hermopolis in a lotus-flower. What more natural

(1) Published by Turayeff, *Ä. Z.* 1895, p. 120 ff.

(2) The gods and goddesses are, probably, the dead who were buried in the necropolis. They would be deities as identified with Osiris.

(3) Pyr. 397. Here the dead is spoken of as the "bull of heaven" — which may possibly be Thoth (as moon-good).

(4) Pyr. 265: Lacau, *Textes rél.*, *Recueil* 27, p. 218 (Book of Dead 174).

than to suppose that it was in the Hermopolitan  that the sun-god appeared? Later this "Isle of Flame" would be transferred to heaven.

In the Book of the Dead (Nav.) 17, 5 we are told that "Re was on the  (the high-place of him who is in *Ḫmnw*), before that which Shu raised aloft (*i. e.* heaven) came into being". (1) Similarly, in the inscription of the Great Oasis (Brugsch, 26, 22—23) we read that the primitive deity, Amon, was on the high place of *Ḫmnw* before any other being was formed. The coming forth of the primitive deity from a lotus-blossom flowering in the *Nwn* is also, as has just been said, localised in Hermopolis. So in Dendereh (Mar. I, 55 b) it is said: "Thou didst come forth in *Wnw* between its five plants". We have already discussed an important form of the ancient legend of the birth of the sun-god, the scene of which is also laid in Hermopolis. (2) There is an interesting modification of this legend to be found in the texts of the Graeco-Roman period which Sethe has analysed for the *Wörterbuch*. According to these texts the Ogdoad, the eight primitive deities were formed in Thebes. *Ṯnn* created them in *ʾIpt*: there they descended to their "home", the Isle of Flame. Then they, in turn, created light on the *Ḳ3i* (*i. e.* probably, the high-place of *Ḫmnw*), (3) and took their place in *Wnw* (*i. e.* Hermopolis) beside their father *Špśi* (probably Thoth). This form of the legend is, obviously, due to an attempt to connect the creative activity of Ptah-*Ṯnn* with the idea of a creation of light in *Ḫmnw*. The Ogdoad had a special shrine in Thebes, and, therefore, are represented here as having been fashioned in Thebes. Their appearance in Hermopolis is looked upon as their shining forth from the "Isle of Flame" — and this idea is probably borrowed from the

(1) It is not possible to determine the precise position of the "high-place of him who is in Hermopolis"; but it is probably correct to hold that it was in Hermopolis, and it may be conjectured that it stood in some close relation to the Hermopolitan necropolis.

(2) *Supra*, pp. 115 ff.

(3) See Sallier, IV, 8, 3—4 where a fragmentary text speaks of the ibis  and the ape, 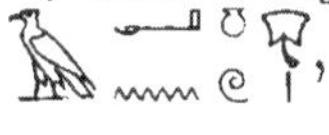, as having been sent to the *ḳ3i* of *Ḫmnw*.

legend of the coming forth from the *Nwn* of Re, the god of light. (1) The saying of the Book of the Dead, c. 17, 4—5 that the 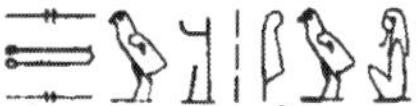 ("that which was raised up by Shu", *i. e.* the heaven) was not yet in being when Re was ruling on the "height of Eshmunein", connects the thought of the creation of heaven and its separation from earth with Hermopolis. (2)

There are many indications that Hermopolis was a centre of cosmogonic speculation. Mysterious passages in the Book of the Dead indicate its importance in the funerary literature of Egypt (cf. Book of the Dead. [Naville], 56, 3—4 ; 64, 8—9 : ch. 5 ; cf. also Lepsius, *Totb.*, c. 146, 31—35). It was known also as a source from which could be derived the most important and powerful magical formulae (Book of the Dead, Nav. 137 A, 23—24). Even in the days of Menkaure sacred formulae were sought in the "City of the Eight" and were found "under the feet of this god" (*i. e.*, probably, Thoth ; cf. Book of the Dead, Nav. 148, 15—18).

The name of Thoth's city, the "City of the Eight" has often been accounted for by reference to the cult, which existed there, of eight beings represented as having the forms of serpents, or frogs, or apes. There existed in Hermopolis — at least in the latter period — a shrine of the Ogdoad beside that of Thoth. (3) The Eight are often mentioned and variously depicted — but not in very ancient texts. The familiar designation of Thoth and of his chief-priest in Hermopolis — "Great of the Five", makes it unlikely that there

(1) Note that in the "high place of *Ḫmnw*" Re won some sorts of victory over rebels. Cf. Book of Dead, c. 17 (Grapow's edition in *Religiöse Urkunden*, 1st pt., Leipzig 1915).

(2) Shu is primitively the light-filled space between earth and sky. Hence he is the god who raises up the sky by coming between it and the earth. In the darkness of night and greyness of dawn earth and sky seem to be merged in a close embrace. Between them comes the light, and raises up the heavens. Shu is thus the support of heaven : he is also, obviously, a light-god. Thus he came to be identified, on the one hand, with Re, and, on the other, with Chons in Thebes. It is probable that "the raised up of Shu" (the heaven) was thought of in the legends of Hermopolis as having been brought into being in Eshmunein by the shining forth in that ancient centre of the light which separated heaven from earth (*i. e.* by the appearance of Shu).

(3) Cf. Pianchi-stela.

was primitively a cult of an Ogdoad in Eshmunein. The "Five" of Hermopolis were, probably, Thoth and four others. The Ogdoad may have developed from the four. An indication of this is the fact that of the names of the Eight four are feminine forms of the remaining four. Thus the four female deities may have been merely supplements made to the original group by priestly speculation. The name *Ḫmnw* for Hermopolis does not seem to go back into the ancient period. The possibility cannot, of course, be excluded that the name *Ḫmnw* is ancient, and that from the name itself has arisen the legend of the Hermopolitan Ogdoad. (1)

It would be possible to set up several hypotheses to account for the introduction of an ibis-cult into Eshmunein. Such hypotheses, however, could not be tested. The comparative absence of ancient archaeological material in the Delta makes it practically impossible to determine whether the northern or southern Hermopolis is the older centre of Thoth-cult. It can scarcely be doubted, however, that there was a shrine of Thoth in the Delta in the most ancient period. It is the existence of such an ancient cult-centre in the Delta that, as we have seen, explains, in part at least, Thoth's association with the Delta-drama of Osiris. The "northern *Wnw*" (Pyr. 191) is probably Thoth's centre in the Delta — but this designation affords no sound basis for a theory of the priority of the shrine in Middle Egypt. It is simply impossible, working with existing knowledge, to determine anything in reference to the mutual relations of the sanctuaries of Thoth in the Delta and in Middle Egypt.

The chief town of the Ibis-nome in the Delta was 
. (2) The town (or the nome?) is written in

(1) The cult of Thoth in *Ḫmnw* explains such a puzzle-script as  to represent the numeral eight. See Düm., *Geogr. Inschr.*, 2. *Abtlg.*, Taf. 80.

(2) Steindorff, *Die ägyptischen Gaue und ihre politische Entwicklung* (*Abhandlungen der königl. sächs. Gesellsch. d. Wissenschaften*, Vol. 27, p. 866). Steindorff conjectures that it is identical with the modern Ṭanaḥ, near Manṣûra. Naville (Ahnas 24) says that the chief town of the Delta Ibis-nome was also called *Ḫmnw*. According to Brugsch (*Dict. géogr.*, p. 188 f.) *Rḥwi* and *Bʿḥ* had the same position in Lower Egypt as *Ḫmnw* in Upper Egypt. Ahmed Bey Kamal says (*Annales du S.* 7, p. 231) that Thoth was worshipped in *Rḥwi* as an Ibis, and in *Bʿḥ* as an ape. Cf. Pierret, *Études ég.* (Paris, 1873), p. 61.

Graeco-Roman texts . This town is probably the same as  (Vatican, no. 16), which, according to Ahmed Bey Kamal (*Annales du Service*, tom. 7; *Rapports sur quelques localités de la Basse Égypte*), lay a kilometre to the north of the modern Baḳliya. "The House of Thoth *wp-rḥwi*" was probably the sacral name of the chief town of the Ibis-nome. The profane name of the town may have been 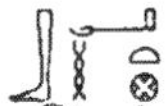 or  (Brugsch, *Dict. géogr.*, p. 962, 188 and 459 f.). Strabo mentions three towns named Hermopolis in the Delta, — so that we may, perhaps, conjecture that Thoth has several shrines in the Delta.

In Dendereh a "Temple of the Bull of Maʿet — , is mentioned in connection with the Hermopolitan nome. There may be here a suggestion of Thoth's epithet "Bull of Maeʿt". (1)

In the Middle Kingdom we hear of temples of Thoth in other districts in addition to El Bersheh and Hatnub. A funerary stela of the M. K. in Munich (Glyptothek, 40) mentions a temple of Thoth; so also does a Turin stela of the same period (Turin, no. 107). The El Bersheh reference to the temples of Thoth in the north and south (*supra*, p. 151, n. 2) justifies us in assuming that there was a fairly widespread public cult of Thoth in the Middle Kingdom.

With the XVIIIth Dynasty a period of exceptionally intense veneration of Thoth begins. That is evident from the extraordinary popularity of personal names having "Thoth" as one of their constituents, throughout the duration of that dynasty. We hear in this period also of the building of different shrines in honour of the god. Queen Hatshepsowet boasts of her zeal for the worship of Thoth. She doubled the offerings usually set apart for his cult (*Urk.* IV, 389. Inscription from Speos Artemidos), and erected new sanctuaries for the god. Apparently she built a shrine for Thoth in the valley at Speos Artemidos (near Beni Hassan). It is probably from this shrine

---

(1)  is mentioned on the stone of Palermo. Brugsch assigns it to the neighbourhood of . It suggests Thoth's function of defending Osiris against his foes.

that Thoth's epithet  (1) is derived — if Maspero's suggestion that 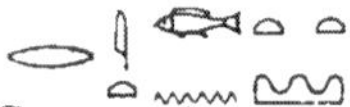 is the valley of the sanctuary of Pacht (*i. e.* Speos Artemidos), (2) is correct. With this shrine should also be connected Thoth's epithet in Leyden V, 1 (N. K.) — Thoth *k3 m R3-in·t.*

The designation of Thoth in a Dendereh text (Mariette, I, 26 o) 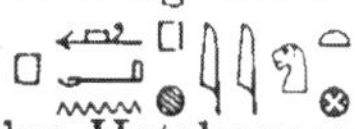 may also be derived from the shrine set up by Hatshepsowet at Speos Artemidos. Maspero points out (*Études de myth. et d'arch.* V, p. 363) that *r3-in·t* and *Pḫit* were situated close together. (3) Speos Artemidos was known as *Pr-Pḫ·t* or 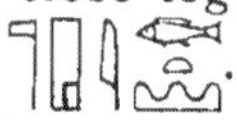.

Other rulers of the XVIIIth Dynasty were, like Hatshepsowet, zealous in erecting shrines to Thoth. Thotmes III and Amenhotep IV built shrines of some kind for Thoth in Hermopolis — as we learn from the inscriptions of those kings. (4)

The cult of Thoth is very prominent in the temple-inscriptions of the entire period of the New Kingdom. His cult was carried also in that period by Egyptian leaders and kings beyond the borders of Egypt. Horemheb, we are told, built a shrine to Thoth in  — the present day Abahûdeh, near Abu Simbel, in Nubia. From this shrine is derived the epithet "*Thoth of Imn-hri-ib*", (5) which Thoth receives in Abu Simbel.

The royal residence of the reformer-king Amenhotep IV — Amarna, lay outside the limits of the Hermopolitan nome. It would be of great interest, from the point of view of the history of Egyptian religion, to determine how the religious movement towards concentration on the cult of the solar disc

---

(1) Horus-myth (Naville), pl. XI.

(2) Maspero, *Études de myth. et d'arch.* V, p. 363,

(3) See Brugsch, *Dict. géogr.*, p. 225, 226. Sethe (*Zur Sage vom Sonnenauge*, p. 23) shows that a 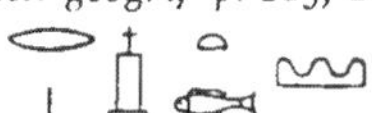 stands in clos. connection with *Pwn.t* and *Bw-gm*, and that it lay on the way which led from *Bw-gm* to the Red Sea, Thoth is described as  (*i. e.* "dweller") in *R3-int. Ibid.* note 2.

(4) See *Annales du Service*, VIII, 1907, p. 211—223. (Excavations in Eshmunein, by Mohammed Effendi Chaban).

(5) Weigall, *Report*, p. 139.

inaugurated by Amenhotep IV affected the worship of Thoth. We have, however, no reliable materials to form a judgment on the matter. It may be assumed, however, as highly probable that the art of Amarna, which is so different in certain features from the conventional art of Egypt, was, to some extent, at least, the work of artists of Thoth's city. The "City of the Eight" was an important centre of art as well as of religion, even in the Middle Kingdom, and the tomb-paintings of the 11th. and 12th. dynasties from Sheikh Sa'id to Minieh, and in El Bersheh, were the work of the Hermopolitan School. (1) The peculiar methods of the Hermopolitan artists can be traced also, it is held, in the art of Amarna. (2) It is not legitimate, of course, to argue from the presence of Hermopolitan artists in Amarna, either that Amarna was influenced in any way by the religious news of Thoth's city, or that the worshippers of the sun-disc at Amarna were more kindly disposed to the cult of Thoth than to that of Amon. Possibly, however, it might be fair to infer from the traces of Hermopolitan art at Amarna something as to the style and method of temple-decoration in Thoth's city in the Amarna period. From the connection between Thoth-cult and Egyptian colonisation and propaganda, which we see in the work of Horemheb in Nubia, it is obvious that the cult of our god lost nothing of its importance through the politico-religious activities of Amenhotep IV.

The period of the 19th. Dynasty furnishes us with unmistakable evidence of the popularity and influence of Thoth in the Egypt of that dynasty. The great builders of temples Sethos I and Rameses II erected several shrines in his honour.

In the time of Sethos I we find Thoth designated 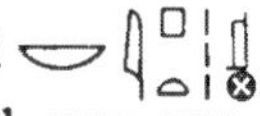 "Lord of Karnak". (3) In Thebes at this period Thoth was pro-

(1) Maspero, *Biblioth. ég.* XXVIII, p. 201.

(2) Cf. Davies work on Amarna. The whole outlook of Egyptologists on the art and religion of Amarna, and on the supposed reform of Amenhotep IV is likely to be changed greatly in the near future. That either the cult of *'Itn* in Amarna or the artistic methods of those who set up the royal buildings there contained features which were quite unconditioned by anything that preceded them in Egyptian culture is not likely to be maintained so stoutly in the future as it has been in the past. See *Mitteilungen d. D. Orient-Gesellschaft*, 1917.

(3) Cf. Champollion, *Not. descr.* II, 100.

bably identified with the Theban moon-god Chons who had an important temple and cult in Karnak. We see the identification formally expressed in the composite name . (1) To the time of Sethos belongs the origin of Thoth's epithet "Dweller in the temple of *Mn-mȝʿ·t Rʿ*", which is familiar in texts of the late period. (2) In the same "Temple of Sethos" Thoth was designated "Bull of Maat". (3)

In the time of Sethos we find Thoth as god in the town (Mar. *Ab.* I, 44, l. 19): and to this period belongs also his epithet Thoth, "Thoth under his tree in the temple of Nefertem". (4) In the reign of Sethos Thoth was worshipped also at Hermonthis (Champ. *Not.* I, 860: Leyden V, 1; etc., etc.).

Rameses II built a temple for Thoth in Memphis which was called (5) or . (6) We hear also of a monument to Thoth in "the house of Rameses" (Mar., *Ab.* II, 206), The Memphite temple is, apparently, referred to in the Pap. Bologna — a letter dating from the 19th. Dynasty, which speaks of . In Tell-om-Harb in the Delta traces of a temple-cult of Thoth as ape-god, which date from the time of Rameses II, have been found (*Annales du Service* XI, p. 3). In far-away Nubia, too, Rameses showed his veneration for the god, for, in the temple which he built at Derr, Thoth is said to dwell, — to be . There too Rameses speaks of Thoth as his father. (7)

---

(1) Karnak, Hypostyle, North Side. Sethe, 19, 62. The identification of the two gods is almost complete in the Graeco-Roman texts.

(2) See Mariette, *Abydos* I, 52; 53: Appendix B, Tableau 23 (A. B.).

(3) Mariette, *Abydos* I, Appendix B; Tableau 23 c.: I, 27.

(4) Mariette, *Abydos* I, 38, c. Cf. Thoth of Pnubs *infra* p. 170.

(5) See Recueil III, 224: Turin Pap. (P. and R.) 19, 1—3: *Memphis*, I, 4.

(6) Pap. Tur. 19, 6; Sethe (*Sage vom Sonnenauge*, 23 note 2) speaks of a sanctuary erected forThoth by Rameses II in El Hammâm. Cf. Mariette, *Ab.* II, 206.

(7) Blackman, *Temple of Derr*, p. 12. Thoth had a shrine in the temple of Ptah built by Rameses II at Gerf Ḥusen in Nubia (Weigall, *Report*, p. 81). The temple of Gerf Ḥusen was a poor copy of Abu Simbel.

Rameses III was a still more eager worshipper of Thoth than his predecessor Rameses II had been. In the Harris Papyrus we are told (I, 58, 4—5) how the third Rameses built two temples to Thoth and equipped them most splendidly with all the apparatus of sacrificial worship. Probably these temples were built in Hermopolis. Elsewhere, too, in the same period we hear of public official worship of Thoth. The Harris Pap. (I, 61 c, 8 f.) speaks of a which seems to be ϕΟΥⲰΙΤ in the 17th., or 18th., nome of Upper Egypt. (1)

In the later periods we hear frequently of temples of Thoth — but very rarely do we hear anything as to the individuals by whom those temples were erected. The shrines of Thoth in this later period are not confined to any one district of Egypt: they exist everywhere, showing thus the universal popularity of the god. On an interesting ostracon of the New Kingdom published by Gardiner (2) there is a list of shrines of Thoth which gives a good notion of the diffusion of his cult in the New Kingdom period. The ostracon speaks of a sacrificial offering to Thoth in six centres: 1. *Ḫmnw*: 2. , Cusae: 3. , Bubastis: (3); 4. , Meir, (4) 5. : 6. . (5)

Thoth often appears in connection with Abydos. (6) He is sometimes called — "dweller in Abusir-el-Melek", the necropolis of Ehnas (Vatican, 99). (7) In the texts of Dendereh he is called "the great god who dwells in Heliopolis" (Brugsch, *Thes.*, 757). In a text on a statue of the late period

(1) So Brugsch: cf. Turayeff, p. 148.

(2) *Theban Ostraca* c.2., Hieratic Text p. 15 f. (University of Toronto Studies).

(3) Herodotus says that Thoth had a temple at Bubastis (II. 138): See, Naville, *Bubastis,* p. 60—62: Turayeff, p. 149.

(4) According to Maspero (*Et. de myth.* V, p. 354 f.) it is Etlidem, or Kum-el-Rahâleh, on the northern frontier of the hare-nome.

(5) Gardiner puts it somewhere beetween Ptolemais and Aphroditopolis. Its chief divinity (according to Medinet Habu) was *Špsi* (— an epithet of Amon, and also of Thoth). See Turayeff, p. 150.

(6) Mar., *Ab.* I, 24 a: Wreszinski, *Ägyptische Inschriften* I, 25 (p. 89), etc., etc.

(7) In the same Vatican text Thoth is called Thoth . What does this mean?

at Florence (Florence 1784) he is called (so also in a Saitic text in the Bibliothèque nationale at Paris; no. 34).

A shrine of Thoth in the late period existed in . A Faiyum Papyrus of the late period (Lanzone V, LI) says that the place called *R3 Snti* is the seat of Thoth *wp rḥwi* . Turayeff locates this shrine of Thoth in the Faiyum Labyrinth. (1) A Leyden funerary stela of the N. K. (Leyden, V, 1) speaks of Thoth Lord of Eshmunein as . A cult-centre of Thoth in the late period, which probably lay somewhere in the Delta, is . (Turayeff, p. 149). Thoth is called in a text of the museum of Aix-en-Provence (no. 14). In the temple of Sethos at Abydos Thoth is called . He gets the same epithet in the text, Mariette, *Abydos* I, 44, 6 and on an altar-piece in Turin, where the text occurs:

Thoth is further called (Mar., *Ab.* I, 44, 3). Late texts connect him with Ombos. So, in a text published in *Catal. des mon. et inscr.*, Kom Ombos, 2nd. part, 3rd facsicule, p. 294, he is called "the Great, the Lord of Eshmunein, the great god . (2) There is, of course, no connection between the presence of Thoth's cult in this Ombos and the circumstance that Thoth supplanted Set in so many of the liturgical ceremonies of ancient Egypt. (3)

In the latest periods of Egyptian history we hear comparatively little about the erection of temples or shrines for Thoth. In the 30th. dynasty we find that king Nechtharheb built a temple for the "Lord of Eshmunein". (4) Brugsch quotes (*Ä. Z.* 1867, p. 91) an inscription of Nektanebos II in the quarries at Turah in which the king speaks of having opened a quarry at Turah to procure building material for the erection

(1) Cf. Brugsch, *Dict. géogr.*, p. 730.

(2) Compare Junker, *Auszug der Hathor*, p. 66.

(3) *Vid. supra*, p. 143 f.

(4) British Museum, 523. 524.

of a temple to "Thoth *wp rḥwi*, the great god of *B*ʿ*ḥ*". Naville thinks (*Ahnas*, p. 25) that the great stone blocks which are still to be seen at Baḳliya are portion of the building material which Nektanebos brought from Turah for the temple of Thoth. It seems, however, that the temple was never actually built.

In the Ptolemaic period the Pharaohs developed a new and intense interest in the maintenance of the older Egyptian cults. Numerous temples were built in this period all over Egypt. The cult of Thoth was affected greatly by the Ptolemaic religious revival, and it would seem as if the ancient god of ritual enjoyed in this period of Egyptian renaissance a greater popularity and exercised a greater influence, than at any other period of Egyptian history.

In the great temple of Hathor at Dendereh Thoth appears as one of the most important deities : he had there a special shrine and a special cult, as we can see from his epithets  (Brugsch, *Thes.* 760) and 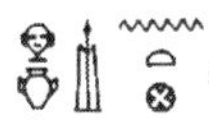, "Dweller in Dendereh" (Mar., *Dend.* III, 68 u) (1) In the temple of Horus at Edfu Thoth was still more important. In that great sanctuary he was revered as one with Chons the moon-god, and in that character was identified, in some sense, with Horus himself. He is called there: 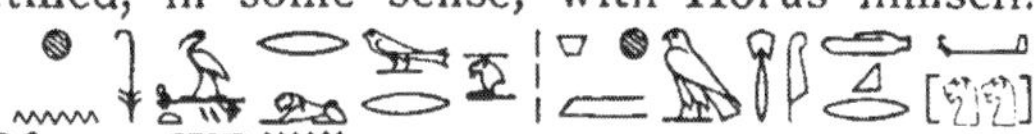 , "Chons-Thoth, the lion, mighty in power, the ʿ*ẖm*, many-coloured of plumage, the great in strength, the mighty of limb, who makes a slaughter among the enemies of the *wḏ*ꜣ·*t*-Eye" (2). The god is here represented, at one time, as a falcon wearing the solar disc (like Horus), and at another, as a lion. This idea of Thoth as a lion is suggested often, as we shall see, in the later Nubian temples. It is possible that it is ultimately derived from the identification of Thoth with Chons-Shu in Thebes. Thoth is connected in a very special way with one portion of the Temple of Edfu. This is the "*Śbḳ·t*-house", the *Ḥ·t śbḳ·t*. It was, apparently, some kind of shrine or chapel of the moon-god which formed part of the temple of Horus. In this shrine were kept statues (or other representations) of Chons and

(1) See Turayeff, p. 149.

(2) Edfu, R. I. 263.

Thoth, and also a sacred staff or sceptre of Chons. (1) The *Śbḳ·t*-shrine was at the east side of the temple of Edfu. (2) The god Shu who (as god of light) is often identified with Chons (thus occasioning, it would seem, the representation of Chons as lion) was also somehow present in the *Śbḳ·t*-shrine of Edfu. (3) That the *Śbḳ·t*-house was connected with moon-worship is clear from the fact that the lunar-eye, the moon as eye of the god of heaven, is called *Śbḳ·t* (Edfu, R. I. 77). (4) Chons is called in a Ptolemaic text (5) 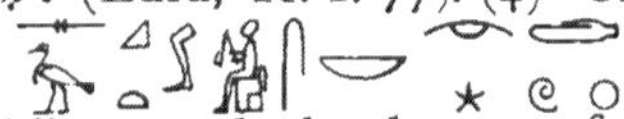 "the glorious *Śbḳ·t*, lord of the month" — and the lunar reference of *Śbḳ·t* cannot here well be doubted. It is likely that special ceremonies were carried out in the *Śbḳ·t*-shrine on the various feasts which marked the phases of the moon. Possibly the Edfu-epithet of Thoth  (Edfu, R. I. 53) may be somehow connected with the celebrations in the *Śbḳ·t*-shrine on the month-days, — or it may point to the existence of still another shrine which belonged to Thoth in Edfu. But the exact meaning of the epithet is obscure. (6)

An interesting shrine of Thoth existed in the Ptolemaic period in Thebes. A remarkable Edfu narrative of the birth of the Ogdoad (Edfu, R. I, 77) speaks of an  of Thoth in ϪΗΜЄ (Medinet Habu). (7) This shrine of the god was erected by Ptolemy IX (Euergetes II). Thoth is entitled there "Lord of Eshmunein", and often in the inscriptions of this shrine he recives the title . (8) In the same temple a god of healing, named  (= Τεῶς) was honoured, and in the texts the two deities Thoth and *Ḏḥr* are, apparently, sometimes confused

(1) Edfu, R. I, 559. For the *Ḥ·t-śbḳ·t* see Junker, *Onurislegende,* p. 148.

(2) Piehl, *Inscr.* II, 91.

(3) Isis as Seshat "the Scribe" and companion of Thoth was also in the *ḥ.t-Śbḳ·t.* See Edfu, R. I. 378. For texts which associate Shu with the shrine see Roch. I, 257: 259: 270: 278.

(4) In a text of Bab-el-Abd (Karnak) of the Graeco-Roman period (Sethe, 20, 103) the 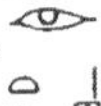 of Horus is put in parallelism with his , "*Śbḳ·t*-eye".

(5) Dümichen, *Tempelinschr.* I, 39.

(6) See above p. 27, note 1.

(7) Cf. Champollion, *Not. descr.* I, 603.

(8) The inscriptions of this temple are published by Mallet in his *Kasr-el-Agouz*; the temple lay to the south-west of the great temple of Medinet Habu.

with each other. *Dhr* is called sometimes 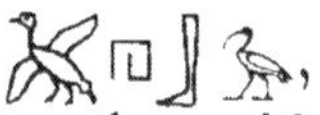, and the name of Thoth is sometimes thrown together with the name *Dhr* in a strange fashion, as, for instance,  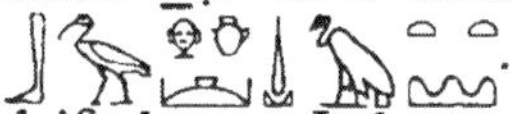. (1) It is to be noted that the ancient deified sage Imhotep was also honoured in this temple. This has led Sethe to conjecture (2) that Teos (= *Dhr*) is really a deified priest of Memphis. (3) The epithet *Śtm* Sethe regards as belonging to the deified priest. Mallet (4) thinks that the epithet  is equivalent to the priestly title , and  he belives to be a specific title (5) of the Memphitic priests of Ptah. Sethe is of opinion that this deified *Śm*-priest of Memphis may possibly be the Theban Hermes whom Clement of Alexandria mentions along with Asklepios of Memphis, as an instance of a deified man. (6) Against this view of Sethe, however, stands the fact that the epithet *Śtm* is used in the inscriptions of the temple in question only in reference to Thoth: it is not used in connection with the name Teos (), and Thoth is called *Śtm* only where he does not appear as identified, or confused, with Teos. (7). The very familiar personal name of the late period "Thoth-*Śtm*" suggestes that *Śtm* was regarded generally as en epithet of the oracle-god and healing god Thoth. It would be very natural that a human sage (Teos) should be honoured, when deified, in the same shrine as Thoth, the god of wisdom. The fact that in this temple Imhotep and Amonhotep appear as

(1) The personal name *Dhr-p-hb* is found in Theban tombs of the Ptolemaic period. See Parthey, *Ägyptische Personennamen*, p. 116.

(2) Sethe, *Imhotep*, p. 8 f.

(3) A priest of Memphis named Teos is actually known. See Brugsch, *Thes.* V, 866 f.

(4) *Kasr-el-Agouz.*

(5) For the equivalence of *Śm* and *Śtm*, cf. Brugsch, *Wb.* 1221: Griffith, *Stories of the High Priests*, p. 4.

(6) Clement, Strom. I, 21, 134, p. 399. See Sethe, *Imhotep*, p. 6 ff.

(7) Reitzenstein (*Poimandres*, p. 118 f.) refuses to identify the Theban Hermes of Clement with the *Teos-p-hb* of these texts. He says rightly: "*Der Thotkult zu Theben stammt sicher nicht von diesem einen Heroenkult her, und die Worte des Clemens lassen sich kaum so pressen*". The cult of Thoth was well known in Thebes long before Ptol. IX built the temple in question. Thoth was identified with the Theban moon-god Chons in the New Kingdom.

paredroi of Thoth is similarly to be explained. (1) Imhotep, Amonhotep and Teos are all deified sages, and Euergetes II who, even more than other Ptolemies, was a lover of Egyptian wisdom, did not think to do dishonour to Thoth, the Hermes of Egypt, in setting up beside him as gods three Egyptian sages.

In the text of the Dedication of the shrine (2) it is said that Thoth (or possibly Teos) was wont to descend on the temple each evening in the form of an ibis; and every morning, according to the text, the god went forth again from the shrine. It would thus seem that the temple was looked upon as a centre for night-oracles received through incubation; and it is probable that the chief worshippers in the temple were the sick who came to get comfort in their pains from such dreams as the night-abiding god of healing might send to them. The peculiar epithet of Thoth in this shrine, — *Śtm*, "he who hears", would fit in well with the customs of such a temple. (3)

The cult of Thoth in the later period in Nubia seems to have developed just as steadily as his cult in the Egypt of that period.

In the great sanctuary of Philae Thoth was very specially venerated. He gets there the title "Lord of Philae": (4) he is also styled in the texts of Philae, "Lord of Eshmunein", "Lord of ", "Thoth of the Abaton" (*i. e.* island of Bigeh) and "Thoth of Pnubs". He appears here as one of the triad, Arhensnuphis, Thoth, Dedwn. The epithet "Thoth of Pnubs" is the special designation of the Nubian Thoth. The texts of Philae are quite clear as to the identity of Thoth of Eshmunein with Thoth of Pnubs. (5) In spite of this recognised identity,

(1) Cf. Reitzenstein, *Poimandres*, p. 120f.

(2) Mallet, *op. cit.*, p. 91—101.

(3) Compare the prayers to Amon published in Ermans *Denksteine aus der Thebanischen Gräberstadt* (Sitzungsber. d. p. Ak. 1911, pp. 1088, 1091, 1092 etc.) in which Amon is invoked as 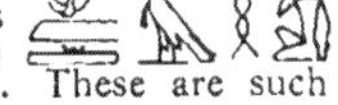 and 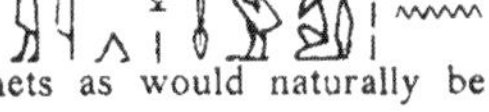 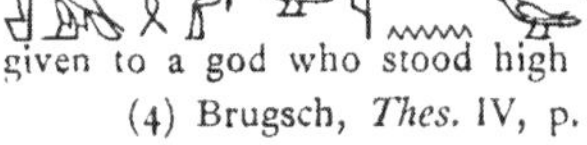. These are such epithets as would naturally be given to a god who stood high in the estimation of ordinary folk.

(4) Brugsch, *Thes.* IV, p. 765.

(5) So in the *Wörterbuch* — Zettel, Philae, 970. (Photograph. 1434); 949 (Phot. 1447).

however, the Nubian Thoth possesses characteristics which do not normally belong to the Thoth of Egypt. Thus he appears, for instance, in Philae as "the god of wine who drinks abundantly" and, again, as "the lord of drunkenness and festivity". He appears here, further, as "the living lion which overthrows the evil ones, mighty in strength, lord of victory". (1) In Philae, as in Dendereh, Thoth is identified with Shu: he is said to be "the mighty Shu, Lord of wine". (2)

The epithets of Thoth in Philae, "great and splendid god in Bigeh ( )" (3) and "He that pacifies the *Nsr·t* in Bigeh, (4) and "He that pacifies the *Nsr·t* in the Abaton ( )" point to the existence of a special cult of Thoth in the island of Bigeh. Here again, as at Philae, it is the Nubian, rather than the Egyptian Thoth that is honoured. (5)

The chief shrine of Thoth of Nubia was the temple of Dakkeh (Pselkis). This temple was built by the Nubian king , Ergamenes, who was a contemporary of the second, third, and fourth Ptolemies. Ptolemy IX, who built the shrine of Thoth in ⲬⲎⲘⲈ built also a Pronaos for Hermes Paotnuphis (*i. e.* Thoth of Pnubs) at Dakkeh. The shrine built by Ergamenes at Dakkeh seems to have been specially dedicated to Thoth of Pnubs ( ). (6) The name *P-nbś*, or *Pr-nbś* ("House of the Sycamore") reminds one of the old name of the village which is now called Ofedwineh (about 10 kilometres distant from Pselkis). This village was known in the Roman period as Hierasykaminos. In the temple of Ofedwineh the sacred sycamore is frequently depicted, and there also the goddess Isis is represented as seated under a tree, while Thoth stands beside her. (7) It is possible that the

---

(1) *Ibid.*, Zettel 958. (2) *Ibid.*, Zettel 947.

(3) Zettel 930. (4) Zettel 816.

(5) Another peculiarity of the Nubian Thoth is that when he is identified with Shu, he is sometimes represented as completely human in figure (cf. Champ. *Mon.* II. Pl. 132, 2).

(6) A Greek inscription of the temple says that its pronaos was built in the 35 th. year of Ptol. IX, and dedicated to Hermes Paotnuphis. (Weigall, p. 521 f.).

(7) See Weigall, Report, p. 85 ff. The *nbś*-tree appears as sacred tree in nearly all the necropolis of the list of nomes in Edfu. In Ed. R. I. 335 means "necropolis".

place-name Pnubs may have derived its origin from the sacred Sycamore of Ofedwineh. (1) There was however, another Pnubs in Upper Nubia (2) where Ergamenes lived in the early period of his rule. It is, therefore, likely that "Thoth of Pnubs" at Pselkis and elsewhere derived his title from the Upper Nubian town where Ergamenes began his reign. (3)

Thoth of Pnubs is represented at times as an ape seated under a tree (probably the *nbś*-tree). (4) It is a reasonable conjecture that the Nubian Thoth was somehow associated with tree-worship. It is rather as ape than as ibis that he appears in Nubia, and an ape-cult would stand, perhaps, without difficulty in close relationship with the worship of a sacred tree. But it is not possible to indicate clearly the process by which Thoth came thus to be worshipped in association with a sacred tree. In Dakkeh, the chief Nubian shrine of the god, his identity with Thoth of *Ḫmnw* is implied in some of the epithets ascribed to him. The epithets of Thoth which recur most often at Dakkeh are "Lord of Pnubs in Takens" (*i. e.* north Nubia), "Lord of Dakkeh", "the Twice-great of *Ḫmnw*", "Lord of Bigeh", "Lord of the southern lands", *jwp rḥwi, śḥtp nṯrw*.

Both in Dakkeh and in Dendûr Thoth of Pnubs appears as a form of Shu. (5) In the temple of Dendûr Thoth is represented in human form, seated, wearing a crown of plumes (the crown of Onuris) and holding in the right hand a -sceptre (round which a serpent coils itself) and a scorpion. (6) The text accompanying this representation of the god calls him "Thoth of Pnubs, Lord of Dakkeh 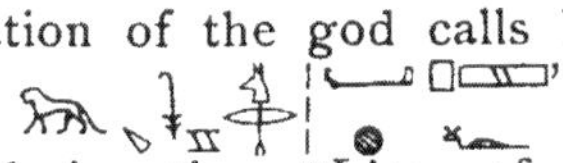" (7) The crown of Onuris and the designation "Lion of the South" are features which really belong to the Nubian equivalent of Shu — Arhensnuphis. (8) The serpent-encircled sceptre

(1) Or, perhaps, Maḥaraḳa.

(2) Ptolemy mentions this Pnubs. Cf. Brugsch, *Sieben Jahre der Hungersnot.*

(3) Cf. Weigall, Report, p. 20.

(4) For a good representation of Thoth of Pnubs See *Bibl. ég.*, vol. 27, plate IV.

(5) Brugsch, *Thes.* 761, 39 (Dakkeh).

(6) Blackman, *Temple of Dendûr* Pl. XLII.

(7) Blackman, *Dendûr*, p. 54.

(8) Brugsch, *Thes.* 765, 62 c. For equation Onuris = Shu = Arhensnuphis, see Junker, *Onurislegende*, p. 7.

suggests the magic, and, particularly, the healing powers of the god. (1)

In the Nubian temple of Debôd (which, like the shrine of Dakkeh, was also built by a native Nubian ruler) Thoth of Pnubs is represented as a man in a standing position who holds in the left hand a 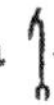-sceptre together with a serpent and two scorpions. (2) It is to be noted that, just as Thoth is frequently identified with Shu in the Nubian temples, (3) so we find in Dakkeh an identification of Shu with Thoth. In Dakkeh we hear of  "Shu, the venerable, the dweller in Eshmunein". (4) This identification of the two gods is based ultimately, as has been already said, in all probability, on the Theban identification of Shu and Chons. (5) The ap-

(1) It would seem to follow from Mar., *Dend.*, IV, 43 that Thoth of Eshmunein could of himself, and, as it were, in his own right, be represented in serpent-form. We hear in that text of "the first serpent-form of Thoth *wp rḥwi*". For the connection of the scorpion with magic see a discussion by Gardiner, PSBA, 1917, pp. 34—44 on the official who is known as *Kherep srḳt*.

(2) Roeder, *Debód*, I, p. 39: II Plate 106). For a similar representation of Thoth in Kalabsheh (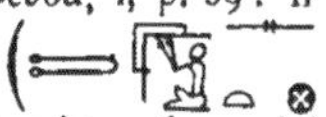 Talmis) see Gauthier *Temple de Kalabchah*, 2me fascicule, Pl. 114, where the god is styled Thoth of Pnubs, *ˁꜣ ˁꜣ wr*, "Lord of Dakkeh".

(3) In Debôd Thoth is identified clearly with 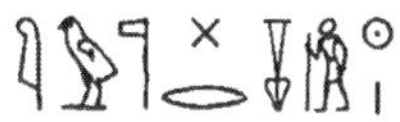 who comes forth from *Kns·t*.

(4) Champ, *Notes descr.* I, 73.

(5) In Mariette, D. II, pl. 44 there is a remarkable representation of Thoth and Shu holding up the heavens in which can be seen the sacred *wḏꜣ·t*-Eye. This would suggest, perhaps, such equations as Herakles = Chons — Shu = Thoth. (Cf. *Recueil*, 1906, p. 181 f.). Herakles in the Greek legend supported for a while the universe. Shu as the light-space which separates earth from heaven performs a similar function. As gods of light Shu and Chons, were readily identified (cf. ÄZ, XXI, p. 79: Wiedemann, *Herodot*, p. 200 f. Pauly-Wissowa, Article, Chons). The descriptive epithet  "the shining one" is applied to Chons in Edfu-texts, and it is possible that the word *šwi* may also have helped to bring about the identification of Chons and Shu. An interesting example of the identification of Chons and Shu is to be found in Dendereh (M. II, pl. 76) where a falcon-god is called "Chons-Shu dweller in Edfu 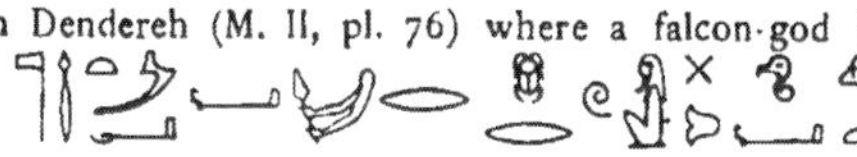
".

Junker in his *Onurislegende* pp. 7—11 undertakes to prove that the connection of Thoth and Shu in Nubia is due to the circumstance that these two gods play practically the same part in the legend of the bringing home to Egypt of the

pearance of Tefenet as the spouse of Thoth in the Nubian temples is due to the assimilation of our god with Arhensnuphis — Shu, and therefore, partly to the rôle of Thoth in the legend of Onuris.

---

angry goddess. The real god of Pnubs, according to Junker, is the warrior-god Onuris, and through Onuris Thoth and Shu are equated. In proof of this theory Junker carefully examines the representations of Thoth of Pnubs at Philae, Dakkeh and Dendûr. The scorpion and serpents which are described in the text above as coiling themselves round the sceptre held by Thoth of Pnubs, Junker regards as a late addition to the original simple 𓌀-staff. In some instances the god holds instead of the 𓌀-staff a staff on which is set a falcon-head bearing the sun-disc — the familiar sceptre of Onuris. Further Junker points out that Thoth of Pnubs seldom or never is shown as receiving gifts such as are generally offered to Thoth of *Ḫmnw* — writing-apparatus, bread, symbols of moon-worship etc. The epithets "Lion of the South" "He who comes forth from Nubia", "Lord of the southern lands" which are assigned to Thoth of Pnubs prove, also, according to Junker that the connection between the ancient god of *Ḫmnw* and the god of Pnubs is merely external and secondary. When Thoth of Pnubs is called "Lord of wine who drinks abundantly", "Lord of drukenness and gladness" he is identified again with Onuris of Nubia who was looked on as the "Lord of wine".

When Thoth of Pnubs is called "Lord of Maˁet, Lord of judging who dwells in the House of books" (Philae, *Phot.* 1356), and again, "the Scribe of the Ennead" (Kalabsheh, *Phot.* 1776), the ascription to him of these *Ḫmnw*-epithets may be due, according to Junker, either to some fundamental agreement in character between Thoth of *Ḫmnw* and the local god of Pnubs, or, more probably, to the fact that Onuris also was looked on (even in the N. K.) as Lord of laws and judging. That Onuris, however, came to be regarded as judge and legislator needs itself to be explained. Junker admits that the representation of Thoth of Pnubs in ape-form makes a difficulty for his theory — suggesting that the primitive local god of Pnubs was an ape-god with which Onuris came somehow to be identified. Junker is certainly right in maintaining that Thoth and Onuris-Shu are associated at Pnubs largely through the legend of Onuris. It is, however, not yet clear in spite of his painstaking statement of the evidence for theory that Thoth of *Ḫmnw* is related in purely external and secondary fashion with the god of Pnubs.

Appendix A.

List of proper names in which the name of Thoth appears.

, Ahmed Bey Kamal, *Tables d'offrandes*, p. 178.

, *Rec.* 1898, p. 88. Florence, no. 1676 (N. K.).

, Pap. Turin. P. and R. 96, 6 (end of XXth Dyn.).

P3 šri Ḏḥwti (Psenthotes), *Rec.* 42, p. 45, l. 3 (Erbach Pap. Ptolemaic).  — Psenthotes.

P3 Ḏḥwti Spiegelberg, *Dem. Pap.* (*Catal. du Mus. d. Caire*: no. 31163). *Rylands Demotic Papyri* III, pp. 283. 194 (: παθωτης). .

, (Μανεθώθ, Μανεθώ). *Rec.* 1903, p. 169.

 Daressy, *Cercueils* (*Cat. du Mus. d. Caire*), nos. 61018 (Rams. I); 61019 (XVIIIth Dyn. Seti I); 61020 (Rams. II).

Μαιθωτις, *Rylands Dem. Pap.* III, 275. This may represent ; or it may be the same as *Mri-Ḏḥwti.*

, Turin, no. 92 (Funerary Stela of late period). Leyden I, 350, *verso*, col. 4, 23 (written ): Anast. III, 5. Gardiner, *Theban Topographical Catal.*, p. 321 (Rams. II).

, Florence, Ushebtis (Sala III).

, Naville, *Deir el Bahari*, 79.

, *Rylands Dem. Pap.* III, no. 4, *verso*, I, p. 211 (*Esḥarthowt*), cf. *ibid.*, p. 453.

, *Rec.* 1903, p. 195 (*Esthowt*).

, *Catal. du Musée*, Kamal, Stèles ptolémaiques, no. 22150.

, Petrie, *Hawara*, Pl. V, 5 (Greek period), cf. *Rylands Dem. Pap.* III, 14, p. 264.

, Florence, *Catal.* 1553. Stela of M. K. (The man's sister is . appears as a proper name, Cairo 20025; and , Wien, Kunsthistor. Museum, no. 13. Stela of M. K.)

, Spiegelberg, *Demot. Inschr., Catal. du Musée d. Caire*, no. 31144; Spiegelberg, *Demot. Pap.* 30710. Cf. *Rec.* 33, p. 152. The Greek form is Χεσθώτης, or Χεσθωυτες (*Rylands Dem. Pap.* III, 189). The Mahaffy-Petrie Pap. has also Χεσθωθης. Cf. P. S. B. A. 23/300. For the Upper Egyptian form Χεσθώτης see Wilken, *Ostraca*, no. 1194.

, Brit. Mus. 772 (N. K.). [Whether represents *Ḏḥwti* is not certain. Cf. the forms of the name and , *supra*, p. 10, note 2. Cf. p. 204].

Mission, V, 346: Petrie, *Hawara*, Pl. V: Petrie, *Kahun*, 28. Cf. Cairo, 20198 (M. K.): Turin (Stela, XVIIIth Dyn.), no. 171.

, Cairo, 20237 (M. K.). (This may be *Śbk-Ḏḥwti*).

, (*Śr pꜣ Ḏ.*), Hilton Price, *Catal. of Eg. Antiquities* II, 1622. Cf. also in the same vol. 1622 a, b: 1626: 125—128.

, Quibell, *Ramesseum*, XX, 4: XXI, 9 (cf. *Rec.* 21, 13—16).

, Berlin, 7272. Tombstone, XVIIIth Dyn.

, Pap. jud. de Turin, 19, 10 (name of a criminal).

, Cairo, *Wb.* 386 (Sethe, 24, 56); a woman's name.

, Cairo, Sinuhe-Ostracon; letter of N. K.

, Cairo, *Wb.*, no. 61.

T3 bw Ḏḥwti, Rylands Dem. Pap. III, 277.

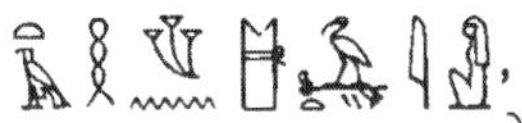, Pap. *Nś Ḫns*, Maspero, *Monum. roy.* Pl. XXVI. Cf. 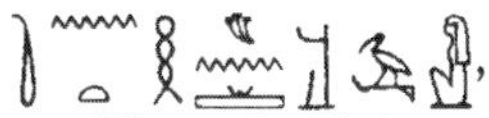, Masp, *Études de myth.*, vol. 4, p. 188: *Rec.* II, 13 f. This may be a contraction for  *T3 šri·t t3 ḥnw Ḏ.* See *Mission* III, Pap. Nesikhonsu: XXth—XXIth Dyn. Cf. the name, 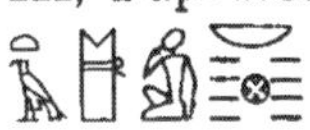 Daressy, *Cercueils des prêtres d'Amon*, p. 15.

, *T3 šri·t Ḏḥwti śtm* (*Stèles ptol.* 22136). For *T3 šri·t Ḏ.* see *Sphinx*, 13, p. 239. Pap. 1201, Brit. Mus.

, *T3 Ḏ·Ḫmnw.* P. S. B. A. 1911, p. 109.

, *T3 Ḏḥwti*, Vienna, Kunsthistorisches Museum, no. 172 (Ptolemaic)  *Catal. du Musée d. Caire*; *Stèles ptol.*, 22238. The Greek form is Ταθωτις. See *Rylands Dem. Pap.* III, pp. 265, 462.

 Cairo, 20258 (XVIIIth Dyn.): Leyden V, 51 (Stela of N. K.). (The name is frequent in the time of the XVIIIth Dyn.). It seems to have been often given to scribes. It is used as a name for women as well as

men. See Legrand, *Repertoir général*. 639. It occurs in M. K. also. So Louvre, Cat. 186. In the Stèles Ptolémaïques it appears as (no. 22145).

, Carnarvon and Carter, *Five years exploration at Thebes*, p. 21 (Ushebti; XVIIIth Dyn.).

, *Rylands Dem. Pap.* III, 262. Cf. P. S. B. A. 23/298. The Greek form would be Θοτευς. Cf. *Rec.* 1903, p. 20. ЄΥϹ = ЄΥ, ΗΟΥ — ps.-participle: a parallel would be Αρευς = *Ḥr iw*. With this name *Ḏḥwti iw* seems to be identical *Catal. du Musée d. Caire*, Kamal, *Stèles ptolémaïques*, 22029: Spiegelberg, *Dem. Pap.*, no. 30664: Glyptothèque Ny Carlsberg (Schmidt), Fig. 67. Another variant of the name is . Berlin, Pap. 3162, 5, 7 (in the same text 15, 1 the name is written clearly).

, Berlin 7731 (M. K.).

, Cairo Ostracon, *Wb.*, no. 7 (XXth Dyn.).

, *Urkunden*, IV, 448 d.

, Louvre, Apis Stela, no. 189. Parallel to this is the name

, *Rylands Dem. Pap.* III, 262, 272, 463. The Greek form would be Θοτορταιος (*Ryl. D. P.*, p. 189, 193) like Αμορταιος, Εσορταιος. Θοτορταις also occurs (cf. Assyrian, *Ti-hu-ut-ir-ti-šu*, Ranke, *Keilinschr. Material*, p. 41). The name is found again in Spiegelberg, *Dem. Pap.* (*Catal. d. Mus.*), no. 30704; and Spiegelberg, Erbach Pap. *Rec.* 42, p. 43. Schmidt, *Glyptothèque Ny Carlsberg*, no. 2428. A woman's name, is found in a Louvre funerary stela of the late period.

, *Ryl. Dem. Pap.*, pp. 124, 463. According to N. Reich (*Rec.* 33, p. 152) the Greek form is Θοτρωισις. It is a name of the Ptolemaic period.

, Leyden, V, 108 (N. K.).

, Turin Pap. P. and R., 165, 5 (name of a sailor, XXth Dyn.).

, Thebes, Tomb of Chonsu (A): Copy by Sethe 12, 115 (Period of Rams. II). *Ḏḥwti pꜣ šps̀i.*

, Turin Pap. 91, 1 (P. and R.).

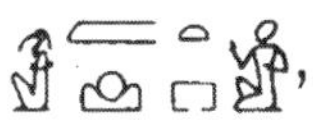, Brit. Mus. 2 (stone coffin of late period).

, Cairo 20198 (Tombstone M. K.).

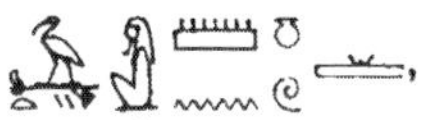, *Rylands Dem. Pap.* III, pp. 262, 272: Spiegelberg, *Demot. Inschr.* (*Catal. du M. d. C.*). no. 31134. The Greek forms would be Θοτμηνις and Θετμεν. Cf.  Ahmed Bey Kamal, *Tables d'offrandes*, p. 98.

, Cairo 20025, 20387, 20068 (M. K.).

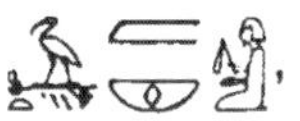, Gardiner, *Topographical Catalogue*, p. 34 (XIXth Dyn.). Leyden, V, 17 (XIXth Dyn.): Harris I, 61 b: Louvre, Apis Stela, no. 10: Lyons, Funerary Stela of N. K.

, Gardiner, *Topogr. Cat.*, pp. 18; 38; 34. This is a very common name in the XVIIIth Dyn. (Greek form Τεθμωσις). The name is especially common at Edfu which is not far from El Kab, where the first beginnings of an Egyptian political awakening in the XVIIIth Dyn. are, perhaps, to be sought. See *Rec.* 1901, p. 130.

, Pap. Mallet (Rams. III): published by Maspero in *Études d. myth.*, vol. 4, p. 37.

, Quibell, *Ramesseum* XI: Gardiner, *Topogr. Cat.*, p. 22 (time of Amenophis II). The name is frequent. In Spiegelberg, *Dem. Pap.*, no. 50012 it is written .

, often in El Bersheh in form . See, also, Pap. Kahun (Statuette of M. K.): Bauer, Berlin 3023, 42 f. It is a popular ancient name.

, Florence, *Catal.* 1500; Statuette of M. K. (cf. Florence, *Catal.* 1549).

, Leyden, V, 15 (N. K.): Leemans, *Monum. funér.*, plate XXIV (*Monuments égyptiens du Musée d'antiquités des Pays-Bas à Leyde*, III).

, Pap. jud. de Turin, 5, 3, 6 (cf. *ibid.*, 46, 3).

Urkunden, IV, 547 (time of Thotmes III).

, *Catal. du Mus.* Reisner, *Amulets*, no. 12209: 12214.

, Brit. Mus. 827. Stela of M. K. This name is frequent both for men and women in M. K. Cf. Blackden and Fraser, *Hatnub*, I, 11: Leyden V, 109, etc. etc.

, *Annales d. Service*, III, 277--280 (coffin of) M. K. A frequent script of preceding name in M. K. Cf. Cairo, 20235. Brit. Mus. 805 etc. etc.

, Ahmed Bey Kamal, *Tables d'offrandes*, p. 129.

, Louvre, Ushebtis, no. 1121: Brit. Mus. 266 (N. K.). Cf. , Brit. Mus. 28 (N. K.).

, Spiegelberg, *Sethosrechnungen*, plate X, col. IV, l. 11. The name is also written .

See Borchardt, *Saȝḥure,* I, p. 124 (name of Ramesside period).

, Louvre, Stela, no. 3936 (Pierret, *Inscr. ég.* II, p. 124).

, *Urkunden,* IV, 465, 16: L. D. Text IV, 94 (XVIIIth Dyn.). Cf. Cairo (*Wb.*), no. 204 . See the name Thebes, Tomb of *Ḥri* (Sethe, 11, 82). The Greek form is Σενδοτευτῆς, according to Spiegelberg (*Griechische Namen,* p. 42). Cf. the name L. D. III, 9 f.

, *Ryl. Demotic Papyri,* III, 282: Spiegelberg, *Mumienetiketten,* no. 90, and *Demot. Studien,* I, 8, 15, and *Demot. Inschr.* (*Catal. du Mus.*), nos. 30704, 31057 b: Hölscher, *Hohes Tor von Medinet Habu,* p. 47. For the Greek forms of the name Θοτσυτσμ Θυσυτσμ see *Ryl. Dem. Pap.* III, p. 464 and *Rec.* 1900, p. 87 f.

, Quibell, *Ramesseum,* XI. (Is this *Ḏḥwti smȝ*?)

, Brit. Mus. 805 (Stela of M. K.).

, Beni Hassan (Newberry) II, pl. XXIX; XXXVI.

, Beni Hassan II (Ind. Tomb), Plate XIII (= L. D. Text, II, 83—85).

, Hannover, Canopus-jars (Saitic period).

, Quibell, *Ramesseum,* XXV. Cf. the similar names , *Rec.* 1906, p. 155 (time of Sheshonk III), , Quibell, *Ramesseum.* Cairo *Wb.*, no. 77 (Sethe, 25, 14: XXIInd Dyn.). , *Catal. du Mus.*; Legrain, *Statues,* no. 42189.

, Newberry, *Ushabtis,* no. 46532.

Appendix B.

Epithets of Thoth.

, representative of Re; Cairo 20062 (M. K.); Turin 2204 (Coffin-lid, N. K.); Leyden V, 1 (N. K.): Book of the Heavenly Cow, 74, etc. etc.

, representative of Atum; Turin Pap. 23, 2—5 (P. and R.).

, the ancient and great one for the Ennead; Berlin, P. 3049, col. 17, 2—3.

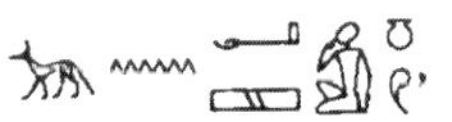, who comes to him that calls him: Philae, Z. 30 (*Wb.*).

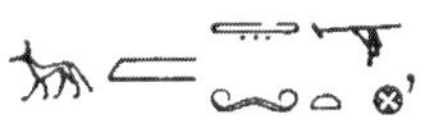, title of Thoth of Pnubs, in Maharraga, Photo 2008 (*Wb.*): in Dakkeh, Phot. (*Wb.*) 1921: 1929: 1925.

(sic)
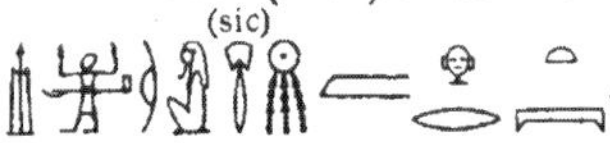, the moon shining in the heavens; Mallet, *Kasr el Agouz*, 82.

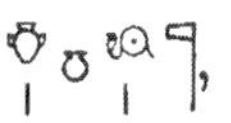, heart of Re: Mar., *Dend.* III, 19 n, and elsewhere often (with Thoth determinative often 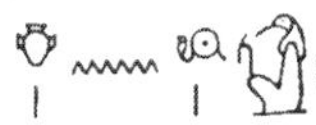; so Mar., *Dend.* II, 65 a).

, the *Ipi*, Edfu, Piehl, *Inscr.* II, 101 (time of Ptol. IX).

, the *Ipi-ib*, Mar., *Dend.* III, 81 e: L. D. IV, 76 e.

, who brings the *i3ḥt*-eye to its owner. Edfu R. I, 25.

, who brings the *wḏ3·t*-eye: Mar., *Ab.* I, 37 a; cf. , Mar., *Dend.* II, 65 a. See discussion of *Ini-św*, *supra* p. 73 f.

, the *Ini-św*; Pap. Leyden, 347, 12, 2—4 (N. K.).

, who brings to Re his eye from *kns·t*: Philae, Zettel 378 (*Wb.*).

, who brings the eye that was far away; Goshen, 2.

, who giveth life to men, *Totb.*, Nav. 182, 11 (according to Af).

, according to whose word the Ennead acts Mammisi (Edfu), p. 14.

, who accomplishes truth (ΜЄ), Mar., *Dend.* II, 62, etc.

, who does what the goddesses love, Edfu, R. I, 63.

, universal benefactor; Turin Pap. 25, 9.

, who does what Re praises in his chapel, *Totb.* Nav. 182, 9.

, who does good; Mar., *Dend.* III, 70.

, who makes slaughter among the foes of the *wḏ3·t*-eye, Edfu R. I, 263 (Chons-Thoth).

, who hath made Eternity; Thebes, Tomb of (Sethe's copy, 13, 87).

, he of the balance; Harris, I, 45, 11.

, the *iḫi* who protects it (the lunar eye), Brugsch, *Thes.* 36.

, throat of *Imn-rnf*; Brugsch, *Thes.* 759, 30 a (Dendereh).

 *iḳr ḏd,* splendid in speech. Naville, *Myth of Horus,* Pl. I.

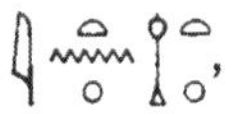, the "silver" sun; Mar., *Dend.* IV, 82.

, the Great One in Hermopolis; Anastasi V, 9, 3.

, the twice great; Mar., *Dend.* II, 4: IV, 41: I, 22: III, 70, 78 n etc. etc.

, the thrice great; Dümichen, *Geogr. Inschr.*, III, 57; Mar. *Dend.* I, 10: II, 37 a: III, 72 a: IV, 33, 74, 89, etc. etc.

, great in fear in every land; Turin Pap. 25, 8.

, great in strength; Philae, Phot. 1448; Z. 958 (*Wb.*).

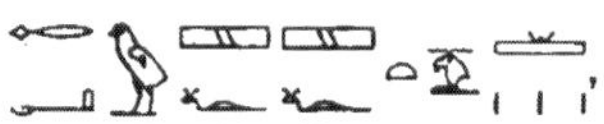, great in power; *Totb.* Nav. 134, 10 – 11: Berlin P. 7518.

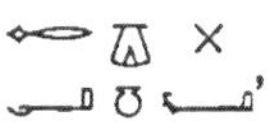, great in power; Philae Phot. 1434, Z. 930 (*Wb.*): title of T. of Pnubs.

, great in triumph; L. D. IV, 58 a (Dendereh).

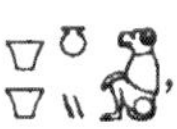, the ape; Mar., *Dend.* III, 81 e: II, 3.

, the great and venerable ape; Harris, I, 45, 12.

, who equipped the Eye for its owner; Mar., *Dend.* II, 65 a.

 *ʿm tȝwi*, he that knows the Two Lands; Mar., *Dend.* I, 57 : II, 30 b. (For reading cf. 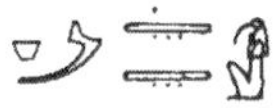, Dümichen, *Baugeschichte*, 42. *ʿm* = ЄΙΜЄ.)

, the beautiful; Turin Pap. 24, 4—6.

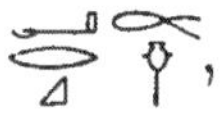, prudent of heart; Karnak, Hypostyle, Sethe 21, 67.

, the eagle of many-coloured plumage; Edfu R. I, 263 (Chons-Thoth as identified with Horus in Edfu).

, to whom is subject life in the Duat; Thebes, Tomb of *Pȝ Šdw*, Sethe, 13, 87 (XXth Dyn.).

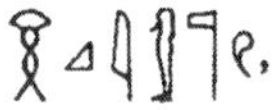, who increased his figure (crescent); Mar., *Dend.* III, 74 b.

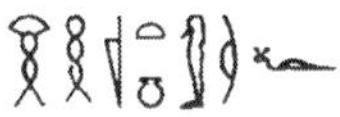, who increases his form (crescent); Mar., *Dend.* II, 31 b.

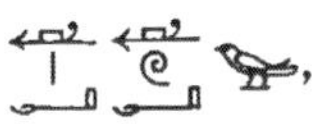, the unique one; Edfu, R. I, 267.

, clean of hands (arms); *Totb.* Nav. 182, 3.

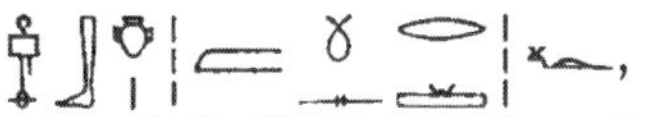, astute (?) in his plans; Dendereh, L. D. IV, 76 e : Mar., *Dend.* III, 70 : Naville, *Saft el Henne* 6, 3.

, the messenger : Mar., *Dend.* III, 81 e : Philae, 2500; cf. Mar., *Dend.* II, 62 b (written 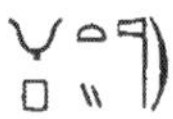). See Junker, *Auszug*, p. 66.

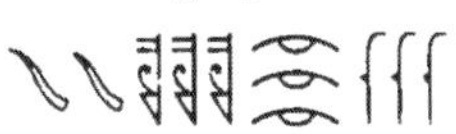 *wp trw ibdw rnpwt*, who distinguishes seasons, months and years; Edfu, R. I, 27.

 *wpiw iḳr*, eloquent judge (?); Mar., *Dend.* II, 3.

, eloquent judge (?) pleased with *maʿet*; Mar., *Dend.* II, 74 b.

, who distinguishes bodies of different countries, Turin Pap. 25, 10.

, path-opener of Re; *Totb.* Nav. 16 (Gate of the underworld).

, porter of Horus; Pyr. 1465.

, the *wn-imꜣ* presiding over the Temple, Edfu Roch. I, 755.

wr, the Great One; Dümichen, *Rezepte* XXI/3: Mar., *Ab.* I, pl. 57. Cf. , Great Amduat, 7th hour (acc. to Sethos IV, 43), and Turin Pap. 125, 2—5.

, great in *mdw nṯr*; Edfu R. I, 27.

, the Great One who came forth from the Nile; *Totb.* Nav. 178, 14 (cf. Pyr. 126 and Cairo 20520, 32 M. K.).

, great in magic; *Totb.* Nav. 182, 8 (acc. to Af): , Mar., *Dend.* III, 67 a etc.

, great in slaughter; *Totb.* Nav. 134, 10 (cf. 95, 3—5).

wḥꜥ ib; Luxor, Stela of Rams. II, *Rec.* 16, 56, Champ., *Notes* II, 161.

, prudent: Karnak, Temple of Chons, Architrave of *Ḥriḥor* (Sethe, 3, 67). Cf. *Urkunden* IV, 554, no. 35.

, who ends (?) the strife; *Totb.* Nav. 182, 9.

, Turin Pap. 25, 2. *Vid. supra* p. 40 f.

, mighty in his words; L. D. IV, 58 a (Dendereh).

, "orderer of fate" on the *mśḫn·t*; Edfu, R. I, 27.

, sound of heart; *Totb.* Nav. 69, 12, 12 (J. a).

, sound of hand; Turin Pap. (P. and R.) 24, 1—4.

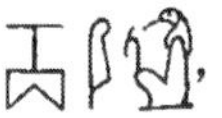, judge of *maʿet*: Mar., *Dend.* II, 74 a (cf. Brit. Mus. 159, a stela of M. K. the reading of which is not certain).

 *wd̠ʿ mꜣʿ·t* for Osiris, Thebes, Tomb of *Nb wnnf* (Sethe, 12, 80).

 *wd̠ʿ mꜣʿ·t* for the Ennead; Luxor, Court-yard of Rams. II, Sethe 2, 105.

, the *wd̠ʿ mdw*; Luxor, Chamber of Chons, *Rec.* 16, p. 55.

, impartial judge; *Bauer*, Berlin P. 30234, 269.

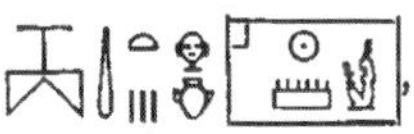, judge in the Temple of Sethos; Mar., *Ab.* I, Appendix B. Plate 23 c.

 *bꜣ* of Re; Turin Pap. 23, 2—5 (P. and R.).

, whose abomination is falsehood; *Totb.* Nav. 182, 3.

, the *bnti*-ape; Mar., *Dend.* II, 71.

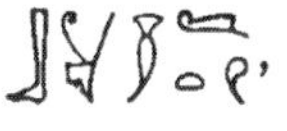, sweet of tongue; Naville, *Horus-myth*, Pl. I.

, the benefactor; Mallet, *Kasr el-Agouz*, p. 30 (Chons-Thoth).

, the Ibis; Anast. V, 9, 2.

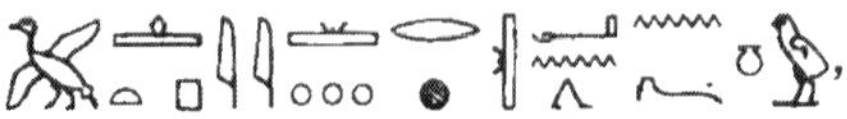, the gracious one who can avert this (evil): Erman, *Denksteine aus der theb. Gräberstadt*, p. 1103 f.

, the silent one; Sall. I, 8, 5.

, Leyden V, 1 (N. K., for ).

, sprung from the *Wr·t*; Edfu R. I, 265.

, sprung from the forehead (?). Turin Pap. 25, 3—6 (P. and R.).

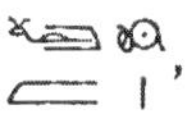, who has come forth from Re; Brugsch, *Thes.* 760 (Dendereh). Speos Artemidos (Hatshepsowet), *Urkunden*, IV, 387.

, the "one with the nose" (or beak), that comes forth from *Ḥmnw*; *Totb.* Nav. 125,3 (confession).

, true (?) of heart; *Urkunden* III, 61.

, the living lion; Philae, Phot. 1448 (*Wb.*).

, lion of the south, mighty in strength; Philae, Phot. 627 (*Wb.*) (Thoth of Pnubs as Shu).

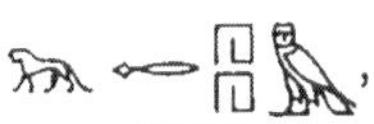, lion with dreadful growl; Philae, Zettel, 217 (*Wb.*).

, whose *i3ḫw* protect his parent; *Totb.* Nav. 182, 8 f.

, whose stylus protected the Lord of All; Thebes, Tomb of Nefer Sechem, Piehl, *Inscr.* I, 122.

, the excellent and impartial politarch; Mar., *Dend.* II, 83.

, who loves *mꜣꜥt*, Turin, no. 101, Funerary Stela (N. K.).

, the *mḥ ib*; Mar., *Dend.* II, 71.

, the *mḥi* who fills the *wḏꜣ·t* for (?) its place; Philae, Phot. 978 (*Wb.*). (Cf. Mar., *Dend.* II, 31 b and .)

, who fills the *wḏꜣ·t* with what it needs; Mar., *Dend.* II, 65 a.

, son of Atum; Edfu, *Mammisi*, p. 116.

, self-begotten; Turin Pap. (P. and R.) 25, 3—6.

, the witness; Leyden V, 1.

, the true witness; Cairo, 20539, 3 (M. K.: king, as compared with Thoth). Cairo, *Wb.*, no. 116, Sethe, 25, 74: Brit. Mus. 581 (Stela N. K.).

, true witness for the gods, *Totb.* Nav. 182, 4.

, lord of gladness; Philae, Phot. 1489—1496 (Thoth of Pnubs).

nb iꜣw·t, lord of old age; Philae, Phot. 1011.

, Lord of wine who drinks abundantly; Philae, Phot. 1434 (*Wb.*): cf. Phot. 1447 (Pnubs).

, lord of life, Edfu R. I, 401.

, lord of life-time; Junker, *Bericht Strabo's über d. h. Falken v. Philae* (*WZKM* 26), p. 46.

, lord of purification; Philae, Zettel 54 (*Wb.*): Philae, Zettel 54 (*Wb.*).

, lord of heaven; Turin Stela, no. 157: *Urkunden* IV, 232.

, lord of judging; Mar., *Dend.* II, 74 b.

nb mdw (or, *ḫrw*), lord of speech; Avignon (*Wb.*), no. 3 (M. K.): Turin, 1031 (N. K.).

, lord of *mdw nṯr*, Louvre A 71 (XXth Dyn.): Pap. Louvre 3238a (letter, XVIIIth Dyn.) and often in late period.

, lord of *mꜣʿ·t*; Mar., *Dend.* II, 71: *Totb.* Nav. 183, 43: Metternich Stela, 22.

nb mꜣʿ ḫrw, lord of triumph; Philae, Phot. 1448 (Thoth's feast on the 19th of the first month of the *ꜣḫ·t*-season is *Ḥb mꜣʿ ḫrw*).

, lord of the gods; Berlin, P. 3049, col. 17, 2—3 (Chons-Thoth).

, lord of laws; *Totb.* Nav. 182, 8 (acc. to Af.).

, lord of the *hdn* (bundle of shrubs used in the *in·t rd*); Edfu, *Mammisi*, p. 76. Cf. Mar., *Dend.* III, 22a: Edfu R. II, 67.

, lord of the *śbḳ·t*-house; Edfu R. I, 63 (Chons-Thoth).

, lord of eternity; Thebes, Tomb of *Pꜣ šdw* (XXth Dyn.); Sethe 13, 87.

, lord of magic; *Totb.* (Nav.) 182, 8 (acc. to Af.).

, lord of foreign lands; Wady Maghara (O. K.), *Urkunden* I, 54; L. D. II, 152 a.

, lord of script; Mar., *Dend.* IV, 74 : II, 17 e: cf. Mar., *Dend.* II, 71. Edfu R. I, 267.

, lord of drunkenness; Philae, Phot. 1447 (*Wb.*) (Thoth as an associate of Tefnut of Nubia).

nfr grḥ, the beautiful one of the night; New York Metropol. Mus. 12, 182, 2 (Stele XVIIIth D.).

, the unknown; Turin Pap. (P. and R.) 25, 3 f.

, who rescues the *wḏ3·t* from him who did evil against it; Edfu R. II, 39 (king as Thoth).

nḫb gnwt n nṯrw nr·t; *Mammisi* (Edfu) 116 (annalist of gods and men).

, Annalist of the Ennead, Edfu, *Mammisi*, p. 21.

, determiner of length of life; Edfu R. I, 27.

, strong of arm; Anastasi I, 10, 6.

nḫt ḫpš, strong of thigh; Edfu I, 263 (Chons-Thoth in Edfu as lion and eagle = Horus of Edfu).

, the strong one of the gods, Pyr. 1237 c.

, tongue of Atum; Brugsch, *Thes.* 759, 30 a.

, tongue of Re; Mar., *Ab.* I, 52.

, king of eternity; *Totb.* (Nav.) 1, 3.

, king (?) of the gods, Turin, Stela 157 (N. K.).

, the unapproachable; L. D. IV, 58 a (Dendereh).

, great god; Leyden, V, 1 (N. K.): Turin, Stela 137 (N. K.), and often elsewhere.

, the great god; Metternich Stela, 49.

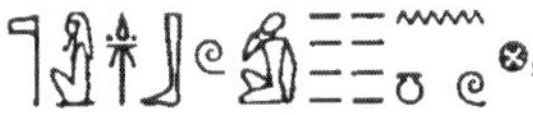, the god for whom *Ḥmnw* longs; Anastasi V, 9, 2.

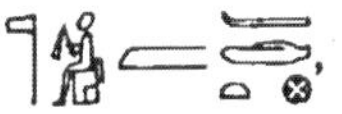, venerable god in Edfu; Edfu R. I, 164.

, Re that shines in the night, *Totb.* (Lepsius) 131, 1.

 *rw wr šfi·t*, the lion great in strength; Edfu R. I, 283 (Chons-Thoth in Edfu = Horus).

, who knows reckoning: Edfu R. I, 63.

 *rḫ mrḫ·t*, who knows the balance (?); Edfu R. II 31.

 Mar., *Dend.* IV, 12. [This is also, apparently, written,  Düm., *Geogr. Inschr.* I/100. Dendereh:  Mar., *Dend.* II, 46: 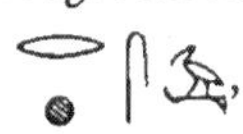, Luxor, Chamber of Chons, *Recueil*, 16, 55; 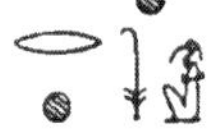 Mar., *Dend.* II, 83.]

, who gives the *wḏ3·t*-Eye to its owner; Leyden V, 1 (N. K.).

, who sets the *wḏ3·t* in its place; Mar., *Dend.* I, 43 a.

, who sets the *i3ḫ·t* in its former place; Mar., *Dend.* II, 65 a.

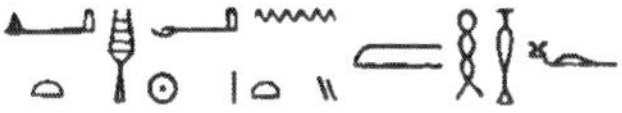, who gives length of life to him who is in his favour; Borchardt, *Saꜣḥure* I, p. 124 (XIXth Dyn.).

, who puts things in their due place; Karnak, Temple of Amon (Rams. IV), Sethe 3, 107 (*Wb.*).

, who gave words and script; *Totb.* (Nav.) 151 a bis, 9 (Acc. to Aa): Mariette, Karnak 16, 27 (Thutmosis III).

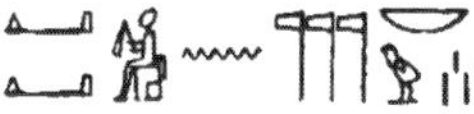, who gives glory (?) to all the gods; *Annales du service*, vol. 8, p. 12 (inscription of Nectanebos).

, the ibis; Turin Pap. (P. and R.) 125: *Totb.* (Nav.) 85, 14.

, the great ibis; Turin Pap. 23, 5 f. (P. and R.).

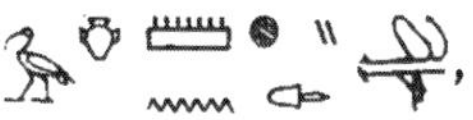, *hb mnḫ ḥkꜣw*, the Ibis splendid in magic; Edfu R. II, 16.

, the venerable Ibis; Anast. V, 9, 2.

, delighting in *mꜣʿ·t*; Mar., *Dend.* II, 41.

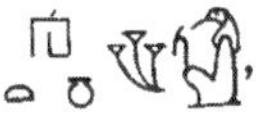, he of the *htn* (see above p. 134); Mar., *Dend.* III, 53 r.

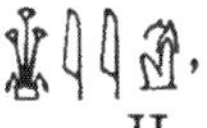, the shining one; Mar., *Dend.* II, 9:  Mar., *Dend.* II, 58. [Perhaps to be read as *mḥi* ?]

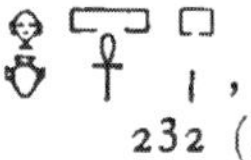, Dweller in the *pr-ʿnḫ* ("library"); Louvre, *Catal.* 232 (Ptolemaic).

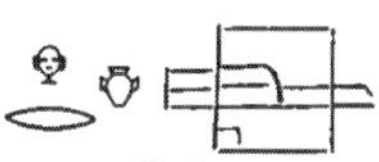, dweller in the *ḥt ibt* (see above, p. 152f.); Cairo 20025 (M. K.).

, he that is on the balance; Vienna, Kunsthistorisches Museum, Sarcophagus Room I, no. XX.

, the great *ḥri ḏꜣḏꜣ* of the gods; Edfu R. I, 295.

, the great *ḥri ḏꜣḏꜣ* of gods and men; Junker, *Bericht Strabos über den heiligen Falken von Philae* (*WZKM.* 26), p. 46. Cf. *ḥri ḏꜣḏꜣ wr* of the Ennead, Mar., *Dend.* III. 68 u; *ḥri ḏꜣḏꜣ wr n nṯrw nṯrw·t,* Edfu, R. II, 80: *ḥri ḏꜣḏꜣ wr* of the Great Ennead, Philae, Zettel 2071 (*Wb.*).

, *ḥri ḏꜣḏꜣ* of *mꜣꜥ·t*; British Mus. 523 and 524 (Nechtharheb).

, *ḥri ḏꜣḏꜣ* of *mꜣꜥ·t* in heaven and earth; Metternich Stela, 49.

, *ḥri ḏꜣḏꜣ* of books; Philae, Phot. 1010 (*Wb.*).

, *ḥri ḏꜣḏꜣ* of Nut; Pyr. 2150 c.

, the great magician, Little Amduat: cf. Dümichen, *Baugeschichte*, 50.

, ruler of the Eye of Horus, *Totb.* (Nav.), c 8 and 9, 5—7.

, lord of judging; Edfu, R. I, 108.

, lord of books; Mar., *Dend.* IV, 74: *Urk.* IV, 53.

, lord of the Ennead; Philae, Phot, 995 (*Wb.*).

, lord of eternity; Hannover, no. 31 (N. K.).

, praised of Re; *Totb.* (Nav.) 182, 8 (Acc. to Af).

, [*r ḥtm b3*] with fierce aspect [to annihilate the *ba*]; Geogr. Pap. Tunis. Two Papyri, Pl. XIV.

, the reckoner; Edfu, R. I, 259 [cf, *Totb.* (Nav.) 100, 10].

, reckoner of gifts; Mar., *Dend.* III, 74 b : II, 41.

, reckoner of time; Philae, Phot. 1011 (*Wb.*). Cf. , Thebes, *Tempelinschriften der griech. röm. Zeit*, Karnak, Bab el Abd, Sethe, *Wb.*)

, reckoner of time for gods and men; Edfu R. I, 112.

, reckoner of years; Edfu R. I, 27.

sic , who reckons all things; Edfu, Piehl, *Inscr.* II, 101.

, pleased with *m3ʿ.t*; Brugsch, *Thes.* 760.

, bearer of the Horus-eye: Philae, Phot. 1398, *Wb.* (Thoth of Pnubs).

, he that is under his tree; Mar., *Ab.* I, pl. 38 c.

, *ḫwi t3wi* who protects the Two Lands; Edfu, R. I, 56.

, he that came into being at the beginning; Brugsch *Thes.* 760 (Dendereh).

, he that came into being at the beginning; Mar., *Dend.* IV, 76 e.

, who leads the throne of the Ennead; Junker, *Bericht Strabos über den heil. Falken von Philae* (*WZKM.*, 26), p. 46.

, who protects Set; Pyr. 1465 c.

(sic)

, he that is on his stairs; Great Amduat, 2nd hour (Sethos IV, 30/31).

, Chons-Horus, Lord of the amulet; Junker, *Auszug der Hathor*, p. 66.

, president of the house of books; Louvre A, 117 (Saitic).

, he that presides over the land of Egypt; Mar., *Dend.* II, 37 a.

, son of Re; Turin Pap. (P. and R.) 125 (N. K.).

, son of Re; Edfu, R. I, 266.

, *sȝb śbḫti*; Mar., *Dend.* II, 37 a: Edfu, R. I, 295.

, the scribe; *Totb.* (Nav.) 69, 11—12 (acc. to Pb.).

, scribe strong of arm; L. D. IV, 58 a (Dendereh).

, excellent scribe; *Totb.* (Nav.) 182, 2—3.

, scribe of *mȝʿ·t*; *Totb.* (Nav.) 182, 3.

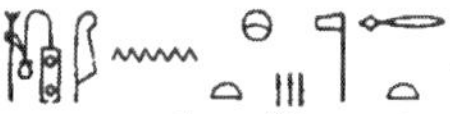, scribe of *mȝʿ·t* for the Great Ennead; Karnak, Temple of Chons, L. D. III, 220 d (time of Sethos I).

, scribe of *mȝʿ·t* for the Lord of eternity; Turin, 912.

, scribe of accounts for Re-Harachtes; Harris Magical Papyrus I, 6—8.

, letter-writer (?) of the Ennead; Anastasi, V, 9, 2.

, scribe of the divine book; Salt, 825, VII, 2—4. Cf. 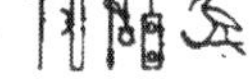 Pyr. 1146 c.

, *ś3ḥ r trwi*; Berlin, P. 3055, col. 8, 9 f

, the knowing one; Stela of Tutanchamon, *Rec.* 29, 166.

, who makes great him that is skilled in his employment; Cairo, Ostracon, *Wb.*, no. 9.

, *śip śbḳ·t*; Mar., *Dend.* II, 65 a.

, who glorifies Osiris with the glorifications of his formulae; L. D. IV, 57 b.

, who glorifies the two Eyes; Mar., *Dend.* III, 19 n.

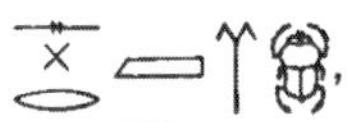, who makes great *m3ʿ·t* in Egypt; Mar., *Dend.* II, 74 a.

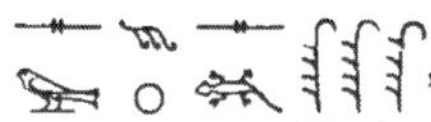, who increases time (*ʿḥʿw*) and multiplies years. Edfu R. I, 27.

, who makes Osiris triumphant against his foes; *Totb.* (Nav.), c. 1, 12—13. (A frequent epithet.)

, who makes splendid his creator; *Totb.* (Nav.), 182, 8 (Acc. to Af.).

, eldest child of Re; Dümichen, *Baugeschichte* XXV: Mar., *Dend.* I, 65 a.

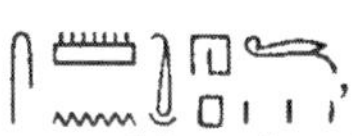, who establishes laws; Edfu R. I, 124. (The king is often thus described as compared with Thoth in Ptolemaic texts).

, a second Re; Edfu, I, 267 (Chons-Thot).

, who announces the morning; *Totb.* (Nav.) 182, 10.

, who gives peace to the Two Lands; *Totb.* (Nav.) 182, 8 (Af).

, who soothes the heart of the gods with his words; Philae, Zettel 91 (*Wb.*).

, commander; Mar., *Dend.* II, 41 a: Cf. , Mar., *Dend.* III, 47 a, b; , Mar., *Dend.* I, 73 b.

, the *śḫm* of the gods; , the divine *śḫm*; Leyden, V, 1 (N. K.).

, the great *śḫm*; L. D. IV, 76 e (Dendereh).

, the venerable *śḫm*; Dakkeh, Phot. 1919 (*Wb.*).

, whose name is mentioned in the birth-house; Philae, Phot. 467 (*Wb.*).

, who inscribes the royal-rule of the lord of the Two Lands; Edfu, R. I, 27.

, who records all that exists on earth; Edfu, R. I, 297.

, who overthrows the foes; Philae, Phot. 1434, 1448, etc. (*Wb.*).

, who overthrows the enemy in every land; L. D. IV, 57 b.

, who pleases (or reconciles) the splendid one with his *śbḳ·t*-eye; Thebes, Temples of Graeco-Rom. period; Karnak, Bab el abd, Sethe 20, 103.

, who reconciles (?) Horus with his Eye; Edfu, R. I, 259.

, who appeases the *Nsr·t*; Philae, Phot. 1448 (*Wb.*) — and often in the texts of Philae.

, who appeases the gods; Mar., *Dend.* II, 37 a, and often elsewhere in Ptol. texts. Cf. Karnak, Temple of Chons (time of Rams. IV), Sethe 3, 107.

, who reconciles the brother-gods; Leyden, V, 1 (N. K.).

, who appeases "the mistress of men" (Hathor) with script; Mar., *Dend.* III, 72 a.

, who pleases the gods with their gifts; Mar., *Dend.* I, 65 a.

, who advances positions; Cairo, *Wb.*, no. 16, Sethe, 25, 74.

, who illumines the Duat in the necropolis; Turin Pap. (P. and R.) 25, 3.

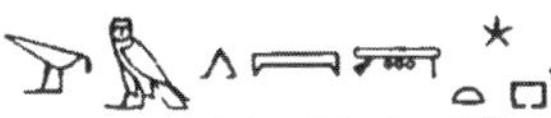, guide of heaven, earth and netherworld; *Totb.* (Nav.), 182, 10—11.

, the guide; Pap. Hearst, VI, 10.

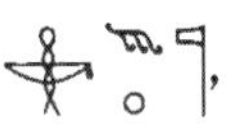, the time-determiner (*śk ˁḥˁw*); Düm., *Tempelinschr.* Taf. 4, l. 3: , Mar., *Dend.* II, 73 c.

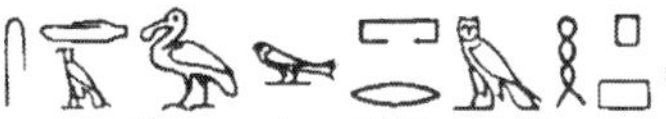, the great *śdꜣ* that came forth from the Nile; Pyr. 126 (identified with Thoth by *Totb.* [Nav.] 178, 13 f.).

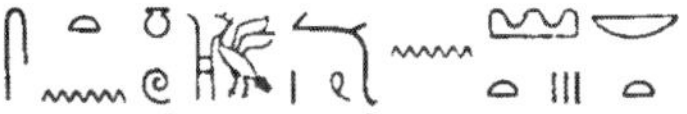, who distinguishes the tongue of every foreign land; Brit. Mus., no. 551.

, who proclaims laws; Stela of Tutanchamon, *Rec.* 29, 166,

, who first fashioned signs and wrote magic (*šꜣꜥ ti·t nḫb ḥkꜣw*); Edfu, R. I, 164.

, the great Shu; Philae, Phot. 1447 (*Wb.*) (Thoth of Pnubs as identified with Shu).

, the great Shu, eldest child of Re; Debôd, Phot. 1691: Dakkeh, Phot. 1921, *Wb.*

, who drives away the evil that is in his neighbourhood; Philae, 1398 (*Wb.*).

, the venerable; Sethe, *Thebanische Tempelinschr. griech.-röm. Zeit*; Karnak, Bab el Abd (*Wb.*).

, skilled in knowledge; Karnak, Hypostyle, Sethe 21, 67.

, acute; Dümichen, *Hist. Inschr.* II, 43 a, 3.

, the mysterious; *Totb.* (Nav.) 116, 6—7.

, cool of mouth; Turin Pap. 24, 1—4.

, who fashioned all things; Edfu, R. I, 289.

, who made all that exists; Edfu, R. I, 164.

, who fashioned things beautiful; *Dend.* Brugsch, *Thes.* 759, 30 a.

, who created purification; Philae, Zettel 54 (*Wb.*).

, bull of Maʿet; Mar., *Ab.* I, pl. 27, etc. etc.

, Bull of heaven; *Dend.* Brugsch, *Thes.* I, 37, 27.

, who beholdeth what cometh afterwards; *Totb.* Nav. 182, 10.

, the great *gmḥś*; Kasr el Agouz (Mallet).

, whose words established the Two Lands; *Totb.* Nav. 182, 4.

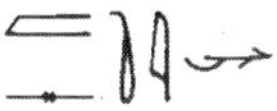, the *gśti*; he of the palette; Turin Pap. 23, 8.

, the ibis; *Dend.* Dümichen, Rez. XXVI/XIII..  *Dend.* M. D. II, 51 e.

, the great ibis; Philae, Temple of Arensnuphis, East Wall, Standards.

, the venerable ibis; Brugsch, *Thes.* 760.

, the venerable ibis that chases away the foes; *Dend.* M. D. IV, 12.

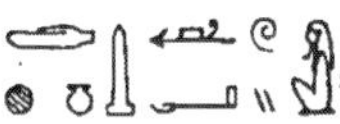, the unique *tḫn*; Edfu, R. I, 270.

, minister of Horus; Lepsius, *Book of the Dead,* 145, 23 (6th Portal of Netherworld. Cf. Mar., *Dend.* II, 33 c)

, who determines fate (*ṯni š3w*) on the *mśḫn·t*; Philae, Phot. 1010 (*Wb.*).

, who gives air to *Wn nfr*; Piehl, *Inscr.* I, 123.

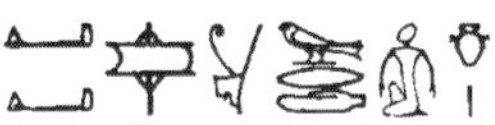, who gives breath to the weary of heart; Tomb of *Nb wnnf*, Thebes (Sethe, 12, 63 *Wb.*).

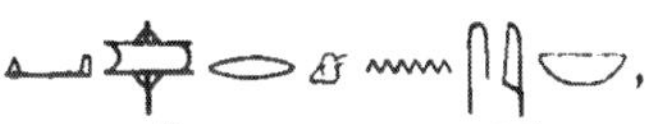, who gives breath to the nostrils of every man; Metternich, 18.

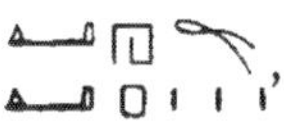, who gives laws; Cairo, *Wb.*, no. 116.

, who gives office to whomsoever he loves; Turin, no. 173 (N. K.).

, *dwn ḥr*; L. D. III, 276 g.

, who purifies the Ennead with his hands; Edfu, *Mammisi*, p. 69.

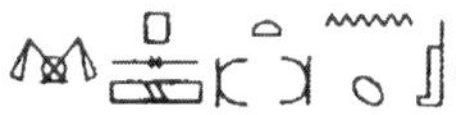, who joins the Two Halves for the son of Isis; Edfu, R. I, 63.

, who makes strife to cease in the eastern heavens; Turin Pap. 24, 10 ff.

, who drives away evil; Nav., *Totb.* 182, 3.

, who drives away the voice [of anger?]; Nav., *Totb.* 182, 9.

Appendix C.

Some divine associates of Thoth.

(a) *Iśds* and *Iśtn*.

In the texts of the Greek period Thoth is very frequently called *Iśds* and *Iśtn*. It has been generally assumed that *Iśds* and *Iśtn* designate two distinct divinities, and possible connections between *Iśtn* and a conjectured Persian *magos* Ostanes have been put forward by Egyptologists in discussing the Hermetic legend of Democritus of Abdera. (1) The truth seems to be, however, that the name *Iśtn* has arisen through a confusion of the sign  (*dś*) with the sign  (*n*). (2) Thus the name *Iśds* determined with the *dś*-jar came to be read as *Iśds-n*, and then as *Iśdn*, or *Iśtn*. This misunderstanding was assisted probably by a confusion between  and , and, possibly also, by the circumstance that there existed a word  (*dni*) which (like *dś*) meant "jar" or "pot". The following list of forms which appear in the texts will help to show how *Iśds* has become *Iśtn*:

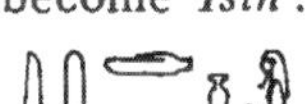 (*Totb.* Nav., ch. 17, 41);  (*Totb.* Lepsius, 145, 39. 81. 86); 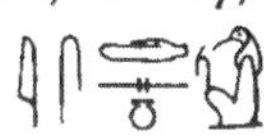 (Mar., *Dend.* I, 39 c);  (Dendereh, Düm., *Rez.* XVII);  (Edfu, *Mammisi*, p. 16);  (*ibid.*, p. 89). The forms 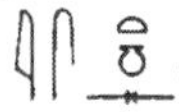, 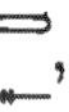, and  also occur in Dendereh.

---

(1) See Maspero in P. S. B. A., vol. 20, pp. 140 ff. *Biblioth. ég.*, vol. 27, 459—464. Cf. *Ä. Z.* 1872, article by Goodwin on the name Astennu.

(2) Cf. *Sphinx*, vol. 2, p. 113; review of *Lebensmüder* by Piehl.

It is obvious that the jar-determinative, where it occurs in connection with this name, ought to be read as *ds*.

The *Iśtn* form of the name is much later than the *Iśds*-form. It does not occur in any early text, while *Iśds* is found even in the M. K. *Iśtn* is variously written:

(Thebes, Tomb of Nb-wnnf, Sethe's copy, 12, 64 *Wb.*); (Dümichen, *Tempelinschr.* I, pl. 26); (Mar., *Dend.* I, 57 b); (*ibid.* II, 18 b); (*ibid.* II, 35 a); (Edfu, *Mammisi*, p. 91); (*ibid.*); (Karnak, Bab el Abd, Sethe, 20, 92 *Wb.*).

It is obvious that all these forms (except those written with the sign) could be explained as arising either from a misreading of the jar-sign *ds*, or from a confusion of with . It must be admitted, however, that the priestly scribes of the Graeco-Roman period probably regarded *Iśds* and *Iśtn* as fairly distinct divinities. Whether in that period the name of a Persian sage Ostanes had any part in helping to set up *Iśtn* as distinct from, and independent of *Iśds*, or whether, on the other hand, the Memphitic Ostanes of the story of Democritus is a double of the Egyptian *Iśtn*, (1) must remain uncertain. We may regard it, however, as practically certain that *Iśtn* is not connected with a verb , to "separate" or "distinguish" (as Brugsch thinks, *Wörterbuch*, pp. 126 f.), and that Thoth's function (Brit. Mus., no. 551) is in no wise connected with his name *Iśtn*. (2)

---

(1) See Maspero on this question, P. S. B. A., vol. 20, pp. 140 ff.

(2) See article on the name "Astennu" (*Iśtn*) by Goodwin, *Ä. Z.* 1872, pp. 108 f. When the crown of Upper Egypt is employed in writing the name we must admit that the scribe intended to write *Iśtn*, for the crown is written *śtn* (Berlin, Amon-ritual 9, 7), or, later, (*Ä. Z.* 15, 99). The name of the crown is probably derived from . See *Ä. Z.* 49 (1911), p. 34, Sethe on "*Das Wort für König von Oberägypten*".

The identification of Thoth with *Iśds* (*Iśtn*) is a familiar feature of the Ptolemaic texts. Descriptions of Ptolemy like that in Mar, *Dend.* I, 42 a: "The good god [the king], the heir of Thoth, the excellent son of *Iśds*", or that in Edfu, *Mammisi*, p. 16: "The splendid god, the heir of Thoth who lives on the good, who judges like *Ḥri Ḏ3d3* (= Thoth), the good god, the son of *Iśds*, the heir of *Wp rḥwi*", frequently occur in the Ptolemaic texts. (1) The determination of *Iśds* with the Thoth-determinative , which is not unusual in the Ptolemaic texts, points in the same direction. In pre-Ptolemaic texts the identification of Thoth with *Iśds* is also found. In the Book of the Dead, ch. 17, 41 (Naville) Set and *Iśds* are put together as the "Lords of Maʿet", (2) and *Iśds* is called , "Lord of the west". (3) This reminds us of Thoth's epithet  in the Catalogue of the Egyptian collection in the Fitzwilliam Museum Cambridge (p. 34), and his other epithet "Bull of the west" (see list of epithets above), and suggests that the identification of Thoth with *Iśds* goes back to the N. K. In the Book of the Dead edited by Lepsius, ch. 145, 86. 87 we read in a prayer to be recited at the gates of the netherworld: "I enter into the house of *Iśds*; I extol (?) the 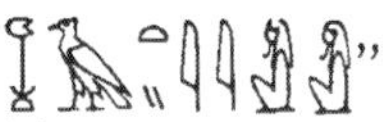" (cf. *ibid.* 81 f.). Since Ḥu and Sia appear in this context we have here a further suggestion of the same identification of *Iśds* with Thoth.

---

(1) In the text Edfu R. I, 508 Ptolemy IV presents a figure of *m3ʿ·t* to eight divinities: (a) Re; (b) *m3ʿ·t*; (c) the Lord of *Ḫmnw* "in his form as *tḫn*, heart of Re, 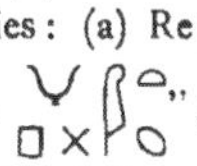"; (d) *Wp rḥwi* 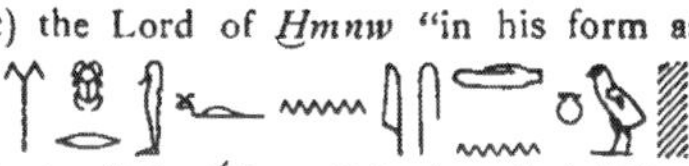; (e) ; (f) ; (g) the great *Śś3·t*: (h) the little *Śś3·t*. *Iśdn* is called *Iśds* in the same context. The offering of a *m3ʿ·t* to *M3ʿ·t* and the separation of different aspects of Thoth in such fashion as to make them almost distinct individualities, is a good illustration of that want of clearness and logic in Egyptian theology to which reference has been frequently made above. (Cf. Edfu R. I, 521 for a similar list.)

(2) For Thoth as *nb m3ʿ.t* see list in Appendix B.

(3) Grapow in his edition of ch. 17 (*Religiöse Urkunden* I, p. 44) reads Thoth instead of Set. For Thoth as  see the tomb of  in Thebes. Champ., *Not.* I, 860.

This identification of Thoth with *Iśds* in the funerary texts of the N. K. and later periods did not prevent Egyptian scribes of the same periods from holding the two beings apart. Thus the members of the *Ḏ3ḏ3·t* mentioned in *Totb.* (Nav.) 18, 24 are Thoth, Osiris, Anubis, and *Iśds* — Thoth and *Iśds* being enumerated as distinct individuals. (1) In the context of Lepsius *Totenbuch* just referred to (145, 81—83) *Iśds* is grouped, as Thoth often is, with Ḥu and Sia, which suggests that, just as Ḥu and Sia are both identical with, and different from, Thoth (*supra* p. 104f.), so also Thoth and *Iśds* were identical and separate for Egyptian religious thought — being regarded, perhaps, ultimately as one divinity appearing in different aspects.

The primary ground for the identification of Thoth and *Iśds* is probably to be sought in the fact that *Iśds* (*Iśtn*) was one of the dog-headed apes associated with the worship of the rising sun in *Ḫmnw*. (2) Thoth was himself an ape-god, and it is not strange that he came to be identified with one of the sacred apes of his own "City of the Eight". (3)

(b) Chons.

Chons was an ancient moon-god whose worship was well established at Thebes, in the Middle Kingdom — and probably earlier. (4) The name Chons means "Wanderer", or "Traveller", (5)

(1) Note that the same *Ḏ3ḏ3·t* in the tomb of *Nb-wnnf*, Thebes, (Sethe's copy, 12, 64) consists of Thoth, Osiris, Anubis, and 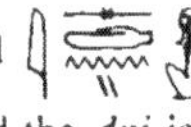 — where  may be due to a confusion between the *ds*-jar and the *dni*-jar, or between 𓈖 and 𓊃.

(2) See Edfu, R. I. 286; Dümichen, Tempelinschr., pl. 26. *Iśds* sometimes appears determined with a jackal figure, as in Düm. Kal-Inschr. pl. 107. This may be due to a confusion between the jackal and the dog-headed ape. Or, possibly, as there is question of a standard, the familiar *wp w3wt* has displaced the ape. Cf. L. D. IV, 55c.

(3) His similar association with the *bnti*-ape may have brought about his connection with the *wn-śb*.

(4) The only reference to any centre of the cult of Chons outside Thebes in the M. K. is Cairo 20481 which seems to ascribe to him a M. K. cult near Gebelên, at  (see *Ä. Z.* 20 (1882), p. 123; 47 (1910), p. 45), *i. e.* Rizagât.

(5) The name is written 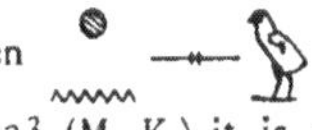 in the O. and M. K. In Lacau's *Textes religieux*, LXXV, p. 123 (M. K.) it is written . In the later periods it is variously written.  is frequent.

and obviously points to the lunar character of the god. It is not possible to explain why Thebes became a centre of moon-cult. It might be conjectured, perhaps, that, in some unexplained fashion, Iooḥ, the moon, was primitively identified with a local god in Thebes, who then took on a special lunar name, and lunar qualities, and, either because his usual symbol had been a human form, or because it was natural to represent the increasing new moon by the symbol of a youth or child, (1) came to be represented in human form as a young man or a child. The association of Chons with Amon and Mut at Thebes as their child is, probably, of secondary origin.

It was inevitable that Chons and Thoth should, in the course of time, be associated and gradually identified with each other. Their identification is not usual, however, until the period of the New Kingdom — a fact from which it may be inferred that either or both gods possessed something more than merely lunar character. What was true of sun-worship was probably true also, to some extent, of moon-worship. The cult of the moon-god was centered in certain shrines by a process of assimilation between the moon-god and local divinities, in which the local divinities retained something of their old non-lunar character. In the case of Chons the old

---

The name is clearly connected with the verb which is written in the Pyramid texts . (Pyr. 130) — a verb used to describe the movement of the moon across the skies. is employed generally in the sense "travel", "journey". (The verb is also written). A text in Edfu (R. I, 267) derives the name Chons from this verb: "Chons . Cf. *Totb.* Nav. 178, 18—20: Acc. to Aa, "who traverses Egypt in order to rule the two halves (of Egypt) in his great name Chons".

Thus the Theban moon-god gets his name like ירח among the Hebrews. In Coptic we have the form ϣⲟⲛⲥ.

(1) One of the standing epithets of Chons in Thebes is *pꜣ ḫrd*, "the child". Cf. the Chons text in Edfu (R. I, 255); "Chons of Edfu, child on the first day of the month, *imꜣḫ* on the 15th, *šwi* in heaven, who takes the place of the *iꜣḫw*, illuminating the night like Re .... Eye of Re who has no equal among the gods". Does suggest a point of contact with Shu? For the title "Chonspechrod", "Chons the child", see Berlin, 17271, Statue, 26th dyn. For the moon as a child see Mar., *Ab.* I, 51, 33.

non-lunar elements, if there were any, practically disappeared, but Thoth retained always much of his local, non-lunar individuality. In the New Kingdom their common element brought the two gods closely together, and ultimately led to their identification. (1) Through this identification the popularity of Chons increased and his worship extended widely outside Thebes. (2) From the 20th dynasty on Chons constantly assumes activities of Thoth, and appears frequently as lord of script and literature, and as judge — like Thoth.

It is to be noted that Chons played no part in the Horus-Set legend, though, as moon-god, he might naturally have been expected to hold some place in the drama of the great struggle between light and darkness. This is one of the many points which go to show that Thoth's part in that legend is not due solely to his lunar character. It illustrates, too, the influence of local circumstance on the development of early sagas. Before the great intensification of Chons-cult in the Ramesside age had begun Thoth, the rival of Chons, had become universally established in the worship of Egypt through his connection with the Osirian drama.

Of the epithets of Chons which belong to him in his own right the most common perhaps, is *p3 iri sḫrw*. (3) This

(1) There is a Cairo ostracon of 20th. dyn. containing a prayer to "Chons-Thoth, the Ibis" (*Wb.* 9). See also Karnak Pillar Hall, Northern half, Sethe, 19, 69, (*Wb.*), where the "Lord of Karnak" is called Chons-Thoth (time of Sethos I).

(2) Maspero has suggested (*Journal des Savants,* Nov. 1902, p. 578, note 2) that the intensification of the cult of Chons in Thebes itself from the 19th. dynasty onwards, which can be inferred from the texts, was not due to an identification of Chons with Thoth, but rather to the local pride of the Thebans who wished to make their own god as important as the widely honoured moon-god and magician of Hermopolis. This is, of course, nothing more than a conjecture. The assumption by Chons of Thoth-epithets, which is a common feature of the N. K. and later periods, is not favourable to Maspero's theory of jealousy between Thebes and *Ḫmnw*. The increased importance and popularity of Chons in the Ramesside period, and later, may be due largely, as suggested in the text, to his fusion with Thoth, but it must also be regarded as possible that Thoth, on his side, derived new importance from his identification with the Theban Chons. Thebes was a highly important political and religious centre in the N. K. period.

(3) He is also described as *imn sḫrw*. This epithet is frequent in Edfu. Cf. R. I, 249, 258 f.; 256. 262 etc. "Chons *p3 ḫrd*" is, perhaps his most usual epithet in Thebes. A fairly frequent epithet of Chons is "lord of gladness". Is it possible that Thoth's Nubian character as lord of wine and gladness may be somehow connected with this epithet of Chons? (Cf Mar., *Dend.* IV, 78 etc. etc.).

designates him as an oracle-god: it is probably derived from his function of measuring time, as moon-god. The measuring of time suggests the determining of fate. The office of Chons as healer or physician (as illustrated, for instance, in the narrative of the Bentresh-stele) may possibly belong to him as moon-god, but more probably it is due either to his identification with Thoth, the physician of the Eye of Horus, or to the pride of his Theban worshippers who wished thus to make him at least as great as the moon-god of Hermopolis.

In the texts of the Graeco-Roman period Chons and Thoth are frequently identified and Thoth-attributes are freely transferred to Chons. In Edfu they are identified not merely with each other but also with the god of Edfu, the winged sun-disc Horus *Bḥdti.* They appear there in falcon-shape and receive the epithets of Horus. (1)

At an early date Chons of Thebes was thrown together with Shu, and the two divinities were there often looked on as one. (2) Both were gods of light and their identification was inevitable when Shu began to be especially honoured at Thebes. Shu is the god of the light-space between earth and heaven: (3) as such he separates earth and heaven at the dawn, (4) and in separating them he seems to raise up and hold aloft the heavens. As bearer of the heavens Shu was identified by the Greeks with Herakles. Chons, then, as one with Shu was also identified with Herakles. Shu was one of the two "lion-gods", and thus, too, Chons came to be represented sometimes as a lion. The identification of Thoth with Shu in Philae, and in Nubian inscriptions generally, may be due, in some measure, to the identification of Chons and Shu in Thebes; but it may be due also — if not solely — to the part played by Thoth in the legend of Onuris. Shu and Onuris are one, and Thoth, like Onuris, is "he who fetches

(1) Cf. Edfu R. I, 275 — where the epithets of Chons-Thoth are very similar to those of the Nubian Thoth-Arhensnuphis (*Onurislegende,* pp. 7—12). Cf. also the long passage about Chons Edfu. R. II, 67 f.

(2) Cf. *Rec.* 1906, p. 181 f.: ÄZ. 21, p. 79: Wiedemann, *Herodot,* p. 200.

(3) The space which the dead traverse on their way to heaven is called *Św* in Pyr. 325.

(4) For this idea see Great Amduat (Leyden), 12th hour, which speaks of "the secret being of Shu who divides earth and heaven at the dawn".

back the Eye that was far away". Since all three gods in the legend of Onuris agree largely in function, they tend to merge into each other. (1)

(c) *Nḥm·t ʿwȝi.*

We find frequently associated with Thoth in the later periods a divinity who is called *Nḥm·t-ʿwȝi* — "She that rescues the plundered". The second constituent of the name was written in the N. K. usually with two final ,  (Leyden, Pap. I, 344: *recto* 2, 9), or  (*Bauer*, Berlin P. 3025, 68). This second element of the name is a passive participle of the verb , to rob, or plunder. It is only in the very late texts that we find the whole name *Nḥm·t-ʿwȝi* written as a single word with a feminine ending —  (See, *Dend.* L. D. IV, 58a etc.), for the feminine ending really belongs to the first part. (2) Sethe has proposed to explain the name as meaning "She who recovers (or rescues) the stolen". (3) Gardiner prefers to take it as = "She who rescues the plundered", (4) referring her activity rather to the person who has been plundered than the property that has been stolen.

Nḥm·t-ʿwȝi is closely associated with Thoth in a variety of ways. In Dendereh (Brugsch, *Thes.* 790) she is called "mistress of *Ḫmnw*, head of Dendereh, daughter of Re and ruler in 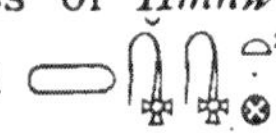" (— *iw nśrśr*, the necropolis of *Ḫmnw*),

(1) Cf. Junker's treatment of this point in *Onurislegende* pp. 7—12, 49, 58, etc., etc.

(2) See for the writing of feminine ending Sethe, *Zur Sage des Sonnenauges*, p. 13.

(3) *Verbum* II, p. 399. Sethe equates her with Δικαιοσύνη and refers to Plutarch, (*I. et O.* 3) according to whom the chief of the Muses at Hermopolis is called Isis and Δικαιοσύνη.

(4) *Notes on the Story of Sinuhe*, p 42. Brugsch (*Rel. u. Myth.*, p. 471) explains the name as = "throwing back the violent". This explanation is excluded by the usual meaning of *nḥm* — *viz*, "rescue". We need not, therefore, seek to connect with the name *Nḥm·t-ʿwȝi* the wearing of a sistrum-headdress by the goddess — as if the sistrum implied her office of "repelling the violent" (*i. e.* Typhon or Set: cf. Plutarch, *I. et O.*, ch. 63). Hence too we may reject Turayeff's suggestion (p. 151 f.) that *Nḥm·t-ʿwȝi* is a mere personification of Thoth's magical power.

She is also called "lady of the *Pr-Ḫmnw*" (L. D. IV, 58a). In Dümichen, *Geogr. In.* III, 87 she gets the title , and elsewhere she is made mistress of the city of Thoth in the Delta, 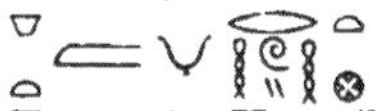 (Mar., *Dend.* II, 27, 15). She appears along with Thoth in *Ḥśr·t* (Leyden V, 1; memorial stela of N.K). In a list of divinities in Edfu (R. I, 53) she appears with Thoth, the Great *Śš3·t,* Ḥw, Sia, *Iśds,* and Onuris.

It would seem that her appearance in the Thoth-shrines at Hermopolis Magna and in the 15th. Delta nome, and otherwise, in close relation with Thoth is due to her character as a goddess of justice, as one whose duty it was to rescue the plundered and oppressed. She was a sort of Egyptian *Justitia* or Δικαιοσύνη. Thoth, as we have seen, was a legislator and judge "whose abomination it was to show partiality". He was thus the most fitting counterpart to, and companion for *Nḥm·t-ʿw3i.*

Nḥm·t-ʿw3i often seems to be no more than a form of appearance of Hathor. In Philae (Z. 964, *Wb.*) she appears with the sistrum headdress (which belongs to Hathor) and is called "*nb·t tḫ* in Philae, Eye of Re, mistress of feasts etc." "*Nb·t tḫ*" and "Eye of Re" are distinctive epithets of Hathor. In the temple of Amon at Karnak (Champ. *Not.* II, 82, 3) Hathor accompanying Thoth is called *Nḥm·t-ʿw3i, nb·t pt.* Like *Nḥm·t ʿw3i* Hathor also is 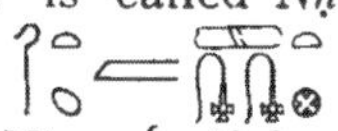 (Dümichen, *Temp. In.* II, XXX).

At times *Nḥm·t-ʿw3i* is represented as if she were identical with *Śš3·t* (as in Medinet Habu, Sethe, *Heft* 14, 31 *Wb.*). This is to be explained, probably, by the fact that *Śš3·t* is often regarded as a form of Hathor, and can, therefore, be equated with another form of that goddess.

When all the evidence dealing with the person and activities of *Nḥm·t-ʿw3i* has been weighed, it would seem as if she were, in most contexts, nothing more than Hathor considered as goddess of law and justice. It is as a personification of justice that she becomes a companion of Thoth, and a dweller in Thoth's chief centres. It is not probable that the Egyptians of the early periods worshipped another abstract goddess of justice or equity in addition to Maʿet. (1)

(1) For *Nfr-ḥr,* son of Thoth and *Nḥm·t-ʿw3i* see Mallet, *Kasr-el-Agouz,* p. 15. Cf. Brugsch, *Rel. u. Myth.,* 483f.

(d) *Sš3.t.*

Śš3.t appears as a divinity in the Old Kingdom. In the Pyramid texts she is identified with Nephthys. In Pyr. 616 a. b Nephthys gathers together the scattered limbs of the dead king *m rn-ś pw n* . In the parallel text (M) the name is written . Though she is thus regarded as one with Nephthys, we yet find that she possessed a priesthood of her own, probably as early as the third dynasty (cf. Mar., *Mast.* A 2). Her name *Śš3.t* means simply "the Writer". The importance of the scribes profession in Egypt at all times must have led very early, indeed, to the setting up of a special divinity as patroness of scribes — a sort of deification of the scribal art. Whether this divinity of the scribes was always looked upon as an aspect, or mode of appearance, of one or other of the great goddesses of the Osirian cycle — Nephthys, or Hathor, we do not know. It is possible that her identification with other great divinities is secondary. In the texts of the later periods — particularly in those of Dendereh — she is constantly identified with Hathor. In Edfu she appears sometimes, just as she does in the Pyramids, as one with Nephthys. (1)

The functions of *Śš3.t* greatly resembled some of those of Thoth. She is frequently described as the "mistress of books", "the president of the library", "the primeval one who first employed writing". (2) Even in the O. K. she is called 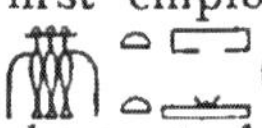 (3) "president of the house of books". Not merely has she control of ordinary libraries, but she is also 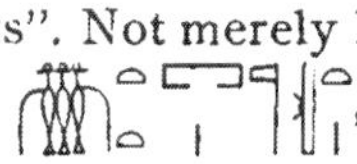, (4) head of the collections of "divine books" (*i. e.* books containing *mdw nṯr*). As "mistress of writing" she must normally be present when there is official writing, or record-keeping, to be done. Hence we find her writing the annals of kings, and predetermining their years of reign. (5) We find her with Thoth

(1) Edfu, R. I, 253.

(2) Mar., *Dend.* I, 57 b.

(3) Berlin, 7721; Mar., *Mast.* B, 16 seems to connect her with *pr ʿnḫ*, the "library".

(4) *Mission,* XV, pl. 75, fig. 185 (time of Amenophis III).

(5) L. D. *Text,* III, 133 (Ramesseum); Mar., *Ab.* I, 34 a.

registering the details of the royal revenue. (1) We find her, further, constantly in the ceremonies of measuring and laying out sites for sacred buildings, for she was, of course, patroness of architects as well as of scribes, and the building of sacred shrines would need to be carried out exactly according to the directions contained in the "divine books". (2)

The similarity of their work brought Thoth and *Śš3·t* together, and sometimes *Śš3·t* is called the daughter, (3) and sometimes the sister (4) of Thoth. Epithets of Thoth tended to pass over to *Śš3·t*, and so it is not surprising to find her called *wr·t ḥk3w* (5) "Scribe of the Great Ennead", (6) and "president of the *Ḥt-ibt*". (7) Neither is it strange to find her acting as a goddess of fate in cooperation with the *Ḥśbw* (the "Reckoner", *i. e.* he who determines the *š3i* = he who decrees fate). (8) The similarity of her work with that of the "Lord of *Ḫmnw*" has made her the "Lady of *Ḫmnw*". (9)

Just as it is unjustifiable to look on *Nḥm·t-ʿw3i* as a divinity invented by the Egyptian priests as a counterpart, or female double, of Thoth, so neither are we justified in accepting the view suggested by Foucart (10) that the origin of a goddess of writing in addition to Thoth was due to the developing outlook of Egyptian science -- it being felt that, as knowledge expanded, one god was not sufficient to deal with it all. The existence of a worship and a priesthood of *Śš3·t* in the O. K. tells strongly against such a theory. *Śš3·t* had her own importance in the early period, out of all relation to Thoth, as the patroness of the ancient scribes.

The most persistent of the epithets applied to *Śš3·t* is *śfḫ·t ʿbwi* which, apparently, ought to mean "She that puts off (or releases) the two horns". The "two horns" are obviously connected in some way with the peculiar headdress

(1) Naville, *Deir el Bahari* 79. *Cf. Śš3·t* in the reliefs of Sahure.

(2) Mar., *Dend.* III, 53 r; Luxor, Court of Rams. II, Sethe 2, 104; *Mammisi*, p. 6.

(3) Mar., *Dend.* II, 74 b.

(4) Mar., *Ab.* I, 51 a.

(5) L. D. IV, 58 a; Mar., *Dend.* I, 33 d.

(6) Leyden I, 350, 6.

(7) Mar., *Ab.* I, 51 a.

(8) Edfu, R. I, 258.

(9) Mar., *Dend.* IV, 34.

(10) *Méthode comparative dans l'histoire des Religions*, p. 196. Foucart, in support of his view compares the case of Ptah and Imhotep.

which she wears, (see above, reference to Pyr. 616 b). The horns are in an inverted position, and it has been suggested that *śfḫ* designates the act of inverting the horns — the process of changing them from the position to the position, which might be taken as equivalent to "putting them off". (1) The other part of the headdress — the grouping of "rays" to form the star-like object in is exceedingly difficult to explain. The number of "rays" is most usually seven and as the word *śfḫ* (= seven) and the verb *śfḫ*, "to put off", etc. are written with the same consonants a connection was sought between the number of the "rays" in and *śfḫ* in *śfḫ·t ʿbwi*. Hence the name could be written as it occasionally appears. It is to be noted however that the number of "rays" in the headdress is not always seven. Besides what could possibly be the meaning of the "Seven of the Two Horus"? *Śfḫ* cannot well be regarded then, as connected here in any way with the word for "seven". (2)

The epithet *śfḫ·t ʿbwi* does not help to explain the association of *Śšꜣ·t* with Thoth. The ground of their association is, however, not far to seek. *Śšꜣ·t*, the Egyptian Clio, is a more or less abstract divinity who was brought into close association with Thoth, the lord of literature, in her character as a personification of the scribal art.

---

(1) See article by Schäfer, *Ä. Z.* 42, p. 72 on Μοῦσα in Horapollo II, 29, and the goddess *Śšꜣ.t*. Horap. says that seven signs held by two fingers signify Μοῦσα, ἄπειρον, Μοῖρα. The "seven signs" are clearly, according to Schäfer, the seven rays, and the two fingers are . The idea of seven has arisen from a misunderstanding of *śfḫ* (taking it as the numeral *śfḫ*). The "rays" must still remain unexplained. *Śšꜣ.t* is Μοῦσα as head of libraries: she is Μοῖρα because she determines the length of royal reigns: she is ἄπειρον, perhaps, because the years of royal reign are predetermined as *eternal*.

(2) Gardiner points out (*Notes on the story of Sinuhe*, p. 105) that means "loosen the arrow" and that *ʿb* may be used metaphorically for "bow". Is it possible to discover any point of connection between the muse of history and a designation, "She that releases the bows"? The seven "rays" of the headdress of *Śšꜣ.t* remind one of the conical crown of the Sumerian goddess Bau, on which stood seven horns narrowing upwards to a point. Cf. Frank, *Studien zur babylonischen Religion*, p. 265.

ADDITIONAL NOTES.

(a)

Page 134, note 3. *Hdn* seems to mean sometimes the calamus of the scribe. In Edfu, Roch. I, 63 the king makes an offering to Thoth with the words:

 "Receive the palette (1) and thy calami." (2) The objects presented to the god are quite clearly the palette of the scribe, and a handful of reeds. That the reeds are writing-instruments follows also from the further words which accompany the offering: "The things dear to thy heart which thy *kȝ* loves. Stretched forth is thy arm when thou performest thy task by means of them (the "task", in the case, being the writing of the royal annals). When, then, the epithet *nb hdn* is closely connected with such other epithets of Thoth as "Lord of script", "Ruler of books", it is probably best explained as meaning simply "Lord of the calamus".

(b)

P. 180: To the list of the epithets of Thoth in Appendix B may be added the following interesting titles of Thoth occurring in Ptolemaic texts.

 *iri ti·t*, who fashioned signs (script, painting, etc.); Edfu, R. II, 67.

---

(1) In Edfu R. I, 377  is used for "palette", and we should read this therefore, in the text above.

(2) That we should read *hdn*, not *hts*, is clear from the parallel, Edfu, R. II, 67:

 "Presentation of the palette to the Lord of the palette,

 and of the calami (ʿr) to the Lord of the *hdn*."

 *iḳr*, the excellent one; Edfu, R. I, 377.

 *mnḫ sḥ*, excellent in counsel; Philae, Phot. 857.

 *n ḫm-n ỉbf*, whose heart is not ignorant; Edfu, R. I, 378 [cf. ibid. I, 63].

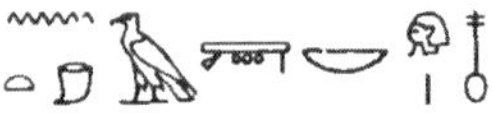 *Ntꜣtꜣ nb tp nfr*, the *Ntꜣtꜣ*, Lord of the good; Karnak, Bab el Amara, Sethe 4, 66; cf. ibid. 4, 51: 4, 91: Philae, Z. 3547.

 *ḥśb nṯr-w rpiwt*, Reckoner of the gods and goddesses; Philae, Z. 3546.

 *śiꜣ ḫpr·t nb·t m p·t*, who knows all that happens in heaven; Edfu, R. II, 68.

 *śmśw wḏ-w*, the first to utter command; Düm., *Baug.* 25; cf. Edfu, R. I, 378: Philae, Phot. 857.

 *śr n mꜣʿ·t*, prince of Maʿet; Mar., *Dend.* II, 14 (and *passim*).

 *śšm n tꜣ nḏ śḫrw·f*, leader of earth, who determines its course; Edfu R. I, 378.

 *ṯꜣti*, the vizier; Philae, Phot. 285.

(c)

As the texts of Philae are not yet widely known, the following passages dealing in the manner of the temples of Philae with certain aspects of Thoth, may be of interest to the reader.

An inscription on the door of the library of the great temple of Philae begins thus:

"This is the . . . residence of the Prince of *Wp-rḥwi* under whose command stand the Two Lands, who sends forth the great ones, and guides the little ones, without whom naught comes into being, the glorious Ibis who came forth from the heart of the god [Re]: tongue of Tenen [Ptah] when he gives command, throat of Him of the Hidden Name [Amun], the Great one is he, too, as ape when . . . . . . the horizon. Great is his name as the Ibis, Lord of the calamus (*hdn*), the first to utter command, excellent in counsel, who fitted together this land (or, this earth), the Highest of the High, the most Hidden of the Hidden, who came into being when naught existed, who of himself alone has wrought all that is: there is no other who is like unto him."

On a pillar in the Great Hall the following hymn appears:

"*Hail to thee,* Chons-Thoth, on this glorious day." ......

"*Hail to thee,* saith Re" — to thee, who rejoicest the heart of Atum, and providest sacrifices for the gods. May thy heart rejoice thereat, on this glorious day when thou shinest forth. Thou art the god that is high on his standard, who came forth from the god himself [Re]; for whom opened the doors of the eastern horizon of Re by whom he was begotten. Every god came forth at his command — what he spoke was accomplished. Thou art the god who protected Horus by his great Eye (*i. e.*, by the uraeus-serpent); do thou protect [also] king Ptolemy, for he is Thoth, the Dweller in *Ḫmnw*.

Hail to thee, Thoth who appeasest the gods; by whose deeds every god is appeased. Thou shinest forth in the eastern heavens: thou smitest the dwellers of the desert. Thou providest sacrifice for every god and goddess.

Hail to thee, thou Eye of Horus which thou [Thoth] didst bring, which thou didst embrace when thou didst rise aloft:

Thou didst set thy arms about it, in "thy" name Iooḥ; because of it thou wast sent forth in thy name *Hb* (Ibis)!"

(d)

It is to be noted in connection with the problem of Thoth's relation to *Ḥw* and *Śiꜣ* that these divinities appear in the legend of Onuris just like Thoth as bearers of the Eye of Horus. For *Ḥw* see Junker, *Onûrislegende,* p. 31, note 1, and Philae, *Zettel* 3544; and for *Śiꜣ*, Philae, *Zettel* 3550.

301014-200-2-60W